Advance Praise for porn.com

"*porn.com* is an outstanding contribution to the emerging field of online porn studies, examining the intersection of online sociability and erotic content, and providing important insights about both.

Online fan cultures and a democratization of production have affected the porn industry as they have all sectors of the communication industry, but these new forms represent a diverse range of practices, values, and challenges that defy attempts at reductive description. The chapters of *porn.com* provide a tour of this new and rapidly changing erotic landscape, and a detailed analysis of the contexts in which these interactions take place.

The collection should be of interest not only to those who are engaged in porn studies, but to anyone who wants to understand the broad range of contexts in which online interaction takes place."

Alex Halavais, Quinnipiac University

"The internet has become the key site of contemporary debates around the effects of pornography on communities and individuals. Anxieties are widespread about the impact of online porn on the sexualities and attitudes of young people and on the capacity of paedophiles to establish networks for sharing images.

Feona Attwood's new edited collection is a timely addition to this debate, bringing together an impressive range of international scholars on porn studies to explore such themes as the production and consumption of online porn, the evolution of the industry, and the content of sex blogging and amateur online erotica. This book is a valuable contribution to an intensifying global debate."

Brian McNair, University of Strathclyde, United Kingdom

"This anthology positions net porn at the throbbing centre of society. If you're ready for some uncensored scholarship on porn cultures in the digital age, this is the reader for you. Beyond good or evil, *porn.com* provides us with a broad overview of topics such as child pornography, the working conditions of porn professionals, Web 2.0 cultures, extreme imagery, image rating, and insights into the online 'swinging' world. So let's praise the researchers and blast the moralists!"

Geert Lovink, Dutch-Australian media theorist and net critic

porn.com

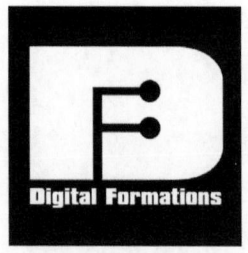

Steve Jones
General Editor

Vol. 48

PETER LANG
New York • Washington, D.C./Baltimore • Bern
Frankfurt am Main • Berlin • Brussels • Vienna • Oxford

porn.com

Making Sense of Online Pornography

Edited by Feona Attwood

PETER LANG
New York • Washington, D.C./Baltimore • Bern
Frankfurt am Main • Berlin • Brussels • Vienna • Oxford

Library of Congress Cataloging-in-Publication Data

porn.com: making sense of online pornography /
edited by Feona Attwood.
p. cm. — (Digital formations; v. 48)
Includes bibliographical references and index.
1. Internet pornography. I. Attwood, Feona. II. Title: porn dot com.
HQ471.P58   306.77—dc22   2009035988
ISBN 978-1-4331-0206-6 (hardcover)
ISBN 978-1-4331-0207-3 (paperback)
ISSN 1526-3169

Bibliographic information published by **Die Deutsche Nationalbibliothek.**
Die Deutsche Nationalbibliothek lists this publication in the "Deutsche
Nationalbibliografie"; detailed bibliographic data is available
on the Internet at http://dnb.d-nb.de/.

Cover design by Clare Harris

The paper in this book meets the guidelines for permanence and durability
of the Committee on Production Guidelines for Book Longevity
of the Council of Library Resources.

Contents

Part One: Porn Practices

Part Two: Porn Styles

Part Three: Porn Cultures

Acknowledgments

I would like to thank the contributors who produced such diverse and interesting chapters for this collection. Many thanks to Clarissa Smith and I.Q. Hunter who read and gave feedback on my own chapter, and to Mary Savigar and Steve Jones at Peter Lang, who were exemplary publisher and series editor, respectively. Thanks are also due to the writers on online porn, especially Katrien Jacobs, Susanna Paasonen, and Dennis D. Waskul, whose work was the direct inspiration for this collection.

The book was completed during a rather frantic time when I juggled too many projects and was not always sure whether I was coming or going. Close friends and family made my life sane and lovely during the process, in particular, Thom White, Adele Stanley, Zander White, and Nick and Ann Creaby-Attwood. Thanks and much love to all of you.

The Cultural and Communication Research Centre at Sheffield Hallam University has given me continuing support in developing my work. Thanks especially to Dave Waddington and Simeon Yates, and to my Subject Leader, Peter Jones.

I would also like to thank the AHRC for providing a grant which gave me space to think about the book and write a proposal for it.

This book is dedicated to Clare and Lesta.

Introduction:
Porn Studies: From Social Problem to Cultural Practice
Feona Attwood

Cyborg Sex

The relationship between sex and technology has long been the focus of cultural fascination, and increasingly in the recent past, a source of speculation about the future of sex and its social and cultural significance. Pornography is often central to debates about sex and, as Henry Jenkins notes (2007), also "at the center of the controversy surrounding any new media as the public adjusts to the larger shifts in the ways an emerging medium shapes our relations to time and space or transforms the borders between public and private." Today it is online pornographies and the related practices of cybersex that provide a key site for moral, political, and legal debates about sex, technology, and media. They are usually framed in two quite distinct ways; as representing a "brave new frontier" for sexual expression, or as a "perilous vortex of danger and corruption"; framings that reproduce the wider competing views of sex and communication technologies as means of liberation or destruction (O'Brien & Shapiro, 2004, p. 118).

In fact, contemporary debates about internet pornography tend toward the second of these views, rearticulating concerns about the bad "effects" of pornography on beliefs, attitudes, and behavior; especially the encouragement of violence against women, the endorsement of sexist and misogynist views, the destruction of childhood innocence, and the commodification of relationships. They also reproduce an older set of anxieties about obscene texts that were frequently seen as violating the distance thought to be necessary for separating subject and representation from their object (Falk, 1993, p. 10). This fear—that porn is dangerously effective at moving us—has been heightened with the increasing accessibility of porn from the late 19th century onward; as Peter Lehman notes, once it could be "enjoyed by the unwashed, illiterate masses ... began the fear that porn could and would be the ruin of us all" (2007, p. 109).

Today, porn is more accessible and mainstream than ever, and still capable of exciting suspicion and concern. Pamela Paul argues that as porn creeps into popular culture it crowds out more positive forms of sexual expression, promoting "shame, humiliation, solitude, coldness, and degradation" (2005, p. 275). Ariel Levy claims that the contemporary fascination with porn represents "a desperate stab at freewheeling eroticism in a time and place characterized by intense anxiety" (2005, p. 199), and Robert Jensen sees pornography as "more cruel and denigrating to women at the same time that it is more widely accepted in our society than ever before" (2007, p. 184). In 2008, Max Hardcore, a porn producer who has been widely reviled for his brand of porn, was jailed in the United States for obscenity (see Kernes, 2009), while a bill to outlaw "extreme" pornography progressed through the British courts and a crack down on internet porn intensified in China. As I wrote this introduction, a radio program on online porn was being broadcast. Typical of the way the topic is covered in the media—with the title, "Online Damage: Porn in the 21st century,"[1] it announced its intention to tell the stories of couples "trying to repair the trust and intimacy dented by the persistent and secretive use of porn sites" and of the young people who are "in danger of having their understanding of sexual relationships damaged by what they see online."

These responses are perhaps not surprising. Since the invention of photography, followed by film, video, and digital media, pornographic images have signified in ever more disconcerting ways, appearing to more thoroughly disturb the categories of the real and representational. Online porn also disrupts boundaries between public and private space in a particularly comprehensive way, becoming accessible to audiences who have traditionally been forbidden it, and potentially, to all. The internet has domesticated porn, and made it impossible to maintain what Walter Kendrick (1996) called the "secret museums" within which pornographic texts were imprisoned in the 19th century. A "visual rhetoric of anxiety" around the connection of body and screen (Patterson, 2004, p. 104) has become fixated on online pornography and other forms of "cyborg" sex and these have also become the focus for discussions about sexual freedom and knowledge, self-expression and harm, and the boundaries of what is acceptable both in sexual representation and sexual practice.

Yet despite this level of concern, there has been a distinct lack of academic work on online pornography. This collection is part of a wave of new publications aimed at addressing that lack. Its approach is not to assume that porn is a social problem but to investigate it as a set of cultural practices. In this, it takes the stance of contemporary Media and Cultural Studies and of critical studies of digital technologies in late modern societies, aiming to make sense of online pornography and contribute to a broader and growing academic literature on sex, media, and technology.

Academics on Porn: The 1990s

Academic literature on pornography is plentiful, although until the mid-1990s it was not particularly diverse in its approach. Early scholarly texts in the 1960s and 1970s established a standard set of responses: "Steven Marcus writing the whole of *The Other Victorians* while seemingly holding his nose," "Susan Sontag ... giving the avant-garde literary, high-serious French treatment to the Sade-Bataille tradition," and "Andrea Dworkin offering the most meticulous descriptions of pornographic writing or images in tones of monumental outrage" (Williams, 2004c, p. 172). A body of work documenting porn's bad "effects" or linking political opposition to pornography to feminism dominated work through the 1970s and into the 1980s.

In fact, until the mid-1990s there was very little work on porn that did not belong either to the effects tradition (see, for example, Donnerstein et al., 1987; Zillmann & Bryant, 1989), or to a discourse of antipornography feminism that equated porn with men's violence against women or institutionalized male power (see, for example, Dworkin, 1979; Morgan, 1980; Griffin, 1981; Kappeler, 1986; MacKinnon, 1993). Notable exceptions included Angela Carter's *The Sadeian Woman* (1979), Walter Kendrick's *The Secret Museum: Pornography in Modern Culture* (1987), Linda Williams' *Hard Core: Power, Pleasure and the "Frenzy of the Visible"* (1989), some of the work in feminist anthologies such as *Powers of Desire* (Snitow et al., 1983) and *Pleasure and Danger* (Vance, 1984), and collections such as *Caught Looking* (Ellis et al., 1986), *Sex Exposed* (Segal & McIntosh, 1992), and *Dirty Looks* (Church Gibson & Gibson, 1993).

This new work was groundbreaking. Kendrick's history of the term "pornography" and its cultural work in defining and regulating texts and Williams' innovative examination of hardcore pornography as a genre challenged an unhelpful view of pornography as a monolithic entity with self-evident characteristics and functions. Carter's book and the collected works on sex and porn provided an opportunity to debate the complexity of pornographic representation in relation to sex and gender politics; a stance also taken by some of the more "first-person" approaches in books by Michael Kimmel (1990), Lisa Palac (1998), Annie Sprinkle (1998), and Susie Bright (1999).

These works marked the beginnings of a paradigm shift in the study of porn (Kirkham & Skeggs, 1996; Attwood, 2002) in which the significance of "pornography" as a cultural and regulatory category and the examination of a diverse range of pornographies both became areas of new interest. Jennifer Wicke has argued that an academic "orgy of publication and commentary" since that time has mimicked the "equally unstoppable flood of pornographic materials into all cultural interstices" (2004, p. 176). In a book written to accompany the U.K. television series *Pornography: The Secret History of Civilization* in 1999, Fenton Bailey, the series' producer, describes the repeated attempts to make such a series over a ten-year period, attributing its eventual commissioning to burgeoning academic interest, and also to the broader cultural shift whereby porn had become a fashionable object of reflection (in Tang, 1999, pp. 9–21). The study of porn itself began to be a theme in academic writing (Curry, 1996; Kirkham & Skeggs, 1996; Kleinhans, 1996).

New work included histories of pornography (Hunt, 1993), its consumption (Hardy, 1998), and its significance for particular sexual communities (Dyer, 1992; Waugh, 1996). Some important new books emerged. Laura Kipnis assessed the cultural significance of porn as transgressive fantasy in *Bound and Gagged* (1996), Brian McNair provided an overview of pornography's place in contemporary culture in *Mediated Sex* (1996), Catharine Lumby's *Bad Girls* (1997) revisited debates about porn, feminism, and the public sphere, and Laurence O'Toole's *Pornocopia* (1998) examined the changing status of pornography in relation to technological development. Jane Juffer's book *At Home with Pornography* (1998) was particularly influential in drawing attention to the landscape of sexual discourses within which porn is situated. Asking "What are the material and discursive conditions in which different kinds of pornography are produced, distributed, obtained and consumed?" (1998, p. 2), she explored the location of porn in relation to other cultural forms and media genres. Her work showed how the various aesthetic claims these make work to position them in relation to particular discourses of sex for particular audiences, with important implications for the ways sex media are accessed, used, regulated, and understood. These new contributions marked a move toward the contextualization of pornography, through the examination of specific porn texts, porn's status as a genre, its place in the wider set of cultural and political frameworks, and in everyday life.

21st Century Porn

New work on porn in the 1990s was enormously important in opening up the area of study, but its development was also driven by a number of social and cultural changes, which have since been characterized as "pornographication," "pornification," "sexualization," or the "mainstreaming of sex" (see McNair, 2002; Attwood, 2006; Paasonen et al., 2007a; Mühlheisen, 2007; Attwood, 2009). The terms describe some of the ways in which sex has become "the subject of public debate, to an extent unprecedented in the history of the mass media" (McNair, 1996, p. 22), and where the expansion of the "pornosphere" has been matched by a growth in "texts citing pornographic styles, gestures and aesthetics" (Paasonen et al., 2007b, p. 1).

These changes are part of the development of sex as an important site for leisure and consumption. Commercial sex products, services, and representations have become steadily more visible and accessible, while some sectors of the sex industry have been mainstreamed, "businessified," or gentrified. Sex work includes an increasingly broad range of occupations and is carried out in an increasingly wide variety of physical, virtual, and media sites (Agustin, 2007). New technologies have provided new locations for sex work. Sex and technology are more thoroughly mixed together than ever before, while mediated forms of sex and "commercially available intimate encounters" (Bernstein, 2007, p. 7) have become increasingly commonplace.

As media and communication technologies become more widely understood as part of the fabric of ordinary life, there has been a general blurring of the "real" and the "representational," reinforced by the dramatic expansion of forms of online self-presentation and social networking. This is part of a broader set of shifts in the ways that the body and identity are represented, understood, and experienced in a "striptease culture" focussed on display, confession, and self-revelation (McNair, 2002). New communication technologies have also become part of people's sex lives, facilitating homemade DIY sex media and new types of sexual encounter in virtual environments. The new visibility of commercial sex, and in particular, porn, has worked to make it appear less disreputable and "other," while the availability of technologies has helped to elide the distinctions between sex producer and consumer and between sex as a set of practices and sex as a set of representations.

As a result, what sex means is changing. It is now strongly tied to discourses of consumerism, style, and therapy; to hedonistic and often autoerotic practices that provide "free-floating sensation" (Bauman, 1999, p. 26); to the expression of self; and to the creation of communities. The increased visibility of sex-positive feminist and queer approaches to sex in political activism, the academy, and the wider culture has worked to reframe the study of pornography. A politics of sex and intimacy, built on an earlier feminist insistence that "the personal is political," and attempts to theorize the intimate aspects of life and reconsider these in ethical rather than moralistic terms (see Weeks, 1999; Plummer, 2003), has provided new starting points for thinking about the ethics of sex media (see also Albury, 2002 and 2003) and created new opportunities for understanding their significance.

From the turn of the century onward, new books on sexually explicit representations have continued to appear. A new anthology on feminism and pornography by Drucilla Cornell was published in 2000. Brian McNair's important book *Striptease Culture* (2002) mapped out the new landscape within which sex media are now produced and consumed, describing the relationship of the pornosphere, art, mainstream media, and the broader striptease culture. Two collections, *Porn Studies* (ed. Linda Williams) and *More Dirty Looks* (ed. Pamela Church Gibson), both published in 2004, staked out the developing area of Anglo-American "porn studies" and identified new themes: the importance of pornography as a subject for research and teaching; the variety of porn texts; the importance of cultural and intellectual economies for understanding pornography; a shift of focus from "women" to "gender" and from straight pornography to a more diverse set of representations; and an awareness of the importance of race and class in the study of pornography.

The researching and teaching of porn has continued to be a theme in academic writing (Jenkins 2004; Williams, 2004b; Driver, 2004; Lehman, 2006; Reading, 2005; Boyle, 2006; Attwood & Hunter, 2009), as has porn as film genre and "on screen" (Lehman, 2006; Andrews, 2006; Williams, 2008; Kerr & Hines, 2010). There have also been ambitious studies of the ways that individual porn texts are produced, signify, and are consumed, for example, in Clarissa Smith's (2007) analysis of *For Women* magazine, *One for the Girls!* The impact of pornography on popular culture has been documented in an impressive collection by Susanna Paasonen et al., *Pornification* (2007a), while a useful and accessible overview of current pornography debates, particularly valuable for its engagement with porn audiences, is presented by Alan McKee et al. (2008) in *The Porn Report*. Studies of young people's relation to porn and sex in the media have emerged (Buckingham & Bragg, 2004; Knudsen et al., 2007), while the issues of pornography as work (Milne, 2005) and in relation to technological innovation (Grenzfurthner, 2008) have also become a focus for writing.

Porn Goes Online

The relationship between sex and technology is an old and established one; technologies have always been adapted for sexual purposes, and it is regularly claimed that sex drives technological development. Yet changes in technology do introduce new ways of doing things and create new environments in which to do them. In porn's transition from material to online spaces, its location is reconfigured as a "private space within a public environment" (Patterson, 2004, p. 120), and its consumption becomes part of a multitasking mode as users move between "socializing, buying commodities and searching information ... chatting, peeping, cruising, masturbating and maintaining friendships" (Jacobs, 2004a, p. 73). As part of the broader trend in which media use comes to be experienced as an interactive and "creative activity" (Kitzmann, 2004, p. 45), the significance of porn shifts, too, becoming part of a wider repertoire of interests and interactions that are simultaneously more public and more private than before.

As Heider and Harp have noted (2002, p. 288), there has been "surprisingly little work by media scholars ... focused specifically on Internet porn" and it has been "almost invisible in academic literature on the information society and digital economy" (Cronin & Davenport, 2001, p. 33). But academic interest in new technologies and sex, and specifically in online porn has grown since the mid-2000s (Waskul, 2004; Jacobs, 2004a, Jacobs, 2004b; Halavais, 2006; Jacobs, 2007; Jacobs et al., 2007). Two collections set out some of the emerging areas for examination. Dennis Waskul's *Net.seXXX*, published in 2004, drew together writings on regulation and technology, cybersex, virtual infidelity, the grotesque, the exploitation of women and children, pedophilia and zoophilia, race and personal ads, and the future of online sex. Three years later, *C'lick Me*, (Jacobs et al., 2007) appeared, drawing on two major conferences in Amsterdam and growing out of "a sense of intellectual and social urgency around netporn" and in response to the rise of global antiporn movements (2007, p. 1). The collection focused on the forces ranged against netporn; on the "small players rather than giant industries or singular porn stars," on representing the alternative, queer sexuality, art and the writerly, feminists and ethnic minorities, and on grotesque sex and warpunk activism.

It is possible to trace several dominant areas of interest in contemporary scholarship. One is the emergence of new "savvy media practitioners" (Jacobs, 2004a), particularly those involved in the production of independent and alternative pornographies, often with a subcultural, countercultural, or queer focus (Magnet, 2007; Attwood, 2007b; Cramer, 2007; Lehman, 2007; Levin Russo, 2007; deGenevieve, 2007). Another is the development of new porn styles that attempt to speak more effectively to new audiences—particularly women and the sexual subcultures and communities who congregate around sexual display in specific kink cultures or as part of a broader interest in cultural and lifestyle issues. Women's involvement in producing online pornographies is another area of study (Lane, 2000; de Voss, 2002; Ray, 2007), and the trend toward DIY porn in which rawer and rougher styles of representation dominate (Barcan, 2002; Messina, n.d; Albury, 2008) has also attracted attention.

Of course, the question of porn's dangerousness has not gone away.

Since the 1990s, this has largely been articulated around cyberporn and cybersex addiction (see Griffin-Shelley, 2003; Attwood, 2007a), or child pornography and the use of the internet by pedophiles to groom their victims. With the odd exception such as Philip Jenkins' ethnographic study (2001), most work in this second area emerges from criminological studies of convicted sex abusers, that tell us relatively little about the prevalence of child porn online, its distribution beyond small communities of child abusers, and what its broader significance might be beyond them.

More recently, porn has attracted attention in discussions about "war porn" or "atrocity porn"—real-life images of torture, combat, and execution circulated online—and about "shock" imagery that often represents the body in excessive and grotesque ways—leaky, uncivilized, hurt, or ruptured (Baudrillard, 2004; Langman, 2004; Pasquinelli, 2007; Jacobs, 2007). Anxieties about the status and significance of these kinds of developments are apparent elsewhere in popular and political discourse, as part of a reemergence of a range of "cyberfears," particularly around "dangerous pictures" and "extreme" porn (Kleinhans, 2004; Jones & Mowlabocus, 2009), but they have also been seen as part of a broader cultural trend toward the depiction of humiliation, suffering, and terror (see Edelstein, 2006; Swartz, 2006; Jensen, 2007; Lockwood, 2009). These developments raise important new questions, potentially opening up porn studies to the broader consideration of the way that corporeality is understood in late capitalist societies in a climate marked by very real concerns with human conflict and dehumanization (Jones & Mowlabocus, 2009), and of what it might mean to engage with media that deal with these themes (Lockwood, 2009).

This collection engages with some of the issues to emerge from the rise of online pornographies. Part One tackles the porn industry, changing technologies, and pornography's significance as a form of production and as a focus of debate. Stephen Maddison describes how responses to the proliferation of pornographies online have worked to intensify views of porn as frighteningly pervasive and oppressive or wonderfully, liberatingly abundant. Both, in fact, work to mythologize porn. Increasingly, the figure of the child pornographer has come to play an important part in these mythologies, sustaining a series of debates about pornography which render important issues of child abuse and protection, regulatory control, civil liberties, and sexual emancipation invisible. Adam Stapleton takes up the issue of child pornography in more detail, examining how it is produced and distributed online, how it is defined and how it is related to pedophilia, abuse, technological development, and to broader conceptualizations of childhood, desire, and representation.

The following two chapters consider the shifting relations of porn and technology. David Slayden examines the development of porn as an industry, focusing on the emergence of a mainstream adult entertainment sector represented by large companies such as Vivid. This sector's success has been built on its ability to exploit emerging technologies and mainstream business practices, but it now faces a new set of challenges posed by the rise of amateur producers and new forms of distribution and consumption in the move toward "Porn 2.0." Sharif Mowlabocus takes up this theme, discussing the new economy of Porn 2.0 in which amateur practitioners make money on the new pornographic "tubes." His chapter explores how these new forms of immaterial labor can be understood in the face of claims that Web 2.0 is "democratizing" pornography and making it more egalitarian. Finally, in my chapter, I examine the labor of new porn professionals and describe the way they blur occupational categories and merge work with leisure, in the process creating new forms of sex work and new conceptualizations of sexual ethics.

Part Two is concerned with the question of porn styles. Sanna Härmä and Joakim Stolpe look at the behind-the-scenes scenarios of straight porn that are increasingly available online as porn texts in their own right. Their chapter shows how, although highly conventional in many ways, these offer glimpses of porn production that present the viewer with things they would otherwise never see; not least, the mechanics of representing heterosexual desire and "porn sex." Alongside these new views of straight porn, gay, lesbian/dyke, bisexual, trans, and queer forms of porn have also proliferated online. Jennifer Moorman's chapter maps the characteristics of this quickly growing set of genres, examining the ways in which they engage with sexual politics and articulate the authenticity of sexual identity, desire and community.

These chapters foreground the ways in which reality and authenticity are central concerns in pornography, and examine the playing out of those concerns in different types of porn. Another kind of engagement with the "real" is explored in Steven Jones' discussion of shock pornography that revels in physicality, displaying bodies that are pushed beyond normal limits and framed as amusing, repulsive, or disturbing. These images function as a shocking interruption of our notions of civility, producing strong and perhaps complicated responses. A very different set of texts is discussed in the following chapter by Susanna Paasonen who considers written pornography—a largely neglected genre. Focusing on the construction and definition of quality in Literotica, an enormous online erotic story archive where amateur writers produce, consume, and rank sexually explicit stories, the chapter shows how erotica and pornography are produced as categories with particular kinds of narrative dynamics, drawing on criteria that are both aesthetic and affective.

Part Three deals more closely with the way people interact around online pornography. Simon Lindgren investigates the online porn fan community of FreeOnes in a context of increased porn accessibility and the expansion of an existing male heterosexual audience. He considers how male porn fans consume and discuss pornography and how pornography is used in social interaction and the construction of masculine identities. In a very different context, Katrien Jacobs focuses on the emerging Web cultures of Hong Kong, Taiwan, and Mainland China, where pornography is often illegal and circulated unofficially through blogs, bulletin boards, and chat rooms. She examines the erotic discourses of female sex bloggers and Lolita Cosplayers against a backdrop of economic expansionism, urban transformation, and government surveillance. In both instances, porn culture seems to reproduce and reinforce existing conventions; the fan site becoming a virtual glory hole where men's pleasure and power is paramount, and the Chinese sexual self-portraits expressing naïve and hedonistic fantasies of lust and attractiveness.

In the final contributions to this section, Dennis D. Waskul and Cheryl L. Radeloff consider the erotic rate-me sites where individuals make and circulate their own representations, offering comments on each others' images, while Alison Rooke and Monica Moreno Figueroa examine the visual cultures of swinging sites. The image plays an important role in both of these new spaces; fusing image and act and becoming a resource for constructing sexual identity and community. In both, sex and gender conventions play an important structuring role, yet gender is also playfully and creatively done and undone as bodies become erotic generators and the possibilities for queering sexual subjectivity are opened up.

As Susanna Paasonen has argued, if we are to understand the specificity of particular pornographies, "we need to remain dedicated to contextualization" (2007c, p. 170). By examining different facets and aspects of online pornographies, it becomes possible to broaden out further what we mean by pornography and to exploit its potential for revealing shifts in the patterns of media and technology use, in regulation and governance, in the performance of identities online, and in the significance of sexual representation and practice. In the concluding chapter, I attempt to draw together some of the themes of the collection, showing how the study of online cultures and practices can be situated in relation to broader configurations of technology, work and leisure, and how they illuminate emerging and conflicting views of sex and reality.

Note

1.   http://www.bbc.co.uk/programmes/b00glc5z. Accessed 5 January 2009.

Part One: Porn Practices

Chapter 1
Online Obscenity and Myths of Freedom: Dangerous Images, Child Porn, and Neoliberalism
Stephen Maddison

The internet offers new forms of communication, data transmission, and community building, and Web 2.0 advocates claim that we are witnessing a new era of user-generated content and devolved, horizontal distribution; one that poses a significant challenge to the business model that has sustained commodity capital since the end of World War II. At the same time, porn users have become used to an increasing range and choice of pornographies, especially in countries such as the United Kingdom, where hardcore has only been legally available for a decade or so, and where it has often been difficult and expensive to obtain. In this context, and set against the view that porn is frighteningly abundant, there is a tendency to consider any legal or political curb on porn as a form of censorship, as an attempt to reinstate so-called Victorian social values, and as a restriction of sexual freedom. However, this also often equates commodity choice with sexual emancipation in a way that needs more careful analysis. In this chapter, I consider the relation of porn to sexual freedom, the operation of myths about porn, and the figure of the child pornographer; a totem that is virtually omnipresent in debates about internet security and the regulation of online porn, apparently marking the limit of freedom.

Myths of Porn

According to Roland Barthes, myth is a type of speech that "transforms history into nature" (1993, p. 140); "Myth does not deny things, on the contrary, its function is to talk about them ... it gives them a natural and eternal justification, it gives them a clarity which is not that of an explanation but that of a statement of fact." Crucially, myth depoliticizes:

"it abolishes the complexity of human acts, it gives them the simplicity of essences, it does away with all dialectics … it organizes a world which is without contradictions" (1993, p. 156). Myth acquires power through devices such as the construction of proverbs, forms of commonsensical scripts, the use of tautology where like is defined by like, and identification, in which we are offered a position of "self" which is defined against and in opposition to an "Other." The function of myths is to naturalize the cultural—in other words, to make dominant cultural and historical values, attitudes, and beliefs seem entirely "natural," "normal," self-evident, timeless, obvious—and thus objective and "true" reflections of "the way things are."

Contemporary debates about pornography are shot through with this kind of speech. For example, in a statement by Concerned Women for America, a right-wing evangelical group in the United States, porn is presented as an "epidemic" that "like a sexually transmitted cyber-disease … widely affects men, women and even children." This crisis is caused by "the instant availability of such obscenity and the lack of enforcement against it," which "entices viewers to consume more and more smut and to delve deeper and deeper into more graphic and obscene material," and which "destroys individuals, families and communities" (Barber, 2008). Here, porn takes on the mythic quality of a biblical plague: abundant, malevolent, mysterious—always ready to entrap the unwary, deadly in its spiral of addiction.

This image of pornographic abundance, mythically malevolent for Concerned Women for America, is mirrored in the notion of pornographic plenitude celebrated by many of porn's advocates. In a typically erudite extract from her book, *Bound and Gagged* (1999), Laura Kipnis suggests that "the abundance of pornography—such an inherent aspect of the genre—simply resonates with a primary desire for plenitude, for pleasure without social limits. Pornography proposes an economy of pleasure in which not only is there always enough, there's even more than you could possibly want." This view of abundance has widespread currency amongst many who seek to defend and promote porn use. For Matthew

Scully (2006), celebrating the 80th birthday of *Playboy*'s founder in the *Wall Street Journal*, "we have Hugh Marston Hefner, more than anyone else, to thank for the great plenitude of porn we take for granted today. There was a dark and joyless time in America when one could actually go about daily life without ever encountering pornographic images." This myth-making, in which symmetrical concepts of abundance and plenitude stand in for freedom of choice, underpins the "tired binary" of the sex wars, as Jane Juffer has described it (1998, p. 2), in which pleasure is set against danger, liberation is set against oppression, and free agents are set against victims.

The notion that porn represents pleasure, freedom, and liberation is exemplified in an Oxford University Union debate in 1998. In this, Tuppy Owens, of the Sexual Freedom Coalition (a coalition of groups campaigning for sexual liberties), offered a number of reasons to support her claim that porn is beneficial to society. She suggested that porn acts as a safety valve; is useful in sex therapy; is educational; spices up physical and fantasy sex lives, and is available and enjoyable by all. Here porn isn't just a palliative for social ills ("people are less likely to commit sex crimes"), but actually improves the health of the heart, lungs, and circulation, offers social catharsis, liberates people with disabilities, and subverts attempts to "nanny" us. Owens depoliticizes sexuality in general and pornography in particular, presenting it as an idyll where bodies frolic in carnivalesque abandon and "sex is beautiful." To be against porn is to be Other; joyless, and repressed, immune to redemption.

The notions of sexuality and porn offered here are mythic in three ways. One level of myth is evident in the sexual pastoral Owens constructs, a "privation of history" in Barthes' terms (1993, p. 151), in its naivety about the relationship between power and sexuality. A second level of myth lies in its concealment of the instrumentalized relationship between the acquisition of pornographic goods and well-being. This relies on an appeal to individuals "to become 'experts of themselves' and to adopt an educated and knowledgeable relation of self-care in respect of their bodies, their minds, their forms of conduct" (Rose, 1996, p.

59). This view of porn's relation to freedom, well-being, and happiness constitutes a myth that is part of a wider process of self-regulation. Owens argues that "Banning porn means society is not free to make our own choices," but, as Nikolas Rose suggests, the individual's desire "to govern their own conduct freely," and to pursue a "version of their happiness and fulfilment that they take to be their own" actually "entails a relation to authority" even "as it pronounces itself the outcome of free choice" (1996, p. 59). The third level of mythic depoliticization in Owens' account relates to the political economy of porn itself. Questions of porn production and distribution are ignored and the pornographic commodity and its consumption are fetishized.

Speaking Sex and Dangerous Images

Although the academic study of porn has developed dramatically since the 1990s, the neglect of questions of production is still apparent. For example, in *Striptease Culture,* Brian McNair associates the "expanding pornosphere" with increasing sexual and political freedom for women and gays (McNair, 2002, pp. 87, 205–207), and a pornographied "striptease culture" is presented as offering "sexual democratization" (2002, p. 207). According to McNair "it has been cultural capitalism ... which has propelled the ... signifiers of what were once marginal, oppositional movements and sub-cultures into the mainstream" (2002, p. 206), a statement that should surely be the beginning, not the end of the analysis. Similarly, in her introduction to *Porn Studies,* Linda Williams states that "pornography is emphatically part of American culture" and goes on to suggest that while "feminist debates about the propriety or danger of pornography marked the 1980s and 1990s, along with larger societal debates about censorship in general, the new millennium ... has become increasingly used to, if never fully comfortable with, 'speaking sex'" (2004b, p. 2).

Despite Williams' skepticism about sexual culture, and her critical erudition, there remains here an implicit recognition of the value of increasing sexual explicitness, evident in the elision between advancing toward the new millennium and advancing toward a more open speaking of sex that strongly accords with Modernist notions of progress. Discussing the 1998 World Conference on Pornography, Williams notes with regret that the published proceedings omitted the "very illustration[s] that had made the conference so lively" and goes on to offer a new critical term, on/scenity, "a more conflicted term ... which ... can mark the tension between the speakable and the unspeakable which animates so many of our contemporary discourses of sexuality" (2004b, p. 4). Here, a preoccupation with the shifting limits of what can and cannot be seen displaces questions of porn production and the wider economic and political conditions in which that production takes place. For Williams, as for McNair and Owens, the fantasy of widening access to a pornographic plenitude comes to represent freedom of expression.

However, we need to consider the politics underlying these powerful calls on the notions of free speech and liberty that are bound up with claims of sexual openness and democratization. Nowhere is this more urgent than in relation to the internet and questions of online obscenity, yet myths of porn are regularly mobilized here. At a time when the culture of the internet offers the lure of "ambient intimacy" (Thompson, 2008), there is increasing concern about questions of privacy and data retention, especially in the context of the counterterrorism imperative and the protection of children. In 2006, the U.S. Republican Senator John McCain proposed legislation that would have required Web sites and blogs to report any child porn and other forms of obscenity to federal authorities and to retain all data for at least six months. In the United Kingdom, the government-endorsed Internet Watch Foundation provides internet service providers (ISPs) with a list of banned sites that they are required by law to prevent customers from accessing. These moves accord with a wider trend toward characterizing the freedom offered by the internet in terms of its apparently unfettered access to porn. They also demonstrate how this is increasingly becoming a means of extending the power of the state to intervene in the private— and especially sexual—affairs of its citizens. In the United States, the Supreme Court has consistently upheld legislation that requires all publicly funded institutions such as libraries and schools to filter sexually explicit material. The implementation of such legislation has had the effect of blocking access to information about women's health issues, gay and lesbian rights groups and sexual education for teenagers (The Citizen Lab, 2007).

In 2007, a proposed amendment to the U.K. Criminal Justice and Immigration Bill included a clause to criminalize the possession of "extreme pornographic images" and thus become known as the Dangerous Images Act. This sought to criminalize possession of representations of extreme sexual activity, which were defined as:

a. an act which threatens or appears to threaten a person's life
b. an act which results in or appears to result (or be likely to result) in serious injury to a person's anus, breasts or genitals
c. an act which involves or appears to involve sexual interference with a human corpse
d. a person performing or appearing to perform an act of intercourse or oral sex with an animal.[1]

The Act responded to a campaign following the murder of Jane Longhurst by Graham Coutts in Brighton in 2003, and to claims that Coutts was inspired by and addicted to extreme online pornography, particularly that featuring asphyxiation and necrophilia. It drew on the established figure of a porn user as a "truly depraved adult male" (Kipnis, 1996, p. 26) and a more recent figure of a cyberporn addict in the grip of a "solipsistic collapse" (Patterson in Williams, 2004a, p. 105). In August 2006 the Home Office published a report on the consultation process it had undertaken before the introduction of the Dangerous Images Act. This report offered an opportunity to assess the competing sets of interests identified as having a stake in the proposed legislation.

The report noted that many of those who wrote in support of the legislation, which included charities such as Barnados, religious groups, and professional bodies such as the British Association of Social Workers, "cited the increased availability of all types of pornography as reasons for the need for stronger legislation. They asserted that even mainstream pornography had a detrimental effect on society ... and that the government should not only legislate in relation to extreme pornography but should also take action against the increased prevalence of pornographic images not only on the internet, but also in top shelf magazines and in material broadcast on television and films" (Home Office, 2006, p. 9).

Many of the Act's supporters took advantage of this opportunity to express their desire to see stricter legislation with a reach far beyond that currently proposed. Their position drew on a popular myth for its characterization of porn as a corrupting flood: an unrestricted abundance in the face of which people, and most especially children, require protection. A key feature of the depoliticization effected by this myth is the way it obscures the extent to which the state already controls access to porn, and child porn in particular, as well as the internet more broadly.

Backlash is a coalition of groups that campaigned against The Act.[2] It ran a lively and informative Web site and successfully lobbied sexual minority groups, academics, and activists. A cornerstone of their campaign rested on the legal advice of Rabinder Singh QC, who suggested that "the legislation as proposed gives rise to real concerns as to its compatibility with an individual's rights under Articles 8 and 10 of the [European] Convention [on Human Rights]."[3] The Web site also displayed this quote from the ex-Prime Minster, Tony Blair, ostensibly to point up the hypocritical nature of New Labour in introducing The Dangerous Images Act: "there are areas in which the State ... no longer has a role ... It is not for the State to tell people that they cannot choose a different lifestyle, for example in issues to do with sexuality."[4]

Backlash pointed out that the acts specified in the proposed law might seem "distasteful," but argued that "it is worth remembering that a majority once took that view on homosexuality,"[5] and that "free societies do not criminalise people on grounds of taste."[6] Its campaign articulated a familiar politics resting on a presumed relationship between sexuality and a freedom anchored in individual choice and set against harm and danger.

It is this very notion of freedom that I want to investigate here. Backlash's rhetoric depends on a notion of sexual repression that has been rendered increasingly irrelevant by greater access to porn in the context of media proliferation and deregulation, and by the rise of ideologies of neoliberalism. The absence of critical and political engagement with the myth of freedom propagated by both the Act's supporters and its opponents degrades our understanding of the relationship between sexual freedom and power. To put it simply, the expanding availability of porn and state governments' ambiguous attitude to regulating it does not mean that we are becoming more sexually free. It is not sexual repression that we need to consider critically here, but the notions of freedom and plenitude bound up in current myths of porn.

The Dangerous Images Act is not the vanguard of a new sexual conservatism but of a continuing sexual liberalism offering choices and opportunities, as well as entailing responsibilities and regulation. The shift from criminalizing producers and distributors to criminalizing consumers accords with a wider trend in neoliberal governmentality: it is an intervention that abdicates State responsibility for the regulation of obscenity. The cornerstone of U.K. porn legislation remains the 1959 Obscene Publications Act—a law so gray as to be practically unenforceable, but one that every government since its introduction has failed to substantially revise. The Dangerous Images Act does not clarify the status of obscenity but, rather, continues to obfuscate the legality of porn. Where the new Act is distinctive is in its emphasis on the actions of individual consumers. As Graham Burchell has noted, whilst neoliberalism entails rolling back the responsibility of the State, it also entails the imposition of disciplinary measures that determine the conditions of selfhood within approved forms (1996, p. 27). Thus, in the context of the U.K. government's "hands-off" protection of online commerce—a trend we can also identify in government policy across Europe, Australia, and the United States—we can see the Dangerous

Images Act as an attempt to instill specific forms of "responsibilization" in "free" and "rational" subjects.

Myths of Freedom

The myth of sexual freedom obscures the operation of power. It is mythic because the freedom it proposes is a technique by which individuals are induced to constitute themselves in approved forms. It is a form of operating government at a distance, apparently dissociating formal political institutions from an enfranchised set of communities of interest, but actually specifying "the subjects of rule in a new way: as active individuals seeking to 'enterprise themselves,' to maximize their quality of life through acts of choice" (Rose, 1996, p. 57).

In a range of ways, neoliberalism offers us subjectivities and choices that propose new sexual freedoms, yet these foreclose sexuality to the sphere of economic enfranchisement. For example, postfeminist ideologies equate consumer choice with the emancipation of women. The power of this ideology can be seen in the extraordinary popularity of texts such as *Sex and the City* (1998–2004), and to a lesser extent *Bridget Jones's Diary* (2001). Rather than emancipating women, *Sex and the City* offers the fantasy of sexual fulfillment as a palliative for having to deal with heterosexual men, through an aspiration to "bourgeois bohemia" (Attwood, 2007a, p. 6) and through the "freedom" of shopping as a rational lifestyle choice. Here, freedom is divorced from material realities, and becomes imaginable only through the acquisition of new skills and responsibilities in relation to the exercise of sexual techniques and of taste.

Another example of an apparent expansion of freedom and choice is the legalization of civil partnership for gay and lesbian couples in the United Kingdom. Entitlement to equality with heterosexual couples is framed by the protection of lesbian and gay consumer power and by their exclusion from the full legal status of marriage. Civil partnerships enable the protection of financial assets, but in 2006 U.K. courts ruled that barring queers from marriage was justifiable discrimination in order to protect the notion of marriage "as a union between a man and a woman primarily with the aim of producing children." Here, access to the limited "rights" of civil partnership depends upon understanding the limits of those rights as defining access to pension and inheritance benefits. Similarly, the supposed rejuvenation of sexual activity offered by a new sexual pharmacology represents a search for new products at the expense of treating life threatening epidemics in the developing world, often also enshrining ideals of female passivity (Marshall, 2002; Marshall, 2006; Maddison, 2007). In the same way, the myth of "unlimited" choice of mainstream pornographies delivers porn as the "killer app" for new technologies and distribution modes: smart phones, streaming media, HD DVD, and so on.

Debates about pornography remain mired in myths of freedom and liberation, danger and threat. But the contexts for these myths and the real politics they obscure are rapidly changing: if we are to produce an adequate politics of porn and sexual expression, we must take account of them. Many activists and academics concerned with the fostering of sexual plurality and the radicalization of intimacy have tended to adopt an optimistic view of porn. But porn is a business, and porn production and consumption can never be separated from questions of economic power.

Since the introduction of the domestic VHS, porn has been a substantial and growing force in the media and entertainment sectors, quick to take advantage of new forms and modes of distribution, and integrated into the business plans and revenue streams of mainstream corporations (Maddison, 2004). Porn companies pioneered models of online commerce and for much of the 1990s were the only sectors of online media that were making money from charging for online content. In 1998 confidence in the profitability of porn was such that the editors of *The Economist* argued for locating "the greater part of the sex business where it ultimately belongs—as just another branch of the global entertainment industry."[7] Porn companies made significant investments in research and development for security and payment software that they marketed to the rest of the industry, and it seemed that pornography was indeed "the handmaiden of new technology."[8]

Porn has been a significant factor in driving the expansion of broadband, which has had a considerable impact on the national economies of the United States, Japan, South Korea, and most European countries. But this success has posed substantial challenges to the very companies who profitably transitioned from VHS and DVD retail and rental to online distribution. As bandwidth has become cheaper and the tools for online publication have become more accessible and easier to use, so the nature of the industry has changed and become less vertically integrated. The economic ascendancy of porn's biggest corporations is currently being threatened by slow adaptation to the challenges of peer-to-peer networks and user-generated content, a trend that can be identified across the media and entertainment sectors. New modes of distribution have spawned new forms of porn as well as enabling the emergence of new entrepreneurs. Commercial "amateur" and gonzo porn, cheaply produced and easily accessible, has become the staple of an ever-increasing plurality of sites, usually based on a subscription model, accompanied by a diverse culture of supporting discussion and fan sites catering for a range of sexual tastes. Of course, in this commercial sector, these diverse and proliferating varieties of porn are in fact assiduously standardized, and limited to predictable sexual desires ("teen sluts," "painful anal," "Asian whores," "bareback twinks," and so on).

As with the music industry, which has been equally complacent in its adaptation to new market conditions, major porn companies have taken an increasingly hawkish attitude to so-called piracy. Greg Piccionelli, a lawyer for porn producers, suggested in 2007 at a Piracy Conference for the Adult Industry, that the U.S. Digital Millennium Copyright Act, designed to protect intellectual property, is problematic for the industry precisely because it attempts to protect freedom of expression. Piccionelli worried that the internet would be "filtered down to the lowest common denominator of scum and villainy" and that this would "totally eviscerate intellectual property rights on the Web" (in Kernes, 2007). As Barthes suggests, myth immunizes the collective imagination "by means of a small inoculation of acknowledged evil" and "thus protects it against the risk of a generalized subversion" (Barthes, 1993, p. 164). Here, the myth of pornographic freedom is secured by an inoculation of acknowledged evil, the "scum and villainy": pirates and file-sharers. What is at risk is that subjects will fail to exercise individual "choice" as consumers of appropriately commodified artifacts.

Thus far, I have considered myths of pornographic plenitude and abundance, and questioned these in the context of neoliberalism. Next, I want to examine what is probably the most powerful and pervasive myth of plenitude in relation to pornography—the myth of child porn.

Myths of Child Porn

As I have shown, in the calls for increased legislation against porn by Concerned Women for America and supporters of the Dangerous Images Act, a conservative antiporn position draws on a popular myth for its characterization of porn as a corrupting flood: an unrestricted abundance from which we require protection. This myth obscures the extent to which the state already controls access to porn and to the internet. It also obscures a contradiction in the way that children and sexuality are represented. On the one hand, the exploitation of "tween" markets by commodity capital rests on an intensification of the sexualization of children. At the same time, discourses of childhood innocence work to configure the family as a "micro-moral domain" (Rose, 1996, p. 57) for the protection of children.

Crucial to the functioning of this unstable and contradictory configuration is the internet child pornographer who is the "figure for emergencies" (Barthes, 1993, p. 166), the abject-outsider. His predatory presence as Other legitimates the routine, "normal" sexualization of children by naturalizing it, and at the same time keeps them off the dangerous streets, at home in front of the TV or the games console, consuming goods and services. But, as a report published in Australia suggests, "One of the more horrifying conclusions to have emerged from the sexual abuse field in the past 20 years is the fact that the least safe place for children is, in fact, their own home" (McCarthy, n.d). In the United States, it is estimated that there are around nine million incidents of child maltreatment per year, and the evidence suggests that most perpetrators are biological parents in two parent households.[9] Three-quarters of all child abductions are committed by family members or acquaintances of the child.[10] In terms of actual danger to children's welfare, the stranger pedophile is a myth.

Despite such clear evidence, Project Safe Childhood, a recent initiative of the U.S. Department of Justice, suggests that the "danger of the production, distribution, and possession of child pornography is … dramatic and disturbing" and that the "response to these growing problems … must recognize the need for a broad, community-based effort to protect our children and to guarantee to future generations the opportunities of the American dream."[11] This rhetoric is symptomatic of "depoliticized speech" and exemplifies what Barthes describes as "the dream of the contemporary bourgeois world" (1993, p. 164). The child pornographer is the Other; exotic and scandalous. He is, in Barthes' words "a spectacle, a clown … relegated to the confines of humanity, [where] he no longer threatens the security of the home" (1993, p. 166). This is effected by a tautology (child pornography is dangerous *because* it is dramatic and disturbing) that doesn't deny reality (children are a bourgeois invention; children are routinely and continuously exploited by and sexualized by capital) but instead "gives [it] a clarity which is not that of an explanation but that of a statement of fact" (1993, p. 156). The specter of child porn becomes a way of securing a state of crisis, against which the American dream must be protected.

The myth of child porn also threatens an already tenuous notion of online privacy, and remains an effective instrument for those who seek the legislative means by which state agencies can gain access to data held by sites and ISPs. In 2006 the European Union (EU) passed the Data Retention Directive, stipulating that telecommunications companies and

ISPs should keep records of all communications for 24 months. Similar moves have been made in the United States, following the U.S. Justice Department's recommendation to ISPs; "You're going to have to start thinking about data retention if you don't want people to think you're soft on child porn" (McCullagh, 2005). In 2007 the U.S. Attorney General proposed a Data Retention law for telecommunications providers and internet service providers, in line with the EU, and in the interest of helping to prosecute child pornographers. In the same year the U.S. Securing Adolescents from Exploitation Online Act was rushed through the House of Representatives. The Act requires anyone offering an open wi-fi connection to report illegal images or face fines of up to $300,000. Its supporters claim that child porn is a $5 billion a year business and a "global epidemic" (McCullagh, 2007a and 2007b). Similar legislation is planned that would oblige federally funded schools and libraries to prevent children from accessing social networking sites. According to House Representative Michael Fitzpatrick, MySpace and its like "have become a haven for online sexual predators who have made these corners of the Web their own virtual hunting ground" (McCullagh, 2006).

In Australia, myths of porn and child abuse have been used to achieve even wider forms of state repression. In 2007, a report entitled *Little Children Are Sacred* (Wild & Anderson) addressed the problems of child poverty, deprivation, and abuse in Aboriginal communities in the Northern Territories. It was followed by the announcement of an Emergency Response, apparently designed to address the problems highlighted in the report. Yet, the report's authors argue that this Response overlooks the systemic causes of indigenous poverty, instead highlighting child abuse, drug addiction, domestic violence, and porn use in order to justify measures that will enable the government to remove land rights from Aboriginal communities. The announcement of an $189 million antipornography initiative accompanied the Emergency Response, to fund ISP- and PC-based filtering, education campaigns, and a consultancy designed to find ways of addressing "the use of social networking Web sites by predators to contact and groom children via the internet" (Ryan,

2007). Here, as elsewhere, the myth of child porn operates as a powerful lever to exploit the resources of the IT industry while appeasing socially conservative constituencies.

The Myth of Freedom: A Politics of Porn?

Uses of the myth of child porn demand a political response, yet current pro-porn and anticensorship activism and rhetoric uniformly accedes to the force of the myth. Backlash's response to the argument that legislation against extreme porn is necessary because children need protection is that there are lots of other things "children shouldn't see." In the context of lobbying against a law that does not directly tackle child porn, such a statement accedes to the common sense of protecting children when the threat to their welfare is mythically external and exotic (what *are* these "things" they shouldn't see?). The mainstream porn industry takes a similar stance: industry lawyer Greg Piccionelli blames child porn on "pirates" who can be defeated by copyright protection (Kernes, 2007). The Free Speech Coalition, the American porn industry's trade association and lobby group, argues that it is antiporn "zealots" who expose children to porn through their extremist rhetoric, and that child porn is "a blight that must be vigorously combated by the public and private sectors working together" (2007, p. 1, 13). These positions strategically negotiate the power of the myth of child porn by assimilating it and rearticulating its meaning in their own terms.

Although governments and politicians have seized the myth of child porn as justification for increasing legislative control of the internet, sexual freedom organizations and anticensorship groups focus on issues of consent and personal freedom. In the meantime, as Zygmunt Bauman has argued, depictions of the family home are increasingly haunted by a "spectre of sex" and children are represented as "always and everywhere sexual objects" (1998, p. 30). Child porn becomes a fetish which, to use Zizek's term (1997, p. 102), is "dissipated": it becomes more apparent and less material, increasingly "spectral," and yet more powerful. There is a morbid fixation on the concept of child porn coupled with the absence of the object itself. Although child porn pervades populist news discourse and political rhetoric, it is literally dematerialized: marked by prurient pixellated images in news broadcasts, and by the hyperbole of politicians (a "$5 billion epidemic"). As a fetish it achieves power through its oxymoronic status: to see it, to know its existence is to be guilty; one can only remain free from its taint by being ignorant of its existence and vociferous in its denunciation. Only the Other knows it, and to see it is to become Other. All the while, the fetish masks institutional and systemic abuses of children in the form of structural adjustment policies, moral and religious conditions placed on development aid, genocide, ethnic cleansing, mass migration, pharmaceutical experimentation, and trafficking.

The myth of child porn is ethically and structurally distinct from a concern for the welfare of the child, in the same way that the U.K. government's concern with extreme internet porn has little to do with a concern for the welfare of women or other alleged "victims" of pornographic representation. Opposing censorship and antiporn legislation on the basis of the individual's right to free choice not only misses the point but also depoliticizes "freedom" and "choice." The myth of child porn works to settle complex tensions in the fabric of subjectification practiced by neoliberal governmentality. Individuals are obliged to govern themselves at a distance from political structures and to bear the responsibility of the contradictions of sexualization and pedophilia. We are encouraged to measure ourselves against myths of freedom rather than within networks of wider social obligation and responsibility. If we are to develop an effective politics of porn, we need a better understanding of the myths that are constructed around it and of the materiality of online infrastructure and the struggles over its control. Myths of pornographic abundance make us subjects of neoliberalism, seeking pleasure and desire in plenitude, and yet subject to a demand for rigorous self-governance. If we are to make significant progress in opposing the forces that diminish sociality and sexual plurality we must develop keener critical awareness of the mythic nature of the freedoms and choices offered to us in the operation of maintaining government at a distance.

Notes

1.   http://www.justice.gov.uk/publications/criminal-justice-bill.htm. Accessed 20 January 2009.

2.   The coalition comprises: Feminists Against Censorship, Unfettered (a BDSM advocacy group), Ofwatch (which represents viewers of adult entertainment), The Spanner Trust (an SM advocacy group set up in the aftermath of the arrests resulting from Operation Spanner in 1990), The Libertarian Alliance, The Campaign Against Censorship, The Sexual Freedom Coalition, The Society for Individual Freedom, SM Dykes Manchester, and the International Union of Sex Workers.

3.   http://www.backlash-uk.org.uk/time.html. Accessed 20 January 2009.

4.   http://www.backlash-uk.org.uk/news.html. Accessed 20 January 2009.

5.   http://www.backlash-uk.org.uk/brief609.pdf. Accessed 20 January 2009.

6.   http://www.backlash-uk.org.uk/summary0610.html. Accessed 20 January 2009.

7.   "The Sex Industry: Giving the Customer What He Wants," *The Economist*, 14 February 1998, pp. 21–23.

8.   BBC News Online Technology Correspondent, "Will Porn Kick-Start the Video Phone Revolution?," http://news.bbc.co.uk/1/hi/technology/2992914.stm. Accessed 1 February 2008.

9.   http://www.villageskids.org/ca_stats.php. Accessed 20 January 2009.

10. http://sexoffenderissues.blogspot.com/2008/03/stranger-danger-shocking-tv-test-flawed.html. Accessed 20 January 2009.

11. http://www.projectsafechildhood.gov/. Accessed 20 January 2009.

Chapter 2

Child Pornography:
Classifications and Conceptualizations
Adam Stapleton

The conceptualization of child pornography is becoming increasingly complex: a complexity related both to the technologies that are used to transmit it, and to the typologies and statutes used to define it. The situation is problematized further by the legacy of a moral panic that has made the subject extremely difficult to discuss and worked to obscure the question of what child pornography is and how it is related to the sexual abuse of children. However, there are important distinctions to observe within the range of materials that have been construed as "child pornography," and it is crucial that we understand these if we are to comprehend the extent to which sexualized images of children have become part of the global mediascape.

This chapter summarizes existing research on child pornography, and describes the range and nature of child pornography materials online and the technologies that are used to distribute them. It examines the construction of the category of "child pornography" and its development alongside media technologies, discourses about perversion, and legislation, highlighting the areas that need to be addressed through further research.

Defining and Framing Child Pornography

As Healy suggests (1996), "the question of what constitutes child pornography is extraordinarily complex. Standards that are applied in each society or country are highly subjective and are contingent upon differing moral, cultural, sexual, social, and religious beliefs that do not readily translate into law."[1] However, generally speaking, the category of "child pornography" depends on a view of childhood as a "natural, universal and biologically inherent period of human development" (Robinson, 2008, p. 115), imagined as an age of innocence that is vulnerable to the threat of deviant sexuality. It also depends on a view of the mass media as having the potential to harm and corrupt children (Kincaid, 1998; Heins, 2001; Levine, 2002; Robinson, 2008). Video games, television, the VCR, comic books, and nickelodeons have all been cast in this way (Postman, 1994, p. 81; Heins, 2001, pp. 52–55, 208–213), but moral panics about child pornography have become particularly powerful because of the ways in which they relate concerns about the innocence of children and the corrupting power of media to a notion of evil embodied in the figure of the pedophile. Individual producers and texts become understood within the parameters of a discursively generated model of pedophilia and child pornography, even retroactively so. For example, Charles Dodgson (also known as Lewis Carroll) has been described as a pedophile because of his habit of photographing young girls (Hacking, 1999, pp. 156–162), although his actions would not have given rise to such a claim during the period in which he lived.

Notions of child abuse and child pornography have been inextricably linked since the 1970s and share a symbiotic relationship that reinforces the evil of each category. Public knowledge of child pornography in the 1970s worked to replace an existing view of pedophiles as "confused individuals succumbing to a warped impulse" with one of individuals with an interest in exploiting and dehumanizing children (Jenkins, 1998, p. 145). The act of producing and distributing child pornography came to be seen as demonstrating the premeditated and systematic abuse of children, while its purchase and collection was seen to imply that pedophiles who did not commit contact offences were encouraging its production, and, by extension, child abuse.

This shift, in conjunction with the efforts of some pedophiles to form associations such as NAMBLA (North American Man Boy Love Association) and PIE (Paedophile Information Exchange), helped to fuel a moral panic around pedophilia and to create a particular figure of the "pedophile" (Jenkins, 1998, pp. 160–163; Critcher, 2003; Angelides,

2005; O'Donnell & Milner, 2007, pp. 9–15). This undermined the emerging knowledge that the sexual abuse of children was something that frequently occurred within the home, focusing attention instead on "stranger danger" and the "pedophile ring" (Kincaid, 1998, pp. 180–185; Kitzinger, 2004, pp. 34–37, 129–136). Concerns about children's vulnerability to kidnapping, serial murder, and organized sex rings were foregrounded and "excessive claims were made about the size and profitability of the trade" and about "vast, tightly organized pedophile rings" (Jenkins, 2001, pp. 33–35).

The moral panic revived in the late 1990s (Thomas, 2005, p. 21), when concerns about sexual predators "increased in number and intensity" and missing children, abduction, and assault narratives became recurring themes in news and television drama in the United States (Kleinhans, 2004, p. 72). Attention shifted from actual acts of sex abuse to their representation, and away from the image "as a document of an event (realism) to questions of intent (communication) and the viewer's act of reading the image (reception, interpretation)" (Kleinhans, 2004, p. 73). Since then, news reporting of pedophilia has increasingly focused on the internet, drawing on a view of young people as "vulnerable and underdeveloped, incapable of informed choice about mass media use or sexual activity" (Critcher, 2003, p. 156).

Today, two accounts of the pedophile—the intrafamilial abuser or ordinary man, and the extrafamilial abuser or strange man, appear to coexist in competition in the public imagination, but they are reconciled to some extent through the image of the online sexual abuser as a monstrous family man who allows strangers to abuse his daughter vicariously through the production and dissemination of online child pornography. He is inherently "evil"; beyond "sick" (Critcher, 2003, pp. 114, 117); "removed from the species, rendered unknowable" (Kincaid, 1998, p. 88). An emphasis on the deviant gaze of the pedophile and on his fondness for all kinds of images of children has also impacted on the way that child pornography has come to be understood; all images of children now have the potential to be seen as child pornography, and child pornography can only be understood in an ad hoc way through the discovery of a collection of images that are in the possession of a "pedophile."

The categories of "child pornography" and the "pedophile" are dynamic and are constructed by groups that have the power to make pronouncements about "normal" and "perverted" sexuality. Their "truth" is established through "a system of ordered procedures for the production, regulation, distribution, circulation of statements" (Foucault, 1984, p. 74). They are produced by government-sanctioned bodies and academic institutions, mainly drawing on the disciplines of criminology, psychology, and legal studies. Law enforcement bodies and related groups such as NMCEC (the National Center for Missing and Exploited Children) and COPINE (Combating Paedophile Information Networks in Europe) also have an active role in disseminating information to the public. Agencies such as NCMEC and Interpol amass large collections of child pornography in order to build databases, primarily for the purposes of victim identification. In the process, child porn becomes knowable in highly circumscribed ways. The roles that are played by institutions and by individuals in the construction of child pornography are framed within an "imaginary scenario" of danger and rescue (Kendrick, 1996, p. xiii). Institutions are constructed as accountable and trustworthy in a manner that is denied to individuals who can only be perceived as villains or victims. The process of recognizing "child pornography" becomes one in which one is either involved in its production or its prohibition.

Child Pornography Materials

What is child pornography? It is spoken of, but not shown, except in brief flashes in the media where there is little to anchor the term, and little in terms of shared cultural experience or knowledge to help the viewer contextualize it. Its definition is constituted through the pronouncements of various professional bodies and groups. The United States and the

United Kingdom have been most active in defining child pornography, while important cases in Australia and Canada have worked to broaden its meaning and application.

Child pornography is outlawed under various state and federal statutes.[2] In Australia, for example, it is defined as:

material that depicts or describes (or appears to depict or describe), in a manner that would in all the circumstances cause offence to reasonable persons, a person who is (or appears to be) a child:

   a.   engaged in sexual activity, or
   b.   in a sexual context, or
   c.   as the victim of torture, cruelty or physical abuse
        (whether or not in a sexual context).

The definition of child pornography is dependent on further definitions, of "child" and "pornography," both of which are contingent, changing over time and across place. These may be supplemented by additional categories; "indicative ... material depicting clothed children, which suggests a sexual interest in children," "indecent ... material depicting naked children which suggests a sexual interest in children," and "obscene ... material which depicts children in explicit sexual acts (Taylor & Quayle, 2003, p. 27). The lack of precision and level of contingency in all of these definitions has been heightened by the increased reliance on the notion of the perverse gaze of the "pedophile" for understanding what "child pornography" is. This makes it enormously difficult to construct a coherent system for classifying child pornography.

A more detailed system, the COPINE scale, devised by Taylor et al. (2001), provides another way of categorizing the range of depictions that may be found in pedophile picture collections, and that, contextualized by the way in which the material is used, may be regarded as child pornography.

Level	Name	Description of Picture Qualities
1	Indicative	Nonerotic and nonsexualized pictures showing children in their underwear, swimming costumes, and so on, from either commercial sources or family albums; pictures of children playing in normal settings, in which the context or organization of pictures by the collector indicates inappropriateness.
2	Nudist	Pictures of naked or seminaked children in appropriate nudist settings, and from legitimate sources.
3	Erotica	Surreptitiously taken photographs of children in play areas or other safe environments showing either underwear or varying degrees of nakedness.
4	Posing	Deliberately posed pictures of children fully clothed, partially clothed or naked (in which the amount, context, and organization suggests sexual interest)
5	Erotic posing	Deliberately posed pictures of fully clothed, partially clothed, or naked children in sexualized or provocative poses.

Level	Name	Description of Picture Qualities
6	Explicit erotic posing	Pictures emphasizing genital areas where the child is either naked, partially clothed, or fully clothed.
7	Explicit sexual activity	Pictures involving touching, mutual and self-masturbation, oral sex, and intercourse not involving an adult.
8	Assault	Pictures of children being subjected to a sexual assault, involving digital touching, involving an adult
9	Gross assault	Grossly obscene pictures of sexual assault, involving penetrative sex, masturbation, or oral sex, involving an adult.
10	Sadistic/ bestiality	Pictures showing a child being tied, bound, beaten, whipped, or otherwise subjected to something that implies pain. Pictures in which an animal is involved in some form of sexual behavior with a child.

Images that are classed at levels 5, 6, and above would come under the legal definition of child pornography in most jurisdictions, although there is some discretion to refrain from classifying an image at these levels as legally objectionable if it can be considered to have "artistic merit" or scientific or educational value. Levels 1 to 4 are more problematic because of the wide range of contexts in which these kinds of images appear. As Higonnet notes, pictures of children "seem to be everywhere, made by everyone" (1998, p. 87), and levels 1 to 4 images are common in family photography or other kinds of "human ephemera" (Richards, 2002, p. 2), as well as in advertising and art. On occasion, these result in tabloid media outrage or arrests, although the law appears to be unable to formulate a coherent statement about them (Higonnet, 1998, pp. 87–107; O'Toole, 1998, pp. 217–245; Rubin et al., 2006, pp. 213–227). However, they remain problematic because the nature of reproduction facilitates the separation of production and intent from the consumption of images, making it difficult to know, conclusively, what purpose an image is meant to have. Instead of making a judgment about the content of such images, we are increasingly expected to "look at pictures as a paedophile would" (Adler, 2006, p. 233) in order to see it as child pornography.

The COPINE scale is a useful tool for suggesting materials that may be construed as forms of pornography for a pedophile. However, its focus on what is depicted, rather than on the level of offence for the person depicted in the image, makes it problematic, particularly in the early levels of the scale, because of the lack of recognition of differences in how and why images are produced. Early legislation, such as the U.K. Protection of Children Act of 1978, explicitly addressed this issue, viewing the production of indecent images as a victimizing process for the participant, and seeing other images, such as those depicting "simple nudity," as clearly distinct from these (Thompson & Williams, 2004, p. 120).

This focus on the relation of images to abuse has become less clear more recently, for example, in the claim that "the crimes of possession, and making or distribution of child pornography, whether virtual or not, are crimes not only against a particular child, but against all children" (Quayle et al., 2008, p. 20). The term "child pornography" has also been criticized for implying legitimacy or consent on the part of the victim, and it has been proposed that "abusive images" is a more fitting description. However, there are a number of problems with this. Referring to "child pornography" as "abusive images" serves to obscure the range of materials that meet the legal definition of "child pornography," and makes it unclear who is abused, and in what way, through their production and distribution. Is the act of recording images of children an inherently abusive process? Is it only when the producer does so for the purposes of sexual gratification that it becomes abusive? Is it an abusive experience for a viewer to either voluntarily or inadvertently be exposed to the material?

This lack of clarity is also found in debates about what kind of artistic images of children constitute child pornography, particularly in the field of photography. In the United States, the photography of Sally Mann, Jock Sturges, David Hamilton, and Robert Mapplethorpe aroused public concern throughout the 1990s. In 2007, an image by Nan Goldin was removed from a U.K. gallery, and in Australia in 2008, the work of Bill Henson and Polixeni Papapetrou attracted controversy (Higonnet, 1998; Atkins & Mintcheva, 2006; Marr, 2008). Images of nudity and the depiction of budding breasts seem to be of particular and continuing concern to some American viewers. Although these do not satisfy the criteria of indecency in a legal sense, they have been regarded as suspect, either because their recording is seen as a betrayal of the subject, irrespective of their consent or the artist's intentions, or because the image could be viewed by the "wrong" kind of person with the "wrong" kind of feelings.

Historically, pornography was a category of writing (Hunt, 1993, p. 13), and although written child pornography is not often the subject of public debate, there is legislation in many countries to prohibit its dissemination.[3] More often, it has been images and videos that have been the focus of concern because of the way they may act as "records of abuse" (Taylor & Quayle, 2003, pp. 21–26). Today, an expanding range of materials are becoming classed as child pornography. Pseudo–child pornography is material that has been digitally manipulated so that images of children are combined with pornography, or are otherwise recontextualized so that they become indecent (Taylor & Quayle, 2003, pp. 37–38). Virtual child pornography is material that has been entirely constructed from an artist's imagination, for example, in drawings or cartoons such as those in "lolicon"[4] and "yaoi"[5] comic books.

Pseudo and virtual forms of child pornography may not be a record of sexual abuse, or the inappropriate, lascivious display of the anogenital region, but they are becoming subject to legislation in some circumstances. Lolicon and yaoi materials are not prohibited in countries such as Japan or the United States, but they fall under the legal definition of child pornography in Canada and in Australia, where, in December 2008, a court found that images resembling minors from the TV series *The Simpsons*, engaged in sexual acts, were child pornography,[6] even though it was accepted that these were depictions of imaginary persons. This development of legislation to encompass not only the actual but the virtual broadens the notion of "child pornography" still further, increasing the difficulty of defining it and obscuring the rationale for its prohibition.

Distributing Child Pornography

Making images of children has a long history. Charles Dodgson, often alleged to be a child pornographer, began his collection of photographs in 1867 (Tate, 1990, p. 37; Jenkins, 2001, p. 31; Cooper, 2005, p. 11; O'Donnell & Milner, 2007, pp. 4, 67), taking pictures of girls as young as six in various states of undress. Dodgson's photographs were viewed as images of "natural innocence," relating to the Romantic conceptualization of childhood that was prevalent at the time (Mavor, 1995, p. 9; Higonnet, 1998, pp. 109–126). Mavor has proposed that "the child and the photograph were commodified, fetishised, developed alongside each other" (1995, p. 3). The development of the definition of the "child," alongside the invention of new ways to capture and reproduce images, also facilitated the emergence of the category of images that would come to be prohibited under child pornography legislation.

There is a significant gap in knowledge between the activities of photographers such as Dodgson and the commercial production of child pornography from 1969 when magazines such as *Children Love, Lollitots,* and *Bambina Sex* appeared in Denmark, the Netherlands, and the United States, where they were disguised as European imports, until the end of the 1970s (Tate, 1990; Jenkins, 1998; O'Toole, 1999, p. 221; Califia, 2000, pp. 77–78). The magazines focused primarily on nudity and genital display, with some images of sexual acts between children and between children and adults (Jenkins, 1998, p. 146), and often contained material that had been produced by pedophiles for their own sexual gratification, as well as for payment or a subscription to the magazine (Tate, 1990, p. 59). Danish companies such as Rodox/Color Climax began to produce pornographic loop films and photographs in 1971 (Tate, 1990, p. 46), fueling a tendency toward increasingly explicit material, as profiteers fought not only to meet consumer demand but also to distinguish their products from those of their competitors. This material was expensive and, although allegedly available in most major cities in the developed world, difficult to find (Tate, 1990; Jenkins, 2001).

Child pornography began to elicit a lot of negative media attention in the late 1970s, initially in response to a feminist critique of child sexual abuse, and later as part of a moral panic focused on "stranger danger" (Jenkins, 1998). It was something tangible to set against the social denial of the prevalence of child sex abuse and was important in making this visible. Materials that promoted sexual abuse became increasingly unacceptable, catalyzing the development of legislation throughout the West to prohibit the production and distribution of child pornography. Child pornography continued to be produced commercially in Japan until 1999 and today it remains legal to possess it, while a large market for lolicon comics and "junior idol" magazines and films remains. Although the former does not depict real persons and the latter is not sexually explicit or even indecent, they would both be likely to meet the legal definition of child pornography in countries such as Australia. There is anecdotal evidence to suggest that commercial material is being produced in other parts of Asia, such as Indonesia, and other areas of the world such as Russia and Belarus, but the exact nature of this material has not been clearly substantiated.[7]

When child pornography was part of a material, analog system, it was relatively easy to ensure that it remained scarce and inaccessible to all but the most ardent collectors. It had to be distributed through the postal service in a clandestine manner and each magazine intercepted by a postal inspector was one more magazine removed from circulation. With the expansion of the internet, child pornography has become virtual, rather than material, circulating through a digital system.

It has been claimed that there are an astounding 100,000 Web sites offering child pornography for sale, although more conservative estimates are given by U.S. Customs of 200–1,700 sites, and by the Internet Watch Foundation of approximately 2,200 sites in 2007[8]. In May 2004, the COPINE database held 700,000 child pornography images that had been retrieved (Holland, 2005). Yet, as Jenkins notes, there is a "stunning lack of available information on the current realities of child porn" (2001, p. 10). His own study, the most detailed account of the trade in child porn to date, suggests that "although pedophile interests and images account for only a small proportion of life on the Web," there is "still a substantial volume, maintained by a small but very active underworld" (2001, p. 51) of perhaps "tens of thousands worldwide," together with "a significant number of casual browsers" (2001, p. 4).

In his detailed ethnography of a concealed site, the "Maestro" bulletin board, Jenkins (2001) described his discovery of a bold subculture of pedophiles. Places like the Maestro board are not easily accessible, its address only becoming apparent after prolonged loitering at other locations such as e-groups dedicated to swapping "loli" images.

Discovering the board would be a positive indication that the participant might have the requisite skills to develop their "hobby." Active engagement on the Maestro board required participants to become familiar with different practices such as disk encryption, IP obfuscation through a proxy server, and joining large files that had been split for ease of circulation. To advance within the subculture required technical ability; to learn how to obtain Web space where illicit material could be uploaded for redistribution, or perhaps hack a site offering commercial child pornography, opening a "backdoor" to the observers at the bulletin board. Unsurprisingly, the most effective way of "rising in the ranks" would be to produce new material for circulation. As one poster at the Maestro board suggested, "don't be shy, get snapping and contributing" (Jenkins, 2001, p. 95).

Online child porn communities like this form a "bandit culture" representing a new kind of organization, "made possible by novel forms of technology and characterized by types of interaction that would have been inconceivable only a few years ago" (Jenkins, 2001, p. 7). They are set apart from other places where commercial pornography is distributed, and from a variety of visible and more accessible porn gift-economies that cater to specialist sexual interests and subcultures. Child pornography is shared within hidden communities, typically through bulletin boards, newsgroups, and message boards (Jenkins, 2001, p. 20). Although newsgroups are relatively accessible to anyone, access to bulletin boards and message boards often require some form of invitation or knowledge that might lead the user to more clandestine areas, unobservable via search engines, for the trading of child pornography (Jenkins, 2001, pp. 59–67).

More recent technological developments have given child pornography even wider distribution through other areas of the internet. Koontz describes a study that put 12 search terms known to be associated with child pornography into the then popular P2P (peer-to-peer) application KaZaA. Forty-two percent of the files obtained in this way conformed to the U.S. legal definition of child pornography (2003, pp. 79–81). The development of P2P technologies has lowered the barriers of access to child pornography (Trifiletti, 2005, p. 623), and has changed the way in which it is circulated. In the past, there was a clear distinction between those who simply consumed child pornography and those who were also involved in its production and distribution. This distinction enabled a clear hierarchy to develop within the subculture and aspects of this remain in groups of contact offenders that share material with one another before it reaches a wider audience on the internet. Progression within that hierarchy is, according to "Pirra8" of the Maestro board, "newbie, lurker, regular, chat member, poster, newsgroup poster, trader, wise one. Takes about a year to get to be a wise one. After that, you might get to be Admin, create your own paysite, or become an underworld guru" (in Jenkins, 2001, p. 94). However, the nature of P2P has undermined the linearity of this hierarchy because users are already sharing portions of files before their download has completed, thus complicating ideas about the point at which a user can be described as "possessing" the illicit material; a radical shift from the structure that Pirra8 describes.

Darknet technologies such as Freenet or other encrypted forms of internet such as Privoxy and The Onion Ring (TOR) are probably the most discreet ways of sharing child pornography with a select group. It is likely that other modes such as File Transfer Protocol (FTP) or P2P clients such as WinMX, Limewire, and eMule are also used for private exchange between producers and traders, with material then released into the wider subculture through Usenet, the World Wide Web, and P2P clients. Various degrees of anonymity are available in all of these.

The threat of social stigmatization and criminal prosecution has made the use of technology to anonymize the circulation of child pornography increasingly complex. There is a view within the subculture that people are only arrested if they behave foolishly, in a way that draws attention to themselves; a "Darwinian function," ensuring the removal of "those least fit to adapt and survive" and ensuring "the efficiency of those who remain" (Jenkins, 2001, pp. 14–17). However, producing child pornography, particularly when it contains details that reveal the likely location of the victim or perpetrator, undermines the utility of technologies to maintain anonymity and disguise (Sher, 2007). Producers of child pornography cannot escape the fact that, no matter how cautious they are, their propensity to share the proof of their crimes may return to haunt them.

Mode of distribution and choice of media affects whether particular materials are categorized as child pornography. Images that may be acceptable within the context of an art gallery may become unacceptable if circulated on the internet (Marr, 2008, pp. 68–69). Images once seen as "innocent" may later become "erotic" (Cooper, 2006, p. 11), while images and narratives that are acceptable in one culture may fit the legal definition of child pornography in another (McLelland, 2005). Internet technologies have added to the complexity of this situation. They have increased the accessibility and visibility of the pedophile subculture. They have also further complicated the distinction between harmless and harmful images, and problematized the notion of possession itself. Technologies such as P2P networks blur the lines between possession and distribution and there has also been some debate as to whether downloading an image is an act of possession or production—individuals who have downloaded child pornography have been charged with "making an indecent image" (Thompson & Williams, 2004, pp. 120–123).

Users and Abusers

The appeal of using the internet for sexual purposes has been attributed to the "Triple A engine" of accessibility, affordability, and assumed anonymity (Cooper, 1998). Users can access a wide variety of media without a high level of technical expertise or income, and the illusion of anonymity may encourage them to indulge desires that they feel unable to express elsewhere. This may explain why child pornography has proliferated so vigorously online; a growth that has exacerbated demands for law enforcement agencies to address the problem effectively.

The growth in demand for enforcement is also the result of media interest in child pornography that tends to fabricate a disproportionate relationship between child pornography and child sex abuse (Meyer, 2007, pp. 123–131; Sheldon & Howitt, 2007, pp. 26–27). Media reports of international law enforcement cooperation to break "child porn rings" and rescue endangered children foster the impression that this is an effective way of addressing the sexual abuse of children. Yet one analysis of 14 investigations found that two were the result of child disclosure, two were the result of public tips, seven came from proactive monitoring of the internet, and three were acquired in the course of other investigations (Holland, 2005, p. 79). Rings such as "W0nderland," "Kiddypics & Kiddyvids," or "Kids—The Light of our Lives" were broken as a result of victim disclosure, which allows agents to access a group and impersonate an arrested perpetrator until a coordinated sets of arrests can be arranged (Jenkins, 2001, p. 78; Sher, 2007, pp. 242–266).

However, the identification and rescue of victims of online child pornography is not necessarily an accurate reflection of the success of child protection efforts. The N-JOV study in the United States in 2000 discovered that almost 90 percent of child pornography production cases began as child sexual abuse cases, and these 402 cases should be compared to the 65,000 arrests that were made in the same year for sex crimes against children that did *not* involve the production of child pornography (Wolak et al., 2005, p. 45). Whilst there were around 87,000 reports of sexual abuse in the United States, approximately 25,000 children were subject to medical neglect, 66,000 were subject to psychological maltreatment, 143,000 suffered "other abuse," 166,000 were subject to physical abuse, and more than half a million suffered from neglect.[9]

It is also important to maintain an accurate view of who the producers of child pornography are. Although the media present child pornographers as strange outsiders, the evidence suggests that child pornography is much more often produced by adults who children know. The images of

"Helena," the discovery of which led to Operation Cathedral in 1996, were allegedly produced by her stepfather (Jenkins, 2001, pp. 2, 78; O'Donnell & Milner, 2007, pp. 38–39). The main victim in the KG/KX series investigated in 2001, "Inga," was the daughter of the perpetrator (Jenkins, 2001, pp. 2, 103–105; Holland, 2005, p. 80), Eggert Jensen, who was later arrested with his wife (O'Donnell & Milner, 2007, p. 53; Sher, 2007, pp. 78–91). Mark Langham, arrested in 2005 in connection with the pornography that he distributed via the Kiddypics & Kiddyvids chatroom in WinMX, made that pornography with his two stepchildren and two other children with whom he was acquainted (Sher, 2007, pp. 242–266). The N-JOV study found that 37 percent of child pornography was produced by family members, 36 percent by acquaintances of the victims, 22 percent by persons related via online relationship, and 5 percent by strangers. This is not surprising, given that an intrafamilial setting is the most common venue for the sexual abuse of children, with acquaintance abuse a close second.

There is significant evidence to suggest that collecting child pornography may be an indicator of pedophilic interest, perhaps more so than committing sexual offences against a child (Seto et al., 2006, pp. 613). Yet the link between searching for and collecting child pornography and the commission of sexual offences against children remains unclear. As child pornography disseminates more widely through the internet, it is increasingly possible for a casual browser to gain access to it without needing to participate in the kind of subculture that Jenkins (2001) describes. At the same time, the evidence suggests that child pornography production continues to be related to the sexual abuse of children by adults who know them.

The problems of building a consensus as to what constitutes child pornography is complicated by narratives that constitute children as "innocent" and "endangered" and pedophiles as "monstrous." A discourse in which sexual danger, the internet, and children are linked has remained intact since the moral panics of the 1990s. Concerns about children and sex have increasingly focused on "sexualised *images* of children, including child pornography," as part of a broader shift in the ways that "discourse around sexuality ... has focused more and more on visual representations" (Kleinhans, 2004, p. 71), increasingly obscuring the material abuse of children.

It has been argued that discourses about child pornography not only fail to protect children, but that they also may work to construct a world "in which we are enthralled—anguished, enticed, bombarded by the spectacle of the sexual child" (Adler, 2001, p. 209). The hypocrisy of the cultural preoccupation with child pornography, alongside the widespread sexualization of children that has been referred to as "corporate paedophilia" (Rush & La Nauze, 2006), or a "Lolita Effect" (Durham, 2008), is evident. Moral panics about pedophilia may well be a way of displacing anxieties about social and technological shifts (Levine, 2002) and about sexualization itself. As Silverman and Wilson note, the "discovery" of the pedophile occurred at exactly the same time as this process of sexualizing children appeared to gain pace (2002, p. 182).

New media technologies, such as digital cameras, webcams, the internet, and mobile phones now enable minors to voluntarily produce, distribute, and collect images that fall within the legal definition of child pornography. This has generated some degree of alarm. Some argue that it is evidence of the way in which children are being sexualized and corrupted through the media. The law has, so far, been supportive of these concerns, and in some cases, minors have been prosecuted for producing or receiving these images, and even charged with the sexual abuse of a minor.[10] As the laws around child pornography are currently configured, teenagers who record themselves in an erotic pose or engaged in acts of masturbation are engaged in producing child pornography; even when they are recording acts that are not illegal in themselves.[11]

The field of images "is not characterised by intrinsic differences between art and pornography or morality and law, but by the contingent and shifting historical configurations of its elements: these forming mobile thresholds for the juridifications, pathologization and aestheticization of erotica" (Hunter et al., 1993, p. 19). A variety of images, from the exploitative to the aesthetic to the banal are criminalized and pathologized through a category of "child pornography" that is imprecise and unhelpful. Recent history suggests that an increasingly wide range of images is now seen as child pornography, and as the speed of the internet and the capacity of computers increases, it seems unlikely that these will be effectively eradicated from either the public domain or private collections (Jenkins, 2001). In order to make progress in this area, it will be necessary to think more carefully about the ways we decide what "child pornography" is, and who has the right to produce and consume images of children. Assuming the perverse gaze of the pedophile in our readings of images will achieve little in terms of child protection. In order to "rediscover the child" (Gillespie, 2008, p. 143) and focus attention on children's safety, we need to rethink the way in which we classify and conceptualize images of children.

Notes

1.   http://www.csecworldcongress.org/PDF/en/Stockholm/Background_reading/
        Theme_papers/Theme paper Pornography 1996_EN.pdf. Accessed 30 March 2009.
2.   See Akdeniz (2008) for a discussion of legal definitions of and approaches
        to child pornography in England and Wales, the United States, and Canada, and
        the policies of supranational bodies such as the European Union, the Council of
        Europe, and the United Nations.
3.   For example, the NSW Crimes Act states that child pornography is material
        that "depicts or describes," while the Canadian Criminal Code Section 163.1
        (1) (b) defines child pornography as any written material or visual representation
        that advocates or counsels sexual activity with a person under the age of eighteen
        years that would be an offence under this Act."
        This detail was the subject of a ruling of the Supreme Court of Canada, R v.
        Sharpe (2001) SCC2. File No. 27376, 26 January 2001. The case suggested
        that it is acceptable to possess written child pornography if the material is
        viewed in privacy and is not distributed to other individuals.
4.   A portmanteau word meaning "lolita complex," a view of pedophilia that is
        sympathetic to the idea of the victim as seductress (Trainer, 1966). Lolicon

materials focus on the sexualization and sexual exploitation of figures that resemble (pre)pubescent females with a primary readership of adult males. Shotacon materials are less popular, featuring (pre)pubescent males.

5. Yaoi are comics that depict romantic love between males, including figures that resemble pubescent males, with a primary readership of young females.

6. http://www.lawlink.nsw.gov.au/scjudgments/2008nswsc.nsf/6ccf7431c546464 bca2570e6001a45d2/ef4625a9db3003f1ca25751500066d48?Open Document. Accessed 30 March 2009.

7. See Akdeniz, 2008, p. 12; Kleinhans, 2004, p. 22; O'Donnell & Milner, 2007, p. 62; Taylor & Quayle, 2003, p. 8.

8. See http://libertus.net/censor/resources/statistics-laundering.html for a list of statistics. Accessed 30 March 2009.

9. U.S. Department of Health and Human Services, Administration on Children, Youth and Families, *Child Maltreatment* 2000.

10. See http://www.news.com.au/heraldsun/story/0,,23959256-24218,00.html. http://www.digitaljournal.com/article/261082. http://www.usatoday.com/tech/webguide/internetlife/2004-03-29-child-self-porn_x.htm. http://www.rottingnation.com/2007/02/09/15-year-old-girl-arrested-for-sexually-abusing-herself/. http://abcnews.go.com/TheLaw/story?id=5995084&page=1.http://www.seacoastonline.com/articles/20090225-NEWS-902250334. All accessed 30 March 2009. Also see Goldstein, (2009) for further discussion.

11. See http://www.news.com.au/heraldsun/story/0,,23959256-24218,00.html. http://proquest.umi.com/pqdweb?did=1263397211&Fmt=3&clientId=8429& RQT=309&VName=PQD http://proquest.umi.com/pqdweb?did=1255845431 &Fmt=3&clientId=8429&RQT=309&VName=PQD. All accessed 30 March 2009.

Chapter 3
Debbie Does Dallas Again and Again: Pornography, Technology, and Market Innovation
David Slayden

In 2007, Goodmagazine published a video that featured Kelle Marie, a 27-year-old Los Angeles woman with statistics on internet porn inked onto her body.[1] These were gradually revealed as she removed first her knee-high stiletto-heeled boots, and then her sexy schoolgirl outfit, piece by piece. They included the following:

12 percent of all Web sites are pornographic
25 percent of all search engine requests are pornographic
35 percent of all internet downloads are pornographic in nature
Every second, 28,258 internet users are viewing pornography
Every second, $89.00 is spent on internet porn
Every day, 266 new porn sites appear on the internet
Sex is the most searched word on the internet
U.S. revenue from internet porn in 2006: $2.84 billion

The statistics cited in the video are not referenced, but they closely resemble those made available through Internet Filter Review, a Web site that recommends content blocking software and offers to "shield your family from pornography."[2] A narrative of porn's economic success and ubiquity has been sustained by the repetition of statistics like this, and increasingly incorporates figures designed to also demonstrate porn's extraordinary growth online since what has been described as a "pornography gold rush" in the 1990s (Lane, 2001, p. 114). Although a study in 1970 estimated the total retail value of hardcore pornography in the United States to be no more than $10 million,[3] by 1996 the *US News and World Report* was quoting a figure of $8 billion (Schlosser, 1997). A figure of $10 billion became quickly established and has been repeated without question in many news stories since then, often to support the view that porn has grown to epidemic proportions since it went online.

This narrative of porn success and growth also restates the close relation between sex and technologies. These have repeatedly been linked throughout history, with each new technological development making possible new types of sexual encounters, interactions and practices (Klein, 1999, p. 2). Sexual images have been used commercially in Western civilization from the making of household objects in Roman and Greek cultures onward (Lane, 2001), but it was only when print culture made writing and pictures accessible to the masses that "pornography began to emerge as a separate genre of representation" (Hunt, 1993, p. 13). In this chapter, I examine the relation between porn and technological adaptation and the development of a porn industry, focusing in particular on the emergence of a relatively mainstream adult entertainment sector, represented by companies such as Vivid. I assess the way in which this sector has responded to the challenges presented by the emergence of the internet, particularly the rise of amateur producers and new forms of distribution and consumption in the move toward "Porn 2.0."

The development of mass pornography began with the introduction of affordable photographic printing in the mid-19th century. It was at this time, too, and under these conditions of wider distribution, that questions of who should have access to pornography took their currently familiar form. Short silent porn films followed in the 1890s, color porn magazines in the 1950s, video porn in the 1980s, and internet porn in the 1990s (McNair, 2002, pp. 38–39). At each stage, concerns about pornography were voiced and can be seen as part of a recurring pattern of anxious discourse about the use of each new technology for sexual purposes (Stern & Handel, 2001, p. 1). Building on older attempts to exclude the obscene—images capable of inciting passions and provoking the imagination (Falk, 1993)—"pornography" became a term used to categorize and contain certain cultural artefacts (statues, amulets, frescoes, paintings, novels—and later more modern media), much as the establishment of "Secret Museums"—19th century collections established in the Museo Borbonico in Naples, Italy, and in the British Museum, to house sexually explicit finds from Pompeii, had (Kendrick, 1996). The resulting "melodrama" in which objects are defined as "pornography" has worked since then to construct porn as a special category of representation and a secret to be controlled by society's moral guardians and kept from certain social groups—particularly women, children, and the lower classes, although, of course, it has increasingly gained wider and wider attention in the process.

Google "internet porn" and many hits are expressions of concern about the dangers of porn and how we can be protected from it. In this discourse, those most endangered by porn are typically represented as young, but there are also plenty of adults confessing to porn addiction and the need for treatment. XXXChurch, which describes itself as the "#1 Christian Porn Site," offers a variety of services to help cure people of porn addiction and merchandise to protect them from porn itself. Filtering software and hardware, such as the Clearplay DVD player that "filters sex and more" from movies are recommended for this.[4]

Because they are parables, porn addiction confessions are remarkably similar, following a trajectory of moral weakness followed by financial ruin.[5] In one, a 56-year-old man confesses that he has been fascinated by porn for 30 years. He describes how this fascination used to take him down back alleys where he could purchase porn in brown paper bags and sneak home to look at it. Porn was his secret life and he was delighted by the emergence of online porn because it meant that he could access it from the privacy of his home. But his consumption spiralled out of control and he soon had financial problems with both credit card and telephone bills totaling several hundred dollars a month. He stole to fund his habit, was arrested, and sentenced to several years in prison.

For conservative Christians, internet porn may be a recruiting and financial godsend. The use of the internet for sex has also been an area of concern for some psychologists and a rash of publications appeared around the 2000s, stressing the dangers of addiction to cybersex (see Griffin-Shelley, 2003). These built on a rhetoric of anxiety around online porn apparent since the mid-1990s and focused on the figure of a cyberporn addict representing "the danger of the dissolution and fusing of man into machine" (Patterson in Williams, 2004a, p. 105). But internet porn stimulates discussion much more widely about what is permissible and what is not, where it may be seen and by whom, and who should make decisions about this; unsurprisingly perhaps, given the threat that the internet poses for regulators, as part of "a larger decentralizing trend in communications over the last few decades," which may be as earthshaking as the democratization of media consumption by the development of the printing press (Coopersmith, 2000, p. 34).

The Quietest Big Business in the World

As Stephen Maddison notes, assessing the success, growth, and value of an industry, much of which operates independently of the authorities through which business activities are usually tracked (2004, p. 49), is genuinely problematic. The problem is compounded by the difficulty of deciding what to include in an assessment of porn revenues, especially since porn producers began to diversify in terms of their products and distribution methods (Simpson, 2005, p. 31). What we do know is that, from print through photography, film and video to digital media, the porn industry has been quick to exploit each new technology, and that it has continued to grow as a whole since the commercialization of the internet and the accompanying rise in digital culture. Pornographers are "lead users of any new communications technologies" (Jenkins, 2007) and have been associated with the development and success of key technologies such as DVD, 3G mobile phones, and broadband (Maddison, 2004, pp. 51–52). With the development of each technology, porn has become cheaper and therefore potentially more profitable to produce, and the industry has become increasingly more accessible to independent and amateur makers.

With technological advancement, porn producers have been able to maximize their profits by generating a number of commodities from the same basic production. A single film shoot may generate video titles which can be sold, rented, and distributed through pay-per-view and subscription sites, while stills can be plundered for print media and for posting online (Cronin & Davenport, 2001, p. 39). This repurposing of product has been further aided by the development of the internet for commercial use, and it has also become much easier to successfully cater for specialist tastes and niche markets which would be impossible to sustain offline (ibid.). A range of providers have made money from online porn, from small-scale and speciality producers through to the large corporations whose online success has been based on "diversifying, refining and integrating services and products to produce multiple revenue streams" (Maddison, 2004, p. 52). Matt Rosoff has dubbed online porn "the quietest big business in the world," and Frederick Lane has argued that "pornography has been the World Wide Web's major economic success" (2001, p. 34).

Indeed, it is often claimed that porn drives technology and that sex has shaped the internet as it currently exists (Johnson, 1996; Perdue, 2002 and 2004). Consumer demand for porn has driven the development of servers, streaming software, chat forums, and e-commerce payment systems (Perdue, 2004, p. 260). As early users, porn consumers accelerate the diffusion of new technologies by increasing sales and reducing costs for subsequent buyers (Coopersmith, 2000, p. 28). Porn has been important in sustaining new media forms until significant revenue can be generated from nonpornographic content (Maddison, 2004, p. 52). What is more, the adult industry's experimentation with new business and delivery models has helped to demonstrate the potential of the internet for retail, thereby "greasing the rails" for other businesses such as Amazon (Bennett, 2001, p. 381), as well as sustaining media hardware production and a range of online businesses such as hosting, router, server, and bandwidth companies. As Stephen Maddison notes (2004, p. 36), just as porn has moved to the center of popular culture, it has also become more central to the global entertainment business. There has been a corresponding "businessification" in which the business models and economics of porn—and often its spectacular successes—are increasingly the focus of interest (Bennett, 2001, p. 382). In the process, porn is reframed as a form of cultural production rather than a social problem. At the same time, the construction of porn consumption as "seedy, lonely and furtive" has begun to be replaced by "sophisticated online experiences of the contemporary industry" where easy access, convenience and "fantasies of personal technological power" coincide (Maddison, 2004, p. 44). In these ways, some types of porn have become more and more a part of mainstream culture.

Debbie Does Dallas ... Again and Again

Debbie Does Dallas (1978), one of the most well-known of 1970s porn films, features the sexual exploits of Debbie, a cheerleader, as she attempts to raise money to fund her trip to Dallas to try out for the Texas Cowboys. The film was made during what O'Toole has called porn's "golden age" (1998, p. 75); an era in which porn first became chic. Feature-length porn films integrating a variety of the "sexual numbers" that had become standard in hardcore porn into recognizable film narratives emerged. These were shown in legitimate theaters and thereby "joined the entertainment mainstream" (Williams, 1989, p. 120). Made on a shoestring budget, the initial success of *Debbie Does Dallas* can be attributed to the wholesome and unknown face of its star, Bambi Woods, combined with an enduring porn fetish for cheerleaders. Other than the hardcore sex, the film exploited the same girl-next-door concept that differentiated *Playboy* from most other skin magazines of the era. In a survey of 1,000 porn consumers in Australia in 2003, 38 percent of respondents noted the existence of "classic" porn texts, frequently naming *Debbie Does Dallas* as one of these (McKee et al., 2008, p. 35), and the film also appeared in the bestselling list of porn videos and DVDs in Australia for the same year.

Three sequels of *Debbie Does Dallas* followed—*Debbie Does Dallas 2* (1981), *Debbie Does Dallas 3* (1985), and *Debbie Does Dallas 4* (1988). There were also a number of spinoffs such as *Debbie*

Does Dallas 99 (1999) and *Debbie Does Dallas: The Revenge* (2003). There was a musical in 2001 and an off-Broadway version in 2002. A documentary about the film, *Debbie Does Dallas Uncovered,* appeared in 2005. The longevity of this particular text is useful in demonstrating how porn content can be repurposed in a range of genres and for a variety of audiences. For example, as McKee et al. note, scenes from the original film that showed sex acts that were not clearly consensual (for example, a woman being spanked against her will before beginning to enjoy it) disappeared in the 1999 version, and the original storyline in which the cheerleaders took on low-paid jobs as a way of earning money in order to see their team play was modified. Here, the women track down members of the opposing team and have such vigorous sex with them that they are unable to play properly. Women's power and pleasure are foregrounded in this later version; a clear attempt to appeal to the couples market (McKee et al., 2008, pp. 56–57). The most recent outings of the story as musical and documentary also show how some porn texts have increasingly become mainstreamed in format, both as light-hearted, tongue-in-cheek entertainment and as the focus of critical investigation.

In 2007, the film was remade yet again by "one of the world's largest producers of adult entertainment": Vivid, a privately owned corporation, which has been described as the "Microsoft of the porn industry."[6] Vivid is associated with technological innovation, with the use of a range of delivery systems to provide a "single, homogenized sex product to a variety of niche markets," and with the quest for a larger, mainstream audience (O'Toole, 1998, p. 213; see also Keegan, 2003). Founded in 1984, Vivid has consistently invested in diversification, both in terms of format and technology. It has needed to, given the challenges of the business. The number of hardcore cinemas grew massively during the 1970s when *Debbie Does Dallas* first appeared, but they were closing in the mid-1980s because of the emergence and success of hardcore video porn (O'Toole, 1998, p. 103). During the 1990s, there were further challenges as profit margins were threatened by increased competition, the falling price of video (O'Toole, 1998, p. 215), the beginnings of a "product-glut" of adult movies (O'Toole, 1998, p. 214), and the establishment of porn subscription channels on satellite and cable and pay-per-view by hotel chains (O'Toole, 1998, p. 181).

Vivid has responded to these historical and technological shifts by moving into each new area as it has emerged. Its move into cable porn began in 1999, dramatically increasing the company's profits shortly afterward in 2000 when its cable channel, the Hot Network, began to be carried by AT&T (Simpson, 2005, p. 28). More recently, it has offered downloadable versions of its most popular releases and online chat with its porn stars, the "Vivid Girls," and moved into providing material for other online porn sites. In the process, it has gained greater exposure, a larger audience, and increased revenue (Simpson, 2005, p. 29).

According to Nicola Simpson, Vivid's success is based on its emulation of the old Hollywood Studio System, especially in its emphasis on branding—both of its products and itself, its quick adaptation to new technology, and its centralized ownership and management systems that exert tight control over the marketing and distribution of its products (2005, p. 33). Today, these are "distributed on videotape and DVD, on pay-per-view and video-on-demand cable and satellite television, over the internet, via wireless programs in 20 countries, and around the world through a network of partners and affiliates." Vivid is a global presence with a business that extends to "advertising, apparel, book publishing, supplements, condoms, snowboards, calendars, comic books, and a variety of other ventures."[7] Its success in marketing nonpornographic products and services qualifies it as a lifestyle brand, rather than simply a porn producer.

Vivid exemplifies what Cronin and Davenport (2001) have described as the "maturing market" of pornography as "adult entertainment," characterized not only by economic success but also by professionalism and the adoption of legal and representational norms. Co-chairman Steve Hirsch described Vivid's main goal in 1998 as "brand name recognition as a quality company" (in Simpson, 2005, p. 25), and this has been pursued through the creation of a distinct and glossy aesthetic that contrasts with the increasing number and rougher style of camcorder shot films (Simpson, 2005, p. 27). The upscale Vivid aesthetic marks out its products as safe and mainstream, and thereby accessible to the largest possible audience. Its star system counters the critique that porn exploits women—the Vivid Girls are the best paid and most powerful performers in the industry. In this way Vivid's branding works to overcome public resistance to porn on both aesthetic and moral grounds and to build mainstream acceptance.

Like other successful adult businesses, Vivid has gained wider legitimation through the diversification and reframing of its products, through neutral or positive coverage in the mainstream business press, increased reliance on public relations, professional management, partnerships with mainstream lifestyle traders, and increased self-regulation (Cronin & Davenport, 2001). The incorporation of adult entertainment into the revenue streams of large and recognizable corporations such as AT&T, Time Warner, Marriott, and Holiday Inn (Maddison, 2004, p. 46), coupled with the development of a purchasing environment that looks like "a virtual shopping mall, or a glossy magazine," has also worked to reposition porn as a form of popular culture like any other (Maddison, 2004, p. 44). It has taken on new significance "as entertainment/infotainment, as therapy, as a hobby, as a life-style good, as an art form" (Cronin & Davenport, 2001, p. 35), moving from marginal locations such as adult bookstores and video arcades to a central position in the global image economy. Vivid's G-rated packaging of XXX-rated DVDs allows distribution in retail outlets that are not exclusively providers of adult content—the Virgin Megastore, for example.

Vivid's "blockbuster" remake of *Debbie Does Dallas* in 2007, directed by Paul Thomas, was accompanied by a second film, an altporn version, *Debbie Loves Dallas*, directed by Eon McKai, the filmmaker recruited by Vivid in 2006 to launch its alternative brand, Vivid Alt. The making of both films was chronicled in a Vivid-produced reality TV miniseries, *Debbie Does Dallas Again*, which premiered on Showtime (Sullivan,

2007). Vivid also chose to release its version of *Debbie Does Dallas* simultaneously on HD DVD and on Blu-ray so that they could "test the market for both formats before deciding whether to continue producing movies in Blu-ray" (in Gonsalves, 2007). As *Information Week* reported, a Blu-ray disk cost at least three times as much to produce as a disk for HD DVD, but this was an expense that Vivid was willing and able to take in order to test the market for both products (Gonsalves, 2007). This demonstrates the continuing willingness of some porn producers to experiment with new technology formats ahead of mainstream content producers, and a profitable understanding of its market, which allows them to successfully deliver content across different media platforms. The integrated online/offline promotion for the movie is also exemplary of the adult industry's ability to exploit a variety of channels, while its use of alternative and reality formats shows a determination to repurpose and reposition a single text according to a variety of generic conventions for potentially new audiences. For its 2007 versions of *Debbie Does Dallas*, David Peskin, Vivid's national sales director, reported "consistent reorders," "amazing reviews," and an unusual amount of mainstream publicity as a result (in Adams, 2007). *Debbie Does Dallas Again* was not simply a production; it was a market test that would provide valuable information into consumer preferences in format and genre in the future.

Zack and Miri Make a Porno

The storyline of the film *Zack and Miri Make a Porno* (2008) is that the titular characters, more or less failing in Pittsburgh and facing their tenth high school reunion, plot their rise out of debt via a porn movie that they will both make and star in. The film demonstrates the extent to which porn themes have become mainstreamed—it is a romcom and is directed by the award-winning director, Kevin Smith. Its plot draws on the assumption that porn accommodates grassroots efforts and is readily available to amateurs because of the increasingly affordable technology for producing content and the availability of the internet for marketing and distributing it. It thereby capitalizes and comments on a general trend in both the mainstream entertainment and porn industries, the rise of reality content created by amateurs.

The rise of the amateur and the proliferation of new technologies have been seen as indicative of "the commercial imperatives and tensions within pornographic industries" (Esch & Mayer, 2007, p. 99). Amateur porn has proliferated, along with more independent and alternative porn varieties as part of the broader emergence of user-generated content. The amateur representations that Sergio Messina (n.d.) has called "realcore," that is, "pictures of real people with real desires, having real sex in real places," originated in BDSM (bondage and discipline, dominance and submission, sadism and masochism) communities that traditionally have been poorly served by the porn industry, appearing online in the late 1990s. They have been accompanied by the growth of all kinds of contemporary fetish representations which have themselves been made more visible and accessible by new technologies.

The rise of user-generated content, of which both are part, has attracted an enormous amount of media attention, exemplified by *Time* magazine's naming of "you" as the person of the year in 2006, a reference to the popularity of sites such as Wikipedia, MySpace, and YouTube, and the potential of Web 2.0 as "a tool for bringing together the small contributions of millions of people and making them matter" (Grossman, 2006). But, as Peter Lehman argues, this accolade is rather belated. Porn sites such as Voyeurweb, set up in 1997, relying on user-generated content, allowing viewer feedback, and providing spaces for discussion were "way ahead of the game," whereas *Time* and YouTube were actually "late getting on board" (2007, p. 109). Indeed, as Henry Jenkins also notes (2007), "there is and has always been a large sector involved in user-generated porn content," aided by the development of digital cameras and camera phones that have made it much easier to produce and share images.

Although DIY amateur porn emerged outside the established industry, it has become "a healthy part of the pornography economy" (Esch & Mayer, 2007, p. 104). Many of the larger porn producers have responded by swallowing it up, mimicking its style in its own productions to the extent that it has become a contemporary commercial subgenre (O'Toole, 1998, p. 181). Indeed, amateur porn has become so prevalent that the annual pornography award show hosted by *Adult Video News* now incorporates categories for Best Amateur Tape and Best Amateur Series, and amateur porn producers can be found "in the largest numbers," although in "the least visible part" of the Adult Entertainment Expo, the adult industries' annual event (Esch & Mayer, 2007, p. 100). This inclusion encourages content innovation and profits from it, allowing the bigger companies to identify and field test new trends without incurring research and development expense.

All the same, amateur porn has offered a challenge to the industry, and has worked to put pornography "back into the realm of social relations as compared to the anonymous images that circulate in commercial pornography" (Jenkins, 2007). Online porn sharing has also worked to recontextualize porn in this way. New economies of distribution have emerged in file-sharing communities that originated in Usenet newsgroups and IRC chat rooms, then graduated to P2P software clients and later to the BitTorrent format. These "communities of exchange" challenge the existing commercial structures within which porn has traditionally been understood to operate. Traditional forms of pornographic production and consumption are reconfigured as a form of gifting (Phillips, 2005).

As broadband and the accompanying increases in bandwidth and power become more widely available, and as media are increasingly shared online in sites that provide a communal context for consumption, the context of porn use has shifted, providing further new challenges for producers. Regina Lynn (2007) has argued that as Web technology evolves, "porn is falling further behind the curve," and that the porn industry is failing to recognize "the centrality of community, interactivity and personalization." This, coupled with industry paranoia about piracy, has led to a lack of engagement with 2.0 technologies in some sectors of the industry, but elsewhere porn producers are "ushering in a new era in online adult erotica: Porn 2.0" (Morrison, 2007).

The most recent indication of the rise of Porn 2.0 lies in the emergence of pornographic "tubes" such as YouPorn, XTube, and PornoTube, based on the hugely successful YouTube, as a platform for hosting and streaming material. In 2006, Adult Video News reported that "total DVD sales in the adult entertainment industry fell 11 per cent, to an estimated $3.8 billion" (Hoffman, 2007), a decline attributed to new sites such as YouPorn, which, according to *Portfolio* magazine, had 15 million users nine months after going live in 2006, and were growing at a rate of 37.5 percent per month (ibid.). According to Quentin Boyer (2008), managing editor at *XBiz World Magazine*, "free sites have made it harder for subscription websites and DVD companies to sell their products and have driven the price of adult product down, industry-wide."

The scenario is reminiscent of earlier advances in porn distribution. Just as video replaced film and subscription sites challenged DVD consumption, so, too, does streaming and sharing challenge the subscription model. The current situation is also comparable to that in the music industry and chronicled by Steve Knopper (2009) who details the industry's failure to adjust to the challenge of file-sharing technologies. This offers a cautionary tale for all content providers facing the operation and success of the tubes. Through ever more powerful, adaptive, and accessible social software, the power of consumers is likely to increase and to confound business models shaped by top-down management of the way content is distributed.

If content generation and distribution become further democratized, they will become increasingly difficult to control. In 2008, Vivid filed a lawsuit against Adult Entertainment Broadcast Network, claiming that its PornoTube Web site was engaged in "wholesale copyright infringement and unfair business practices" (Brewer, 2008). This followed Viacom's earlier $1 billion copyright-infringement suit against YouTube on the grounds that it was contributing to the piracy of video clips from Viacom properties such as MTV, Comedy Central, and Nickelodeon. Although it is not yet known what the long-term impact of the tubes will be on porn production and consumption, there is widespread concern about the shifts in porn revenue.

Sites such as PornoTube, XTube, and YouPorn are particularly challenging, not only because of the issue of copyright infringement but also because of the huge volume of user-generated content that they make available. It has also been argued that they are likely to bring about dramatic changes in the way that porn consumers think about the porn they consume (Brewer, 2008). The huge amount and variety of material on sites such as YouPorn—certainly in comparison to those of more traditional producers—and the speed with which it can be got to market threatens to reduce the life cycle of porn products and make it possible for users to develop their tastes much more quickly, becoming much more discerning and demanding consumers in the process. The porn industry is potentially facing a future market that demands more content, greater variety, better quality, and reduced costs, if any, effectively placing porn business in the context of a deal culture. This may be a giant step backward for companies such as Vivid that have carefully built a brand out of adult entertainment.

The Vivid versus PornoTube lawsuit is predictive for mainstream businesses that depend on the protection of intellectual property as well as the adult entertainment industry. But Reed Lee, an attorney (in Boyer, 2008), argues that it is important to consider the development of new technologies in the context of porn history: "This happened when the phonograph came in, and everybody was convinced that the phonograph would kill the market for live musical performances, and it happened when motion pictures came along, and then the thinking was that motion pictures would kill live theater. ... This is just another iteration of that same progression; it's painful for a lot of the people involved, and some of them will not survive, but others will adjust and they will continue to make money and prosper."

The fortunes of the porn business have risen with the internet, helping to characterize it as an industry that is innovative in its ability to adapt new technology to its advantage, combined with an exceptional understanding of its markets. It is ironic, but not, finally, surprising, that a company such as Vivid that deliberately and successfully cultivated a mainstream image for its brand should now be suffering the same copyright infringement problems as other mainstream content providers as it considers the future. What will that future look like and what will it mean for the dynamics of interaction that Web 2.0 will allow between porn users and the adult industry? According to Boyer (2008), the question "is not whether the new technologies can be harnessed by adult producers and used to improve, instead of undermine, adult producers' profits, the question is how to do so." In the context of Web 2.0 and its emphasis on participation, affiliation, collaboration, economy, and user-centric benefits, this looks likely to be a difficult lesson to learn, not just for the adult industry, but for the entertainment industry as a whole.

Notes

1. http://www.good.is/?p=11826. Accessed 14 January 2009.
2. http://www.internet-filter-review.toptenreviews.com/. Accessed 14 January 2009.
3. President's Commission on Obscenity and Pornography (1970) *Report of the Commission on Obscenity and Pornography*. Washington, DC: U.S. Government Printing Office.
4. See http://www.clearplay.com/. Accessed 22 January 2009.
5. http://xxxchurch.com/gethelp/confessions/. Accessed 14 January 2009.
6. *Details* Magazine, quoted at http://www.vividentertainment.com/. Accessed 25 January 2009.
7. Vivid Overview, http://www.vividentertainment.com/. Accessed 25 January 2009.

Chapter 4
Porn 2.0? Technology, Social Practice, and the New Online Porn Industry
Sharif Mowlabocus

This chapter seeks to plot a critical route through the amorphous and shifting terrain of "Web 2.0," a vague and sometimes misused term, which has lately been employed as a euphemism for applications and services that are considered "on-trend" and fashionable. My focus is on the emergence of a new economy within online pornography made up of practitioners who are, often for the first time, making money out of their own sexually explicit material. These subjects are living proof of Brents and Hausbeck's claim that "recent changes in the economic infra-structure of mass consumption and the values and attitudes of consumer culture are affecting how the sex industry is organized and sex as a product is marketed" (2007, p. 426). Through a consideration of this new economy, and the questions of representation, labor, and agency that it raises, I examine the notion that Web 2.0 is "democratizing" pornography, and that this new era of online communication and practice supports more egalitarian, less objectifying pornographies. The continuing development of digital communications means that this exploration can and must be treated as a snapshot of digital porn, taken at a particular time and in a particular place. It is from this position that I begin my discussion as to what lies behind the claim that Porn has gone "2.0."[1] Similarly, the case study employed in this chapter should be seen as indicative of wider shifts occurring in digital pornography, rather than an isolated or unique example in an otherwise static landscape of adult entertainment.

"Tubing" the Web

In recent writings, scholars such as Skiba et al. (2006), Noam (2007), and Lee and Li (2007) have identified the economic dimension of 2.0,

and articles in the press have demonstrated a slow awakening to the
political and economic dimensions of this networking "revolution."[2]
Although difficult to define,[3] "Web 2.0" remains an enticing new
development for academics studying the internet and technoculture(s),
not least because of a sense that it builds on the dreams of an earlier
generation of commentators such as Rheingold, who imagined the
formation of an "electronic agora" back in 1993. This notion of a "new"
form of democracy and of a revitalized "public" continues to permeate
the field of Internet Studies (see Warf & Grimes, 1997; Dahlberg, 2000;
Papacharissi, 2002; and Travers, 2003 for further discussion).

Web 2.0 has reenergized these arguments. For example, with its call
to "Broadcast yourself," YouTube has sparked new discussions about the
role of the citizen within news production and agenda setting (Thurman,
2008). Blogging, vlogging, and other "You media" technologies have
all been cited as examples of a newer, more *participatory* generation
of media-making (Drezner & Farrell, 2004; Jenkins & Deuze, 2008).
Participatory[4] media incorporate technological practices such as
"folksonomic" search and archiving applications, allowing users to form
new categorizations and aggregations of material. Unlocked editable
content such as that found on Wikipedia makes it possible to add
comments to published objects, raising questions about the ownership
and production of knowledge and suggesting a shift from publishing-by-
individual to participation-through-social-network.

Jenkins and Deuze are aware of the political-economic tensions
caused by the meshing of bottom-up and top-down approaches in this
new era (2008, p. 7), and the economic motivations behind Web 2.0 must
not be forgotten. Web 2.0 has been seen as emerging out of the bursting
of the dotcom bubble, where success depends on both technological and
financial strengths related to new "design patterns" and new "business
models" (O'Reilly, 2005). It is not unsurprising to find pornography
engaging with technological innovation, new forms of production, and a
new economic model. As Lane's study of pornography highlights, porn is
first and foremost an industry—and an incredibly profitable one (Lane,

2000, p. xv), generating huge profits through online sales. In this chapter, I seek to build on Lane's earlier "1.0" understanding of the online porn economy and demonstrate how the "skin trade" is "harnessing collective intelligence" (Jenkins & Deuze, 2008, p. 6) in order to make ever more "obscene profits."[5]

Shake Your Moneymaker: Porn in the 2.0 Economy

XTube launched in 2006 with the aim of providing "an adult version"[6] of the video-driven YouTube. Alongside free-to-view trailers, clips, and photos from commercial pornography, XTube allows amateurs to upload their own material to the site, which is then "broadcast" as on the YouTube platform. In many ways, the Web site embodies much of the Web 2.0 ethos. Movie files are searchable through "tags"; a system of categorization based on information generated by users and one that is infinitely expandable and adaptable. "Tags" allow users to form content-relations between materials on the Web site, creating metadata (Best, 2006), which are used to generate a "folksonomic" categorization process.[7] This "grassroots" organization process is integral to 2.0 thinking, countering the "top-down" taxonomic model of database management of an earlier internet generation. Folksonomic practices generate search results for users looking for particular content and offer radically decentralized search services compared to those on Web sites such as Match and Gaydar where search mechanisms are predicated on the Web site's organization of content into categories (Mowlabocus, 2007).

The Web site also engenders a sense of community that can be aligned with recent discussions of social networking, where individuals are able to express themselves in nonhierarchical and noninstitutional spaces (Livingstone, 2008). XTube encourages users to engage with consumers and producers via profiles, comments, and introductory videos. The ability to comment on a video posted to the site—and to "track-back" and identify the author of that comment—suggests that the video is not experienced on its own, but is embedded within the community that consumes it. These responses are sometimes, but not always, complimentary and inclusive.[8]

Perhaps most important, XTube employs the discourse of "participatory" media, encouraging users to publish their own material, and suggesting that they "let XTube show you the money" and "use [its] massive web presence to promote [their] naughty bits, and earn real money." This focus on user-generated content is central to 2.0 rhetoric. XTube positions itself as a service for pornographers. The site does not produce any original pornography; instead amateurs and professionals create content. It does not seek large-scale sole distribution contracts, nor does it purchase the copyright of amateur material uploaded to the site. XTube thus stands in contrast to conventional porn studios and distributors, establishing itself as a *platform* for exchange. Like eBay, it offers users a system whereby small payments can be made for short video clips or small collections of photos. It *facilitates* transactions, and makes money from providing this intermediary service. In this way, the site "leverage[s] customer-self service and algorithmic data management to reach out to the entire web, to the edges and not just the center, to the long tail and not just the head" (O'Reilly, 2005, p. 21).

In offering "services" as opposed to "packaged software," XTube upholds one of the core values of 2.0, that of *user positioning*. In Web 2.0, "you control your own data" (O'Reilly, 2005, p. 22), and XTube echoes this, inviting users to "take control of your porn with XTube. com." Shifts in user positioning mean that now, more than ever before, "we" are able to create, edit, manipulate and distribute content across a variety of spaces. This shift means that "the former audience" becomes "we, the media" (Gillmor, in O'Reilly, 2005, p. 27). In keeping with the grassroots feel of much 2.0 discourse, it is user-generated content that XTube sets out to celebrate—and profit from.

Technologies of Sexual Representation

XTube upholds the long-established relationship between technologies of media production and sexual representation.[9] In particular, it builds on and extends the shift in production methods begun by the advent of camcorder technologies (Lane, 2000) and VHS recorders, which allowed "private networks of couples [to begin] exchanging videos of themselves having sex" (Hardy, 2008, p. 61). Digital media technologies have worked to create further shifts in the production, distribution, and consumption of sexual representations (see Lane, 2000; Kibby & Costello, 2001; Attwood, 2007b). Recent advances have been characterized by an increasing *mobility* of pornography via wi-fi, mobile phones, PDAs, and laptops, suggesting that if porn came into the domestic space in the 1980s, then the new millennium has seen adult content going back "outside," into the public spaces of the internet café, the work station, and the commuter train. Digital media have also increased the mobility of porn production as digital video takes us into locker rooms, bathrooms, bedrooms, and, of course, outdoors. All of these spaces have previously been accessible using camcorders, but the ability to transmit live streaming footage over the Web means that one's bedroom can be turned into a live amateur porn studio with increasing ease. The internet has also served to further smudge the boundaries between producer, performer, distributor, and consumer. Using the internet for distribution "has changed the relationships between producers and consumers" (Kibby & Costello, 2001, p. 359) and complicated "established ways of viewing cultural production and consumption as a linear process where ordinary people 'receive' media and other products from media professionals" (Attwood, 2007b, p. 442).

Although amateur porn has been available online since the mid-1990s, XTube further dissolves these boundaries as it does not "produce" but instead *facilitates*, allowing the performer who produces the material to sell that content "directly" to the consumer. The user is no longer just a paying punter, but actively organizes and *controls* their porn in ever more individual ways.

High Hopes and Hardcore: Sexual Agency and the
Promise of Pornotopia

Notions of user positioning and control tie in with wider issues of sexual
agency and pornography, a key theme in feminist discussions of porn's
role in the oppression of women (Kappeler, 1986; Dworkin, 2000).
Of chief concern here have been the relationships of power circulating
within and around the pornographic text: the coercive and commercial
power of the producer over the performer, the voyeuristic power of the
consumer over the text, the legal power of the state over the industry,
and the ideological and cultural power of the genre over society as a
whole. Feminist antiporn campaigners unsurprisingly see gender as a key
factor in these relationships, arguing that women inevitably end up as the
objects of these power relations.[10]

While not denying the oppressive power of pornography, Williams
(1992) suggests that a rethinking of pornography and its structures could
lead to the reorganization of its power relations, and the subversive
potential of pornography is also acknowledged by Dyer (1989), Kibby
and Costello (1999), and Mercer (2000). The digital age has become
a catalyst for a plethora of further studies that seek to reposition
pornography as subversive and counterhegemonic, or at the very
least, carrying politically effective and disruptive elements that may
problematize simple "oppressor-oppressed" binaries.[11]

Issues of ownership, specular control, and empowerment have been
identified in women's use of webcam technologies that allow them to
"understand, participate in, and profit from the specular economy"
(Knight, 2000, p. 22). White also argues that "[w]ebcams can suggest
some ways to resist the more submissive aspects of being looked at" and
to reorganize the relationship between spectator and spectated (2003, p.
18). Indeed, she suggests that the webcam cannot *help* but disrupt the
classic gaze of Western visual culture "because the male gaze is usually
envisioned, produced, and controlled by women" (2003, p. 16).

Alt.porn has also been seen as situated at the crossroads between sexual representation and sexual politics (see Attwood, 2007b). Magnet, writing about the alt.porn site, Suicide Girls, states that "[m]any models assert that they enjoy participating on Suicide Girls because it gives them a chance to subvert ... stereotypes about women in the sex industry" (2007, p. 581). She suggests that the model's choice of shots, of how much of their bodies they reveal, and of how they (re)present themselves may provide a feminist intervention into the "male gaze" of pornographic representation (ibid.). Although these positive readings are later problematized, Magnet identifies strong feminist messages within the discourse of the site and the imagery of the models; messages that circulate around, and gain power from, the central theme of self-empowerment and self-government over the pornographic image. Magnet echoes Jacobs (2004a, p. 73) who suggests that new "networks of sexual agency and politics" are being formed via the proliferation of new pornographies and new technologies and spaces of mediation.

In such writing, the internet is constituted as a space, technology, and culture that promotes Williams' vision of a perverse and politically subversive pornography, one that responds to the misogyny of mainstream pornographic representation. This subversion operates at the level of representation, ownership, and economics. Knight (2000), Jacobs (2004a), and Attwood (2007b) all acknowledge the role the internet has played in diversifying the flow of capital generated by pornography and increasing the economic stake women have in this industry. In terms of technology, aesthetics, and empowerment, XTube can be seen as the next step in this rhetoric of self-empowerment. Central to this rhetoric—and to the XTube phenomenon—are issues of agency, control, and power.

XTube: Amateurs on Display

In the three years that the Web site has been operating, thousands of members have signed up to become XTube amateur performers. They include women, men, and trans people, and represent a range of sexualities. Unlike much alt.porn, there is no apparent gender-bias or particular sexual identity promoted within the amateur pages. On accessing the Web site, visitors are asked to state the type of content they are interested in (straight, gay, or both), but beyond this initial statement of preference, a reliance on boundaries between genders and sexualities is not visible.

This is not to say that the pornography featured on the site is not highly gendered or organized through sexual categories. Rather, in this space "anything goes." Models and porn stars appear alongside "regular" folk—people who aren't tanned or toned, or conventionally attractive. Tagging means that a search for "blowjob" or "twink" or "shaved" can result in the user encountering a wealth of images and videos featuring a diversity of body shapes and types. Users are not necessarily democratic and antidiscriminatory in their selection of what they view, but on XTube the professional and the amateur occupy the same space, and the stylized body of the porn star cannot be seen in total isolation; other bodies that do not conform are just as likely to be encountered—and *enjoyed*.

Indeed, a sense of enjoyment is key among the XTube amateur community, and although the Web site discourse frames pornography as a means of generating income, playful, sex-positive language is regularly employed in members' profiles:

> I love sex and I love sex toys so I figured I may as well combine the two. tee hee … we try to have as much fun as possible. Tongue out . . . anyway drop me a line—let's party!

Given her occupation, that of running her own sex toy Web site, it is perhaps unsurprising that this member invokes a sex-positive discourse. However, such affirmative statements are by no means uncommon in amateur profiles:

> I like variety in my life, and am up for anything. I'm very open-minded and have many sexual fantasies that I'm wanting to fulfil.

Hey guys, thanks for checking out my page. If you're tired of skinny guys or guys with the perfect hairless bodies, I'm definitely the guy for you.

Hi Guys!! Welcome to my sexy fantasies! My name is ... I'm a 21 year old sexy girl from Canada! I'm studying ... and I love it! Recently I found a new passion—making movies about my sex life!

Amateur profiles do not need to include any content beyond that generated by the profile software, but where there is user-generated content, the discourse employed is often upbeat and friendly. This is understandable given that these individuals are advertising themselves, but if we contrast this with professional pornography, which regularly employs discourses of objectification and of submission when advertising its performers,[12] we can see that in the XTube community, amateurs present the consumer with more than just sex. Their chatty tone and informal manner position them as embodied subjects whose sexuality, although important, is not their only feature. For example, one member quoted earlier identifies herself as a student, while others talk of their roles as housewives, mothers, business executives, and artists. Pornography is caught up in a constellation of other activities—and identities—within the XTube profile.[13]

Perhaps most important is the fact that amateurs can address their potential audiences *directly*. Profiles regularly include short promotional videos, which automatically play upon navigating to the profile. The effect is a powerful one as the amateur immediately begins addressing the browser, marking the profile as their space, which they then welcome you into. These direct-to-camera introductions often position the amateur as both a performer and a subject beyond the performance. Although the former position—the position being marketed—is foregrounded as an invitation to view the amateur's photo sets, videos, or webcam, the latter position—that of a fully formed subject—resides in the background (often literally as the introductions are filmed in domestic spaces), regularly punctuating the video as the amateur laughs, struggles to operate their recording equipment, and talks about their likes and dislikes. These promotional videos tie in with the written content of many profiles and demonstrate a "breaking through" of subjectivity as the amateur shifts their focus from the camera in front of them and the computer screen (off-camera) to check the quality of the image being recorded. Videos often begin with the hands and face of the amateur retreating from the camera, having switched it on or altered its position or settings before sitting back to address their imagined audience.

It is through such ruptures, accidents, and imperfections that a sense of agency and subjectivity is maintained in amateur introductions, in contrast to professional pornography, which "entails the abandonment of the female sexual performer's address to the client" (Williams, 1993, p. 123). The XTube amateur's sexual performance is intimately tied to their own subjectivity and the browser/customer witnesses shifts between performance and subjectivity, each serving to bolster the other so that "sexual display becomes an important part of individual and collective self-definition" (Attwood, 2007b, p. 443). Furthermore, as Hardy writes, the comparatively low quality of the production values serves to validate and authenticate the performer and the performance, "a signifier of the real, over the glossy and obvious artifice of professional pornography" (2008, p. 62).

If the aesthetics and discourse of the amateur profile suggest a closer linking of subject and performance, then the economic structure of the Web site appears to place the amateur in financial control of these representations. Through a system of micropayments using an in-house finance management system, XTube amateurs are paid 50 percent of the net profit for every download of their material. Irrespective of content, body type or sexual preference, the prices for downloading are standardized (currently $0.20 per minute of video or $0.50 per photoset) and amateurs are paid monthly.[14] They also hold on to the copyright of their material, which is licensed to XTube for sale and promotional use for the duration of the contract.

This is arguably the defining feature of XTube, both for the amateur performer and the consumer, signifying an important shift within the economic structure of pornography. The transactional nature of pornography has never been so transparent. The wiki attached to XTube includes detailed explanations and examples of how income is generated and paid out on the site and the company clearly sets out the fee structure, percentages taken for marketing and overheads, and the net profit paid to amateurs. This transparency, based on delivering service as opposed to content, demonstrates the radical reorganization occurring within some online pornographies as a result of the new technologies and practices of social networking, and new Web-behaviors around user-generated content. It is this economic restructuring of pornography that is of particular importance to the Web site's appeal and to an understanding of its complex and often contradictory politics.

Laboring Under an Illusion? Economies of Affect and Capital on XTube

Writing about the pornography of sex activists, Katrien Jacobs asks the question, "how can we view such agency in light of capitalism's tendency to control ownership, consolidate 'edgy' content and maintain class divisions between cultures?" (2004a, p. 79). In doing so, she identifies a central tension within much alt.porn. If a new type of agency and new economies can be formed through alternative pornographies, how do these emerging forms "fit" with good old-fashioned capitalism? And if these new pornographies are being sold, then how do we address the problematic issues of market forces, consumer demand, and objectification? Doesn't the very process of turning labor into a commodity and selling it on to an unknown consumer thousands of miles away, engender a sense of alienation?

It is within the context of Jacob's question that we might consider Coté and Pybus' work on immaterial labor (2007). Developing Lazzarato's original definition of the term (2001), they suggest a new framework for

understanding the shifts caused by online social networking in relation
to capital, labor, and subjectivity. Using the globally renowned MySpace
Web site as their case study, Coté and Pybus offer a reevaluation of
immaterial labor in relation to a range of practices associated with Web
2.0 spaces:

> What the "2.0" addresses is the "free" labour that subjects engage in on a
> cultural and biopolitical level when they participate on a site such as MySpace.
> ... Immaterial labour 2.0 explicitly situates this subjective turn within the
> active and ongoing construction of virtual subjectivities across social networks.
> Furthermore, we wish to emphasize the role of affect as the binding, dynamic
> force which both animates those subjectivities and provides coherence to the
> networked relations. (2007, p. 90)

This subjectivity—identified as a call to "become"—is formed
through the production of cultural objects and the "work" of multifarious
practices including profile authoring, networking with other users and
uploading/linking to user-generated content. We might think here of
Graham's work on the "social production process," which he defines
as "the entire network of activities and artefacts, with which societies
reproduce themselves from every perspective, and at every level:
materially, socially, relationally, mentally, *and* economically" (2000, p.
137). Graham argues for an acknowledgment of the role of new media
in the development of what he terms "hypercapitalism" and echoes of his
argument can be heard in Coté and Pybus' analysis, where labor becomes
a process of (re)production, in which abstract, nonmaterial "things"
become "increasingly integral to capital relations" (2007, p. 89).

However, there are differences between Graham's argument and that
of Coté and Pybus. The former relies heavily on Adorno and Horkheimer's
reading of culture as industry and in doing so, risks being aligned with a
belief in the naivety of consumers. Rather than writing MySpace subjects
off as "unwitting immaterial apprentices" (2007, p. 95), Coté and Pybus
are attentive to the driving forces behind their labor, a labor which can
also be viewed as skills training in preparation for joining the workforce
of Castell's "network society" (2000):

What motivates users is the composition of bodies with which they can network. Thus an affective dimension is inscribed into a user profile. ... Through the user's built up network of social relations comes a sense of connectivity and belonging amidst the multiple on-line communities. (2007, p. 96)

This model of labor identifies not only the processes of production and commodification occurring within online social networking but also the affective dimension of such labor whereby subjectivities are actively constructed through acts of cultural production, and maintained through dynamic network relations (2007, p. 90). Echoing Lazzarato, Coté and Pybus identify the "higher level and intensity of antagonism" that these new forms of production contain (2007, p. 99). They remind us that "resistance comes first" (2007, p. 104), and this phrase serves to underscore the tensions operating within social networking, which, on the one hand, provides an escape from regimes of disciplinary power[15] and, on the other, involves activities that open up new flows of capital, and engenders new forms of control.[16] "Capital ... increasingly flows through more and more otherwise discrete social relations, and finds passage in different political and social techniques and practices" (Coté & Pybus, 2007, p. 95).

The resistance alluded to here may at first appear to echo utopian dreams of cyberspace and of inhabiting new identities that subvert dominant structures of power. However, as Coté and Pybus state, this reading of the Web's immaterial labor force should not be understood as another "uncritical celebration of the proliferating subjectivities of postmodernity" (2007, p. 101). Such celebrations were endemic within the first wave of internet commentary,[17] but what differentiates this more recent work is a recognition of the relationship between the practices and performances of the individual, and the political-economic contexts in which those practices and performances take place.

As Coté and Pybus argue, in laboring practices, the subject you become "must be compatible with the needs of contemporary capitalist reproduction" (2007, p. 99). This issue of "compatibility" is especially pertinent to a discussion of adult content on the Web, and serves to provide a new perspective on contemporary analyses of online sex sites. For example, a recognition of capitalist need provides a response to Magnet's question about Suicide Girls, "Why are women of color represented in certain ways on the website?" Arguably because the space remains networked into systems of cultural and capital production. As such, it not only responds to commercial pornography, but is also shaped by the discourses of "mainstream" porn, even as it identifies itself as an alternative to such material. This answer also serves to problematize discussions of agency and lays bare the "compatibility issue" between subjectivity and market forces that operate across commercial porn sites. Within the context of XTube, it also highlights the difficult political position the Web site finds itself in. Of course, not all alt.porn or amateur porn sites charge consumers for downloading material. The argument made here is not that all pornography is inherently capitalist, but that when pornography is sold, a discussion of capitalism must be considered.

Immaterial labor operates across XTube, where the emphasis on users not only creating but also selling content, is the driving force behind the Web site and participation in its network. Although the Web site's primary aim is to offer amateurs the opportunity to profit from their laboring, this profit operates on both an affective and economic plane. Amateurs translate their real bodies into (immaterial) digital bodies that can enter the XTube economy and earn capital. In doing so, they simultaneously enter a parallel economy, one that legitimates them through ratings, comments and tagging, and increases their subcultural capital and standing within the social network. As Coté and Pybus note of MySpace, "These series of activities are not recognized in an orthodox conception of work but they are the heart of immaterial labor"; what is more, they are vital to its raison d'être, "to be valorized and to extend one's network and hence cultural capital" (2007, p. 94).

However, the capitalist "imperative" can also be seen in the discourse of XTube, where the focus is not so much on the specific demands of the market as on continual production. Hence, when signing up to become an amateur, the Web site offers advice on being an efficient laborer:

> We can't stress this enough—you need to post new content as often as you
> can because ... if you post more often your videos will be displayed on the
> homepage (more chances to sell; if you only post 2 videos people will get tired
> of them and your sales will drop). (XTube Amateur wiki entry)

Lee and Li (2007) have highlighted that what Best termed a "new amateurism" (2006, p. 19) has implications for the quality of user-generated content compared to commercially produced material. Although the relatively low resolution of video material on sites such as YouTube is somewhat compensated for by the site's free-to-access structure, the quality of videos and images becomes more important when it is anticipated that users will be paying to download material. Given this fact, it seems somewhat surprising that XTube's advice to amateurs does not focus on quality, but on *quantity*.

This might be seen as an unwillingness on the part of the Web site to try and shape content according to a predefined market "standard," thereby providing a truly democratic space for the production of a diverse range of pornographies. However, such a view fails to address the drive toward production that amateurs are strongly urged to conform to. The "constant pressure to produce new effects"[18] is made explicit as the amateur is invited to participate in the perversity of the site, "getting paid for being sexy" and "promot[ing] your naughty bits" (XTube). The site offers the amateur the opportunity to be rated by peers and users, to be valorized through audience comments, and to build up a network based on shared sexual interests and fetishes. However, commerce compels amateurs to generate more content, to talk to more and more users, and to even give away some content for free[19] in order to market themselves—and the Web site—to new and potential customers.

In this mode, the user resembles a casual laborer or "flextimer"[20] as s/he is transformed from a subject with full agency into a worker engaged in piecework, paid only for their productive labor with no opportunity for

wage negotiation, the price always being set by "the company." Further
evidence of this economic imperative is apparent in the final piece of
advice given to amateurs:

> Talk to your fans ... people really like the fantasy that you are a real person, not
> some fake porn star that they could never meet. Talking to them is exciting for
> them. (XTube Amateur wiki)

Perhaps this demonstrates the limits of agency and subjectivity
in online pornography.[21] Aside from the potential risk of on/offline
harassment and harm that such advice engenders,[22] the discourse of the
Web site struggles to position the user as both a producer of content
and an embodied subject. "People really like the fantasy that you are a
real person" claims the wiki, raising the important, but never answered,
question of what the amateur *really* is on XTube—Porn Star? Embodied
user? Laborer? Fantasy?

Of course, it might be argued that multiple positions can be embodied
simultaneously, and doubtless amateurs envisage themselves as both
producers of content and in control of the online subjectivity they
inhabit. However, the discourse of the Web site implies that consumers
have a prioritized investment in such subjectivities, and that this should
be encouraged by the amateur. It seems the customer is always right, and
the consumer's "fantasy" of meeting the amateur should be maintained—
arguably at the expense of the amateur's own agency. In short, the amateur
may create their digital body, but the Web site supports the consumer's
appropriation and objectification and of that body—for the right price.

In early 2008, XTube began promoting a new pay-per-view webcam
facility allowing customers to communicate live and direct with amateur
performers. Significantly more expensive than the "micropayment" system
used for video and image content, these webcam performances further
complicate the discussions of agency, empowerment, and consumption
raised in this chapter. The webcam may in fact serve to demarcate the
point at which XTube's democratizing rhetoric of "Porn 2.0" begins to

retreat into a more hegemonic politics of explicit sexual representation. XTube not only exploits changes in economic infrastructure but also developments in communication infrastructure. The result is the formation of a new economy of sex, one that may at first sight appear to sidestep issues of capitalism, consumption, alienation, and objectification. As XTube increasingly promotes amateurs who are online and "available" for instant chat, video, and sexual performance, however, the promise of Porn 2.0 begins to look tarnished. Along with videos and photo-sets, the webcams may well democratize access and performance. Yet, their appeal to the customer—the fantasy that the performer will do what you want, and do it just for you—increasingly makes the cams resemble other, commercial forms of sex-work including strip shows, sex-shows, and live sex-chat lines. If in their videos, amateurs are asked to maintain a fantasy of the "real," then perhaps the webcams should be read as the triumphing of consumer fantasies over the performer's own embodied subjectivity?

In this chapter, I have sought to illustrate the difficulties, promises, and realities that are encountered when the philosophy of Web 2.0 is appropriated by the adult entertainment industry. That there is a space being created by these new Web behaviors, software, and platforms is undeniable. That this space provides for a reorganization of the power relationships that flow around and through pornography is less clear. As XTube races to position itself at the forefront of this technological revolution, questions of agency and objectification remain. If I perform for my own camera and sell my "wares" on XTube, am I showing off my sexual agency? Or willingly objectifying myself? Will anyone buy what I'm uploading? And has anything really changed in terms of practices of consumption? Undoubtedly the growth of social networking will soon provide scope for a further development and extension of this initial analysis, and perhaps provide answers to these questions in the future. What I hope to have illustrated here are some of the initial promises and pitfalls that can be identified as online pornography begins the transition to 2.0.

I am indebted to the constructive feedback and discussion that reviewers and readers of this chapter have given me, particularly Feona Attwood and Danny Weddup.

Notes

1. "Porn 2.0," although not in common use, is relevant to this study, not least because the main case study identified in this chapter claims to have ushered in this "revolution" in online pornography.
2. See Hodgkinson, 2008.
3. The term "Web 2.0" is generally attributed to Tim O'Reilly, and in particular the paper 'What is Web 2.0: Design Patterns and Business Models for the Next Generation of Software' that he presented at the O'Reilly Media Web 2.0 Conference held in San Francisco in October 2004.
4. I use "participatory" to identify a set of technological practices currently assembled under this term, while recognizing that it can be misleading. Arguably all mediation involves a level of participation, just as it involves a level of interaction.
5. This being the title of Lane's 2000 study.
6. See XTube wiki entry for the full mission statement of the Web site, http://wiki. XTube.com/indexphp?title=XTube&action=purge. Accessed 21 March 2009.
7. Interestingly, this mode of categorization is being exploited by users to increase the viewing of their videos and images. Users regularly include unrelated tags in order to generate more interest in their material. Although this can be frustrating for browsers, such taxonomic "hacking"demonstrates the "open" nature of this 2.0 phenomenon, allowing users to reorganize content according to their own criteria.
8. In the case of videos depicting bareback sex, for instance, comments regularly highlight tensions surrounding this high-risk sexual activity. Notions of what is deemed acceptable sexual practice and what are appropriate levels of risk are played out as viewers comment on and debate (often in a hostile manner) the streaming video.
9. See Johnson, 1996; O'Toole, 1997; Kibby and Costello, 2001; and Lehman, 2007.
10. See Stoltenberg, 1999; Dworkin, 2000; Russell, 1998; and Kimmel, 1990 for illustrations of this viewpoint.
11. For example, see Jacobs, 2004a; Butkas, 2004; and Paasonen, 2006.
12. See Paasonen (2006) for a discussion of commercial porn advertising's invocation of a language of female submission.
13. Of course objectification may at times be a conscious component of the sex act represented, for example in BDSM.
14. Amateurs must earn $50 before XTube issues a check. Should an amateur not make $50 in a month, the money earned is rolled over to the following month.
15. Coté and Pybus suggest that users of MySpace are escaping "the controlled confines of home and school" (2007, p. 94), whereas we might consider users of XTube to be escaping the claustrophobic containment of sexuality.

16. I use the word "control" with reference to Deleuze's work on control societies (1992) in order to identify the role that digital media technologies play in a shift from a disciplinary model to one of control.

17. See MacRae, 1997; Stone, 1998; and Rheingold, 1994.

18. Adorno and Horkheimer, (1993/1973, p. 35).

19. The wiki dedicated to amateur performers suggests that amateurs may want to provide free content in order to entice potential "fans" to the fee-paying content.

20. I use this term with reference to Castell's work on the shifting nature of work and employment in the information age. He refers to the "flextimer" as embodying a "new social and economic organization based on information technologies aim[ed] at decentralizing management, individualizing work, and customizing markets, thereby segmenting work and fragmenting societies" (1996, p. 265).

21. See White (2003).

22. See Magnet (2007) for a discussion of this.

Chapter 5

"Younger, paler, decidedly less straight": The New Porn Professionals

Feona Attwood

In an interview with altporn director Eon McKai, Violet Blue (2007) documents the emergence of a group of new porn professionals— "intellectuals, directors, performers and bloggers" who are "younger, paler, decidedly less straight" than the norm, at least as represented by the "circus of porn stereotypes" at the AVN porn convention where Blue and McKai met to talk. This new type of producer is hip, "real," genuinely turned on by their involvement with porn, and focused on the emergence of a young, sophisticated, media-savvy audience previously neglected by mainstream porn producers; McKai describes "a huge hunger to see people like the girls you'd see in a coffee shop and boys at the record shop." As the discussion between Blue and McKai indicates, they are also characterized by a reflexivity that marks them as thoughtful practitioners, indicating an overlap between critical, artistic, and activist interventions into the production of sex media. The emergence of this group of practitioners is particularly evident in the United States and coincides both with what has been described as the pornification of mainstream culture (see Paasonen et al., 2007a), and the development of participatory online cultures.

McKai, whose first film, *Art School Sluts*, appeared in 2004, and Blue, who is a prolific sex columnist, author, and blogger, are indicative of the group. Like McKai and Blue, the Finnish performer Rakkel Liekki also demonstrates how this new style of porn professional challenges stereotypes of porn performance. Her career has ranged from "painting to hard-core videos, Web presence, mobile phone services, newspaper and magazine articles, and television shows," and she has worked as a performer, host, producer, and writer (Nikunen & Paasonen, 2007, p. 30). Her professional work has often involved a reframing of porn as "recreational fun" and "educational leisure entertainment" (Nikunen &

Paasonen, 2007, p. 40), while her persona has worked to associate porn with feminism, youth, and cosmopolitanism.

In this chapter, I consider the emergence of new porn professionalism and its significance in relation to a variety of cultural trends; creative labor, pro-amateur production, participatory cultures and the postmodernization of sex. In practice, delineating this new "type" is tricky, not only because the producers I consider categorize themselves in a variety of ways, but also because they complicate the idea both of "porn" and the "professional." My examples are drawn from new networked communities of individuals who are frequently young, white, American women making an often precarious living from working with sex in a variety of media.

Katrien Jacobs has characterized new forms of porn as emerging from "alternative producers and activist sex workers, younger pro-porn feminists, queer porn networks, aesthetic-technical vanguards, p2p traders, radical sex/perv cultures, and free-speech activists" (2007, p. 3). These are part of a group of new media makers and connoisseurs who "test new models of e-commerce as production/consumption alongside intimate personal camaraderie, information sharing, fictional storytelling, and cultural debates" (Jacobs, 2007, p. 12).

Clearly, "porn" is meant to signify more broadly here than it has in the past where it referred much more narrowly and explicitly to the established adult entertainment industry or to the illicit production of sexually explicit imagery. New porn producers often operate—at least at the outset—as amateurs and consumers-turned-producers in gift economies such as Usenet alt.fetish groups and peer-to-peer networks. Their interest in experimental forms of sexual communication that make use of chat, instant messaging and Web cameras also appears to blur "the boundaries between porn and sexual self-expression" (Paasonen, 2007c, pp. 162–163). If they turn professional, they often operate independently, outside of the established adult entertainment industry, unlike Violet Blue's interviewee, McKai, who joined Vivid, the world's largest porn producer, in 2006 to produce and promote the "alternative" as a brand,

Vivid Alt.

The emergence of new porn professionals can be understood as part of an unprecedented global growth in sex work, which has been matched by a cultural fascination in the West with sex commerce of all kinds. As Elizabeth Bernstein has noted, sex work in the 21st century has provoked an "explosion of writing … rivalling the obsessive attention that was devoted to the matter by the social reformers of a century ago" and "supplemented by a rapid succession of … accounts of erotic labor by journalists, social activists, self-proclaimed allies, and popularly appointed 'sex-perts'—plus accounts by film-makers, journalists, talk show hosts and fiction writers" (2007, p. 12). Fictional representations of sex workers have become more numerous since the 1990s, in films about striptease (*Showgirls*, 1995; *Striptease*, 1996) or the porn industry (*Boogie Nights*, 1997; *The Girl Next Door*, 2004), and in best-selling novels-turned TV series about escorts such as *Diary of a Manhattan Call Girl* (Quan, 2001) and *Intimate Adventures of a London Call Girl* (Belle du Jour, 2005).[1] Indeed, Diane Negra has argued that "the female sex worker is becoming one of popular culture's most regular archetypes of paid labor" (2009, p. 100).

The emergence of mainstream fascination with sex work and the rise of a broader "striptease culture" focused on "self-revelation" and "public intimacy" (McNair, 2002, pp. 81, 98) has worked to foreground the porn star as an important cultural figure, who, like other sex performers, has become emblematic in critiques of contemporary sexualized culture. Porn performers are more visible than ever before; increasingly elevated to "international celebrity status" (Simpson, 2005, p. 13), and according to Ariel Levy, becoming in the process, "no less mainstream or profitable than Mickey Mouse" (2005, p. 19). The celebrifying of porn is also evident in the playful adoption of porn aesthetics that has been associated with Madonna since the 1990s (McNair, 2002), the pop performance of "kitschy, slutty stereotypes of female sexuality" (Levy, 2005, p. 34), and the exposure of celebrity sex lives as an established form of sexual display.

These shifts demonstrate how the boundaries between pornography and mainstream culture are increasingly becoming blurred and how, in the process, the significance of pornography is changing. As in other media forms, the glamour of celebrity and the rawness of amateur performance have become significant in conveying a closer connection between representation and reality. This demonstrates the increased importance of media as a set of cultural resources for image-work and for the construction of identity and community. As Esch and Mayer note (2007), celebrity branding and the figure of the "amateur" have become more and more important to the adult entertainment industry. Porn stars' lives and personalities are increasingly presented as significant; witness Jenna Jameson's best-selling autobiography, *How To Make Love Like A Porn Star* (2004) and Timothy Greenfield-Sanders (2004) glossy *xxx 30 porn-star portraits* in which porn stars posed clothed and unclothed and, as Greenfield-Sanders notes, "shared their life stories with me and allowed me to see them as real people" (2004, p. 142). Stars and amateurs are both used as guarantors of authenticity and contemporaneity in porn; a move repeated, albeit differently, in the new online alternative pornographies where amateurs achieve a kind of "micro-celebrity"[2] for their select audiences.[3]

Across all of these areas, there is a notable personalization and psychologization of porn performance, manifesting as an interest in the interiority, multifacetedness, and behind-the-scenes lives of porn performers. Here, "the rhetoric of artificiality in classical mainstream pornography—artificial body parts, sterile studios, wooden acting" is replaced with "a rhetoric of the authentic" (Cramer, 2007, p. 174). This move to personalization is particularly evident in the emergence of women's self-published porn sites, which have been seen as "identity projects—spaces where they own and control their bodies" and "appropriate stereotypical notions of pornography" (deVoss, 2002, pp. 76–77). This takes two key forms; "putting bodies that we don't typically see online, and inserting an intimacy not representative of most porn" (2002, p. 85). In this way, the sites create "an intimacy of identity" rather than one "based on the objectification of a generic woman, specifically her genitals and sexuality." The women project "strong, independent, and competent personas" and present "multiple and complex identities" (2002, p. 86); one describes herself as a "39 year old wife and Mother, a marathon runner—camping, playing tennis, riding my mountain bike, and riding our horses in the mountains, modelling for pictures" (2002, p. 87). Similarly, on alternative porn sites such as Bella Vendetta and No Fauxxx where modified, queer and artistic bodies are put on display, the producers double as models, posing as "an expression of their personal and real sexuality" (Ray, 2007b). It is not simply that there is a blurring of porn and mainstream representation here, but of porn and sex, work and leisure, representation and self-presentation. These new combinations of categories are expressed through the use of aesthetics which are not generally associated with porn as a genre and characterized by varying degrees of engagement with the politics of pornography.

Porn Laboratories

Many new porn producers favor forms of DIY authorship that are associated with both artistic and activist movements and evident in a range of subcultures. They have attracted attention because of their tendency toward artistic, critical, technological, and political innovation. They have been credited with developing new porn aesthetics, ethics, and business practices (Mies, 2006) and with the "reclaiming of porn culture and sex education" (Jacobs, 2007, p. 77). Some are associated with experimental forms of artistic and critical production such as Isaac Leung, whose work, "The Impossibility of Having Sex with 500 Men in a Month: I'm an Oriental Whore" (2002), explored gay men's use of webcam sex, and Barbara deGenevieve, whose art work explores issues of sexuality and who has also written about and produced queer porn, most notably at ssspread.com (see deGenevieve, 2007). Another type of radical porn is represented by Sharing is Sexy, an Open Source "sex positive collective" of polyamorous, queer, and transgender people who make porn for love rather than money. They present their work as a response to mainstream porn; a "porn laboratory" where everyone "has an equal voice in what we do and how we do it." They have been praised by Film and Media academic, Constance Penley, for their innovation in bringing experimental porn "up to date with the latest ideas about everything from intellectual property and social networking to collaborative online creation."[4]

These forms of self-expressive sex performance differentiate themselves from traditional notions of sex work—specifically the idea of the bruised and battered street walker—and, indeed, it seems likely that, for many, it is the association of porn with performance that marks it as consensual, pleasurable and acceptable in a way that other forms of sex work are often not. Both amateur and professional forms of new porn production have been associated with queer and female authorship and the challenge this offers to existing porn norms of sex and gender. The presence of women-owned sites has been cited as "a significant trend in the industry" for some time (Lane, 2000, p. 113), while the potential for egalitarian feminist and sex-radical forms of sex work has been explored in anthologies such as Jill Nagle's *Whores and Other Feminists* (1997) and Carly Milne's *Naked Ambition: Women Who Are Changing Porn* (2005). Pioneers such as Annie Sprinkle are often cited as influential for a new generation of female porn professionals, as are the sex-radical politics associated with writers such as Gayle Rubin (1984) and Pat Califia (2000).

In all of these, there is a concern with embracing and shaping cultural and commercial sexual practices, rather than with their regulation and censorship, differing from the approaches of other political ideologies because of their attempt at "honoring sex and desire" (Queen in Nagle, 1997, p. 125). Women's involvement in porn is often seen as "helping shape and change society's views on sexuality" (Milne, 2005, p. xiii), associated with the growing visibility of women's perspectives on sexually explicit representation and with the articulation of female desire in cultural forms.

The most visible manifestation of new porn production online is indieporn or altporn, which in 2007 was described as "the pornography of this decade, if not of the whole century" (Cramer & Home, 2007, p. 164). The terms, "indie" and "alt" porn are regularly used to denote—and often to criticize—the ways in which queer, activist, and alternative sex cultures have increasingly become commercialized, and, as a result, less independent and less alternative. Yet altporn is a broad church, encompassing a wide range of sites, from the relatively mainstream Suicide Girls—"the Wal-Mart of altporn" (in Ray, 2007a, p. 163), to the alternative fetish site, Bella Vendetta, with its "underground kink" images of asphyxiation, age play, body modification, gender fucking and menstrual art, and the queer "hot radical porn" at No Fauxxx, which combines alt, gay, lesbian, straight, trans, kink, and bbw[5] genres.

Despite this variation, altporn sites share a set of characteristics; they feature "models who are real people," are generally "considered woman-friendly and sex-positive" (in Ray, 2007a, p. 160), and are not uncommonly run or dominated by women. Stylistically, they often draw on punk and retro styles, challenging the established aesthetics and address of hardcore industry pornography. Others such as Furry Girl embrace a more natural aesthetic; Furry Girl models unshaved and without makeup. The sites' variation in their adoption of the "porn" and "erotica" labels, and the coining of new terms such as "punk porn" or "subculture erotica" to describe their content suggests a simultaneous challenge to the aesthetics and politics of porn. Varieties of subcultural, countercultural, queer, or feminist politics are frequently evident, though it is altporn's engagement with feminist critiques of pornography that has most often attracted the attention of cultural commentators. This has been particularly evident in discussions of Suicide Girls, especially since 2005 when nearly 40 models left the site amid claims that the site's male president, Spooky, was abusive to models and used his cofounder, Missy, as "a pro-woman front" (Fulton, 2005).

Altporn sites also combine commerce with community, often adopting a subscription model in which prime content becomes available to members for a monthly fee. They often present themselves as sites of community as well as commercial enterprises, as Deviant Nation proclaims of itself on its welcome page:

> We believe that people who love erotica are more than just faceless members sitting at a computer looking at photos of nameless models. We are a community, a cooperative, a society of people that are more than the dollar amount of their site memberships. We are striving to combine community, subculture, artistic expression and erotica all at once.[6]

This combination of previously unrelated elements is a particular feature of new porn production; sexual and nonsexual content are mixed together and sex is located in a broader cultural context alongside music, art, and politics. In this way, sex and porn are repositioned as part of a mix of media, lifestyle, and sexual practices through which the self is expressed and community created, and in which neither is antithetical to commerce. The inclusion of blogs, discussion groups and message boards, camsites and chat rooms on many altporn sites further emphasizes the mixing of sex with social networking, self-imaging, and user-generated content. Here "sex work" becomes a stylish and alternative form of self-expression and a way of developing community.

Porn Professionals and Sex as Medium

Increasing numbers of people involved in new pornographies are attempting to make money from their involvement, and they are found in an increasingly diverse range of occupations. The journalists, editors, educators, photographers, performers, directors, producers, marketers, curators, retailers, product developers, promoters, and sales workers described in Carly Milne's anthology have been joined by online s/experts, sex-cultural intermediaries and sexbloggers, and a group of workers who frequently operate across media forms, genres, and occupations.

Many new porn professionals show "exceptionally flexible media agency" (Nikunen & Paasonen, 2007, p. 30). Violet Blue is a prolific author, sex educator, and reviewer, who runs her own site (Tiny Nibbles) and a technology blog (Techyum), and is sex columnist for the *San Francisco Chronicle*. Bella Vendetta runs her own porn site, where she is both artist and model, and works in fashion, film production, direction, and performance, writes poetry and erotica, and edits zines. Audacia Ray, one of the most name-checked of the new porn professionals, has been a sex worker, a researcher at the Museum of Sex, New York, an author, model, film director/producer, executive editor at sex worker magazine *$pread*, editor of the public education blog, Sex Work 101, cofounder of Sex Work Awareness. She has been described as a "Jill of all media trades"[7] and is "a prolific writer, video blogger, and erotic art curator."[8] She teaches a university class on sexuality, runs workshops on sexual health, sex and technology, and sexual politics, regularly speaks in public, and currently works as the online strategist at the International Women's Health Coalition in New York. The diversity of Ray's work and her collaborations with other women in her networks are also indicative of the way that the new porn professionalism involves the drawing together of sex work, Web technologies, cultural production, education, and more.

Ray's Waking Vixen site includes a list of "heroes,"[9] which neatly indicates the spread of skills and interests represented by porn professionals like herself; they include sex educators such as Ducky Doolittle ("Fabulous NYC sex educator"), Heather Corinna ("Founder of Scarleteen, the incredible sexuality resource for teens"), and Tristan Taormino ("Anal sex guru and sex ed dynamo"); sex-positive writers of both fact and fiction such as Carol Queen ("pansexual pervert and sex radical"), Tracy Quan ("writes novels about the trials and travails of sex workers in NYC"), and Susie Bright ("Erotica writer and editor, sex educator and cultural critic"); and sex/technology experts such as Annalee Newitz ("nerd ... geek ... raging polyamorous queer") and Regina Lynn.

Women are visible as independent, strong, multifaceted beings who are politically astute, sexually desiring, talented, and incredibly hardworking. Friendships are apparent between many of these women, while self-promotion is combined with a sense of community, particularly around sex work as a form of labor.

This drawing together of generic and occupational categories is also evident in the emergence of a new vocabulary. Audacia Ray describes her company Waking Vixen Productions as a "producer of smart sex culture,"[10] while a post at Melissa Gira's Sexerati column on sex writing (2008a) talks about "thinking sex online," "contributing to the sex culture," "talking sex," "working sex," and being one of the "sex people." Noting a tradition in which writing about sex was previously only ever a "stepping stone to some supposedly elevated ground as a real writer, a real journalist, a real contributor to society," Gira asserts the value of sex work that is "not limited to prostitution or porn or what we think of as sex work, but as ... medium," and which might include "Producing sexual media, theorizing and studying sex and educating about sex."

The notions of "sex culture" and "sex as medium" clearly show how, for these new professionals, occupation is linked to identity and sex work may take hybrid forms with all kinds of personal, aesthetic, political, community, and commercial significance. The insistence on the value of the work is in marked contrast to an established view of porn as one-dimensional and of little cultural importance. Entertainment and knowledge production are also often combined in these new networks; a tendency also apparent in the drawing together of the academic/activist/artist roles of netporn conferences such as C'lick Me (Amsterdam, 2005 and 2007), the "unconference" on sex and media, Sex 2.0 (Atlanta, 2008 and Washington, 2009), and the sex and technology conference, Arse Electronica (San Francisco, 2007 and 2008). Organized by Monochrom, a collective dealing with technology, art and philosophy, Arse Electronica's 2007 contributors included Violet Blue; Eon McKai; Timothy Archibald, the author of *Sex Machines* (2005); Mark Dery, cultural critic and professor of media criticism; Thomas Roche, writer of erotic fiction; Annalee Newitz, writer on technology, media, culture, and science; Carol Queen, sociologist and cultural sexologist; and Kink, producers of BDSM movies. Like Audacia Ray's "heroes," they represent some of the many new ways of "working sex" and demonstrate highly reflexive forms of professionalism in new sites of knowledge production.

Labor and Love: Fame without Fortune

Although new porn professionals have attracted a great deal of attention, relatively little interest has been paid to what they do as a form of labor. Stereotypically, porn labor has been understood in terms of illegitimate industries, exploitation, and dirty money, although this view has increasingly been challenged by sex work activists who have argued that sex work should be recognized as "as a job not wholly unlike other jobs," and that the diversity of sex workers' experiences and conditions are often ignored, with the consequence that sex workers are branded and stigmatized as "Other" (Pendleton, 1997, p. 75). The gift economy and amateur origins of much new porn production also provide a different context for understanding porn labor, part of a broader shift from cultural production and consumption to usage and active engagement in participatory cultures (see Jenkins, 2006).

The notion of the pro-am is particularly relevant for the type of labor represented by new porn professionals. The pro-am is "a new social hybrid," disrupting categories of work and leisure, professional and amateur, production and consumption (Leadbeater & Miller, 2004, p. 20). It is particularly associated with the broader growth in forms of creative labor—especially in new media and the cultural industries— which foreground bohemian and artistic modes of work and ways of living. These are often characterized by work practices which are flexible, autonomous, and individually fulfilling (Ross, 2004, 2008; Lloyd, 2005; Gill, 2007a; Gill & Pratt, 2008). For those who work in them, the notion of "lifestyle" is paramount in drawing together work and leisure, as is the "wearing down of the lines between the personal and the professional," as Audacia Ray describes it (2008a). But this type of labor is also insecure, promoting a "feast-or-famine economy," a model of the employee as "capable of self-discipline under the most extreme job pressure," and the survival of only the most "spunky, agile and dauntless" (Ross, 2008, pp. 34–36).

Ray's Web site, Waking Vixen, is a fascinating document of the shifting nature of such labor and of the hybridity of new porn professionalism as it attempts to bridge mainstream and alternative lifestyles, the personal and the political, work and leisure. Begun in 2004, the first post, "A beginning," describes "what this blog is to be about: the process I'm going through as I try to figure out what it looks like to try and create a balance between Straight World and Pervland, in both the professional and filthy senses. You'll get to read plenty of ruminations on sex, politics, history and get acquainted with the inner workings of my brain as I think these things through—but you'll also get to hear funny stories from the daily worklife of a half-time professional pervert. And, of course, you'll also get some dirty stories that aren't about work at all" (Ray, 2004).

Since then, Ray's site has grown and is now linked to her other sites; Live Girl Review, launched in 2007 to review the presentation of sex in art, porn, blogs, books, sex toys, and beauty and health products, and AudaciaRay.com which acts as a work portfolio. Ray has also worked as Community Manager at the online sex community, Peeq (2007), and edited the *Village Voice* sexuality blog, Naked City (2008), producing its weekly documentary video show, "Naked City TV." Both ventures were short-lived, illustrating the precariousness of much of her work.

Marking the fourth anniversary of Waking Vixen, Ray reviews the past four years, noting that, "blogging changed my life … I've met lots of fascinating people … Blogging has brought me the biggest opportunities of my career, and it's shaped a lot of who I am today … it helped me sort my shit out both personally and professionally, and it has created more opportunities than I can count." She concludes, "I think I've pretty much solved the initial problem of this blog—how to live the divide between

Pervland and StraightWorld. The answer, in short, is: don't be such a wimp, kill the divide" (2008b).

Yet killing the divide is not easy. Not only is the work precarious, it is also potentially endless and without boundaries because there is no division between productivity and pleasure. In a post titled, "How I get it all done" (2008c), Ray describes the overlap between work and leisure; "I truly and deeply love the work I do, so that it doesn't feel like work"— work is "what I do for fun," "part of a lifestyle choice." This ensures that she is "always and never working" and her "personal secret to getting things done is a combination of a total driven obsession with producing something that I think will be awesome and total panic that I need to keep making cool stuff or I'll stop being worthwhile and not be able to pay my bills." She notes, the "intense and unhealthy obsession with things I think are interesting and worthwhile, fear of failure, no day job to catch me. That is the wind beneath my wings and the fire under my ass."

At times, this variety and pace become oppressive. In a post titled, "Frustration, Overload and a Little Panic" (2008d), Ray lists the mounting projects that there's not enough time to finish; a new short film she's made, two more porn films in the pipeline, a book waiting to be written, all of which she juggles as a "loner" with "no team" and not enough cash-generating work. The precariousness of this kind of work became even more apparent during a "major shake up in the conjoined worlds of sex writing and sex blogging" as the recession began to grip the United States in 2008 (Ray, 2008e). It included the end of Regina Lynn's well-known "Sex Drive" column for *Wired*, the axing of Melissa Gira's "Sex Trade" column for Valleywag and the firing of Tristan Taormino from her *Village Voice* column, "Pucker Up." A number of reasons were suggested for the shake-up; a "glut of online content" generally, the perception of sex writing as frivolous, and, conversely, a movement away from older, established producers in favor of younger writers willing to write for free (Ray, 2008f). As Ray noted, and as Violet Blue (2008), Melissa Gira (2008b), and Gracie Passette (2008) also acknowledged, the shake-up raised the question of whether and how sex sells, even in a culture apparently obsessed with sex, and what kinds of compromises new porn professionals might have to make between business and activism in the future.

Decidedly Less Straight?

Critiques of new pornographies and other practices that claim to demonstrate contemporary forms of sexual agency often depend on a broader critique of individual autonomy associated with the work of Nikolas Rose (1996). From this point of view, the construction of self is a form of discipline in which the mechanisms of social control are internalized. Individual freedom is seen as a form of self-regulation by which individuals are increasingly made to take responsibility for features of late capitalism over which they actually have no control. As part of this process, genuinely alternative and countercultural politics are assimilated to promote "hip" forms of consumerism (Frank, 1998; Heath & Potter, 2005), while feminist politics are acknowledged only in order to be repudiated (McRobbie, 2004; Gill, 2007b). Forms of bourgeois bohemianism (Brooks, 2000) rework sexual politics as hedonism and the struggle for sexual liberation is caught up in the pursuit of profit.

But to frame the rise of new porn professionalism only in these terms would be to miss the complexity of new forms of erotic labor, which are influenced much more complicatedly by a bourgeois ethic of fun, the alternative values of subcultures, by sex work activism and by feminist, queer, and sex-radical debates, as well as by the more prosaic constraints imposed by the need to make money. It would also be to ignore the real advances that have been made in the arena of sexual politics and "the new freedoms, positive identities, genuine choices" that now exist (Weeks, 2007, p. 132). And it would be to overlook the shifting context in which these changes are taking place—both in sex work and more broadly in the ways that self, kinship, labor, and leisure are imagined and experienced as postindustrial economies become characterized by a "proliferation of forms of service work, the new global information economy, and 'postmodern' families peopled by isolable individuals" (Bernstein, 2007, p. 6). In this context, new configurations of commerce and intimacy, love and labor, sex and technology arise, requiring new ways of thinking, not least about the politics of sexuality.

Indeed, the attempt to develop a sexual ethics beyond existing moral frameworks provides an important context for the development of new porn professionalism because of its refusal of moralistic assumptions that sex should be private, that commercial sex is simply "wrong" or always damaging, that sex workers are inevitably alienated, exploited, or dehumanized by their work, or that porn necessarily "represents a limited range of body types as sexually appealing" (Albury, 2003, p. 198). This attempt has been apparent throughout sex-radical and sex worker activist discourses. It can also be detected in the development of a variety of alternative sexual activities such as BDSM and polyamory which are "bounded by practices of ethical decision-making" (Albury, 2002, p. 171, see also Easton & Liszt, 1998). These depend on the refusal of sexual double standards, on the establishment of a set of values that are explicit rather than implicit and that focus on individual consent, responsibility, openness, turn-taking and reciprocity, and on the ongoing negotiation of rules (Albury, 2002).

Some new porn practices have also provided spaces for developing a new ethics of sex. The reflexivity of these practices is particularly apparent in the community-based processes of amateur porn production and its working out of best practice guidelines, rules, codes of conduct, and forms of etiquette. This is a "conversation, linking bedrooms, lounge rooms, kitchens and garages" (Albury, 2003, p. 208), a form of what Jeffrey Weeks has called an "everyday experiment" (in Albury, ibid.), drawing on material realities rather than abstract principles, and linking sex and sexuality with everyday life.

Some altporn practitioners have also been concerned with developing an ethical framework for new forms of sexual representation. Bella Vendetta's site is "a celebration of sex," but it also aims to "make you question your ethics, question your ideals, question your sexuality and question what it is that turns you on." Furry Girl has argued that porn performance should be a form of self-expression in which performers are portrayed "as multidimensional beings, with interests other than sex." It should defy conventions of beauty, body type and style, and challenge "stereotypes and negative attitudes about race, size, gender, and sexual orientation." It should aim to build a participatory culture, drawing together "people who are a part of each other's lives outside of porn," so that porn becomes "an expression of the people who make it" (in Watson, n.d). No Fauxxx's mission statement describes its attempts to mix "arousal" with "crafty attitudes," "alternative lifestyles" and "political ideas" to "create a community of varied identities," which is respectful toward the cultures it borrows from, to promote safe sex, provide affordable and accessible porn, and adopt "female-friendly," "trans-friendly" and "worker-friendly" perspectives.[11]

What these approaches share, in contrast to abstract concerns about whether sex work, and porn in particular, is "wrong," is a concern with a "responsible hedonism" (Hartley, 1997, p. 57), which is specific and practical; focused on the power relations between producers, how images are produced and distributed, and what kinds of contexts they are consumed in. As Kath Albury notes (2009), by refusing to frame porn production and porn labor in terms of "either/or propositions," it becomes possible to think more productively about *what* the production, consumption and distribution of porn might mean to different stakeholders." The rise of the new porn professionals is of great interest in this respect, for illuminating new developments in porn and its proliferation online, but it is also important for what it might show us about the shifting significance of sex, media, labor, and leisure in the new precarious conditions of late modern societies.

Notes

1. Belle du Jour's novel has been adapted for British television as *Secret Diary of a Call Girl* (2007), and Quan's work has been optioned by Darren Star, producer of *Sex and the City* (1998–2004).
2. The term is from Teresa M. Senft (2008) *Camgirls: Celebrity and Community in the Age of Social Networks* (New York: Peter Lang).
3. Visitor numbers for representative altporn sites in January 2008 were as follows: SuicideGirls 212, 865; Bella Vendetta 3067; No Fauxxx 1594, http://altporn. net/2008/01/28/altporn-a-list-competecom-january-27-2008/. Accessed January 2009.
4. Sharing is Sexy welcome page, http://sharingissexy.org/node/2. Accessed 22 January 2009.
5. Big-boned women.
6. http://www.deviantnation.com/. Accessed 15 January 2009.
7. *Clamor Magazine*, quoted at "About Audacia Ray," http://www.wakingvixen. com/about/. Accessed 5 January 2009.
8. Welcome page, Waking Vixen, http://www.wakingvixen.com/. Accessed 5 January 2009.
9. http://www.wakingvixen.com/heroes/. Accessed 5 January 2009.
10. home page, http://www.wakingvixen.com. Accessed 5 January 2009.
11. http://www.nofauxxx.com/index.php?option=com_content&view=article&id= 51&Itemid=651. Accessed 21 January 2009.

Part Two: Porn Styles

Chapter 6
Behind the Scenes of Straight Pleasure
Sanna Härmä and Joakim Stolpe

In this chapter, we look behind the scenes of straight mainstream online porn, focusing on the blooper reels and other behind-the-scenes materials that are offered by both free and commercial porn sites as "side dishes" to "the real thing." Since the introduction of the DVD format, most mainstream film studios have included this kind of material as additions to feature films and the porn industry has followed the trend so that today it is fairly standard for any full-length adult release to feature at least some behind-the-scenes footage, and in some cases a separately shot behind-the-scenes sequence. Online providers of straight downloadable porn also offer behind-the-scenes footage, usually collected from DVD features, but made available here as a separately downloadable "Behind The Scenes" segment. Isolated from the feature in this way, behind-the-scenes material becomes available for consumption on its own. The growing availability of this material raises questions about the relation between the "front' and the "behind' of straight porn. In this chapter, we examine some of the behind-the-scenes available online in the mainstream vaults of straight feature films that commercial sites such as Dooza, Videosz, and Downloadpass represent.

Behind-the-scenes invites the audience to take a peek behind hardcore porn film, into dressing rooms and toilets, parking lots and lounges, to meet the actors behind the characters and porn star personae, all masks apparently removed. Some footage shows only brief instances of pornographic action, whereas other materials include longer sex scenes, complete with money shot and more kinky elements such as urination and enemas. Often shot by camera operators on their break or, less commonly, by the director of the film, behind-the-scenes material invades the privacy of the actors between scenes, following their preparations and posing a set of questions about porn stars' lives and work: "How long have you been in porn?" "Who have you worked with?" "Who do you like working with?"

Behind-the-scenes is not intended to be seen as arousing in itself. Nonetheless, the clips are circulated and consumed alongside, and maybe even *as* hardcore porn. They clearly contain explicit content and hardcore narratives and they depend on the recognition of porn conventions and settings. Is this material pornographic? Certainly, up until the "punch line," most behind-the-scenes footage looks just like any other porn and indeed its humor depends on the way it interrupts the arousal of the viewer. Behind-the-scenes may be understood as representing a distinct porn genre—on some porn sites it is now categorized in this way—though it shares some characteristics with other new porn forms. Like amateur porn videos, it lays claim to a certain authenticity of behavior and representation, and like celebrity sex tapes, it appears to show how glossy on-screen characters act in private. It can also be related to some SM sites such as Hogtied that use interviews at the end of scenes to confirm the participants' pleasure in the rough encounters that are portrayed. All of these forms can be seen as related to a broader set of reality genres that now enjoy unprecedented popularity, as part of what Brian McNair (2002) has called a "striptease culture" in which the reality of events and experiences becomes the focus of fascination. They are also part of the "orgy of publication and commentary" (Wicke, 2004, p. 176) that has accompanied pornography since the 1990s, speaking about sex in ways that are "closer to anthropology than pornography" in their "focus on the discovery and explanation of sexual phenomena' (McNair, 2002, p. 88).

Amateur videos, celebrity tapes, independent SM productions, and behind-the-scenes material constitute parts of the contemporary discourses about sex that "fit into one another, interpenetrate one another, support one another … and engender one another" (Wittig, 1992, p. 22). More specifically, behind-the-scenes materials constitute a discourse *about* pornography, allowing porn stars, viewers, directors, and cameramen to participate in a discussion about porn, and in particular, about what is to be considered funny in the making of porn.

Porn is often assumed to be solely concerned with reaffirming the mainstream and conventional representation of gender complementarity, depicting men and women as being, in some natural way, "made for each other." In this way, gender is presented as bound to heterosexuality, a construction that has been referred to as heteronormativity (Warner, 1991; Jackson, 2006), compulsory heterosexuality (Rich, 1980), or the heterosexual matrix (Butler, 1993 and 2004). In these accounts, gender complementarity and heteronormativity form the taken-for-granted models of social life, organizing social institutions, the division of labour and resources, and sexual practices and desires.

Our aim in this chapter is to look behind the scenes of straight porn as a possible starting point for posing questions about contemporary representations of straight sexuality in mainstream porn. We ask in what ways representing straight sexuality is bound up with the representation of properly gendered bodies and heterosexual desire. Our interest is also in the ways that the mundane and everyday aspects of making porn glimpsed in behind-the-scenes footage allow us to come across features we would otherwise never see. We claim that these representations might shed new light on understanding hardcore and the ways in which it attempts to portray straight sexuality as a stable and unwavering monolith, while also revealing cracks in the depiction of a cohesive and pleasure-hungry heterosexuality. As a result, we aim to present a much more sprawling and "open" view of what it means to look at and consume online straight pornography. We examine ideas about the "reality" of the material, about its "dirtiness" or "nastiness," about its representation of sexual identity and the way it closes down and opens up questions about pornography and heterosexuality.

Bored and Bothered—The Real Pornographers

Porn is often seen as disturbing the boundaries between reality and representation, part of the reason why it arouses such concern. On the one hand, as a form of sexual practice, porn is criticized as a poor substitute for "real sex." Porn and porn stars are seen as unnatural and artificial; according to Ariel Levy, they *"aren't even people.* They are merely sexual personae, erotic dollies from the land of make-believe" (2005, p. 196). On the other hand, as a form of representation, porn is "too real," because the sex it features is not simulated, and because of the very real response it calls out in its audience. Behind-the-scenes material disturbs the boundary of the real and the representational even further, apparently documenting the reality of porn, unlike the more theatrical performances that make up straight hardcore. By claiming to represent reality, behind-the-scenes footage appears to expose the relationship between porn texts and the claims to reality often associated with pornography, showing what happens when the (main) camera is switched off. This is emphasized by the importance given to sex performed on set but "off camera," and captured by the behind-the-scenes camera operator. Indeed, many behind-the-scenes attempt to convey the feeling that the on-camera sex interrupts the sexual intimacy of the actors off-camera. For example, the director of *Narcassist* (2004) joyously exclaims "We're doing a scene, but no one's filming!" as she receives oral sex from one of her male actors.

Although arousal is generally used as a measure of porn's "reality," both in terms of its production and consumption, behind-the-scenes material shows a peculiar combination of boredom and arousal not usually connected with porn. This appears to do away with the space between "the reality of the porn industry" and the fictional and cinematic features of hardcore films. In particular, the reality of behind-the-scenes footage depends on its representation of the "boring parts" of making porn; posing for stills, fluffing, waiting, picking out clothes, the constant masturbation of the male actors, makeup, the director's choreography of the action. This depiction of boredom serves to open up unconventional perspectives that contradict the porn actor's function of enacting sexual fantasies for the audience.

The degree to which boredom is shown or acknowledged varies in behind-the-scenes materials. The photo sessions that take place before, during, and after every porn scene are eroticized in some films, but most are shown with original audio so that we hear the photographer's instructions, the clicking of the cameras and the subjects' wisecracks. The shoots are generally relaxed as the performers are focused on the still camera and able to joke around with each other, both verbally and physically. Behind-the-scenes footage also shows the tediousness and repetitiveness of the business at hand. In particular, waiting represents a challenge for the performers, not only in terms of holding the scene together, but also in maintaining some degree of visible sexual readiness. This is particularly true for the male performers. Although the introduction of the potency drug Viagra has made this easier, all but eliminating the traditional role of the on-set fluffer, masturbation is very much the main male sexual activity seen in behind-the-scenes footage. However, it is not portrayed as a sign of excitement, but rather as a skill that is part of the job of a porn actor. The only time it is even commented on is during the brief instances when the performers make fun of its mechanical nature by imitating each other—for instance, in *Squirt Factor* (2005), the male actors put on an amusing "air stroking" show, drawing attention to the way that something that is normally considered as erotic behavior is merely part of a professional routine for them.

These "boring" segments are often funny because they show us the impossible acrobatics designed to foreground the male performer's penis and because of the other varieties of physical comedy, particularly those involving porn mishaps. For instance, in the behind-the-scenes footage of *Skeeter's Fresh Asses* (2006), we see the numerous takes that were needed to complete the sex scenes, because of the trio of actresses who keep falling over, even after they are assisted into the acrobatic positions required for the most explicit shots of the sex act. These become increasingly slapstick and the actresses become the butt of many on-set jokes because they have "been smoking way too much pot in the garage."

Humor is crucial for keeping the border between boredom and arousal blurred, as the following examples taken from the behind-the-scenes of *Contract Killers* (2005) show:

Actor entering the shot: Are you ready?
Actress on all fours: I'm so ready, I'm gonna start fucking myself right now.

In this brief exchange it might seem that the actress is playing the role of the horny porn star, but the ironic tone of her voice makes it clear that this is also a statement about the boredom of waiting for the actor to be ready and wanting to get on with her work. In another scene from the same film, two actresses are waiting for an actor to get ready for an anal scene:

Actress on all fours: Slap it in there already!
Actress lubricating her colleague's anus: Yeah. Go!
Actor fervently masturbating: Shut the fuck up!

The actresses are not making a sexual invitation, or expressing horniness, but rather demonstrating their wish to get to work, in the process drawing attention to the effort and labor involved in porn. The fact that they are "only joking" makes it possible to read their requests both as asking to be fucked *and* mocking the male performer for his inability to carry this out. A similar tone is taken by one of the more experienced actresses in *Skeeter's Fresh Asses* (2006) as she is interviewed about her sexual habits by a cameraman who is clearly keen for her to regale the audience with extravagant tales about her promiscuity. "Yes, yes, I am a whore, I fuck everyone," she says. Her ironic reply might be read as a form of resistance through submitting, removing the "security that the words mean only what they say" (Hutcheon, 1994, p. 14) as she displays her boredom at the obvious and repeated framing of her persona as porn star: "Yeah, my home is a dungeon," she continues.

Here the boundaries between the actual circumstances of the shoot and the presentation of sex and sexuality become more visible. These boundaries can be considered meeting places. In particular, they become spaces for speaking about the relations between reality and representation, boredom and arousal, the purpose and pleasure of porn, and the reality and performance of sex in porn.

As a figure, the porn star is often understood as plastic and fake, constructed by fantasy, unnaturally endowed and giving a false impression of how sex is performed and experienced. A porn star look—perma-tanned, waxed, bleached, artificially enhanced with silicon—emphasizes this sense of artificiality. However, this figure also represents what appears as an authentic sexual insatiability—porn stars are always available for sex and "up for it." Nicola Simpson has argued that "the most visible evidence of pornography's success is in the elevation of performers to international celebrity status, even household names." Porn stars "get up close and personal with fans at conventions, video and poster signings, and through copious websites," and increasingly, "the performer *is* the product" (2005, p. 13). Celebrity branding is becoming more and more central to adult entertainment (Esch & Mayer, 2007, p. 99), and porn stars are becoming more visible, both as celebrities and as real people.

In behind-the-scenes material, there is an increased tension between the importance of maintaining professionalism and the porn star image on camera and "dropping the mask." Some porn actors emphasize the gap between the role and the reality ("I fuck for money"), but the importance of maintaining a star image on camera may work in the other direction, to rub out the distinctions between pornographic spectacle and personal pleasure. Yet, alongside performances of the porn star image we get to see performers' frustration, boredom and sometimes even disgust for aspects of their work. The addition of the behind-the-scenes camera threatens to document every embarrassing moment and bring it into the public eye, producing a "losing of face," and a disruption of the boundary between being "in character" and "out of character."

It is possible to read behind-the-scenes performers both as representing the "real people" involved in the porn industry and as performances of the porn star persona, extended beyond the scenes shot in front of the camera and developed and maintained in the public images constructed by performers. In this context, the role of "porn star" might be understood as a form of camp or masquerade that can be turned on and off, which is not to say that it is hiding something. Instead, it might be argued that this role provides the actors with a certain kind of agency. Even as they embrace and embody the role of heterosexual pleasure-hungry porn star, they paradoxically gain more room to operate and the "unconventional" or "surprising" things they do become part of their role, thereby rearticulating its significance. To draw on Judith Butler's model of performativity, there is no "true" person "acting" like a porn star; instead "person," "actor" and "star" are intertwined, often freely shifting between different representations of sexuality.

Filthy Fun

Sex in general and porn in particular are often regarded as dirty and vulgar. Porn's focus on a body that is dirty and disorderly contrasts with artistic representations of bodies which are, above all else, clean and orderly (Nead, 1992, p. 89) and like other forms of "low" representation, porn moves the body (Dyer, 1992, pp. 121–122), whereas art is supposed to stimulate the mind. Laura Kipnis has noted that hard-core porn is "insistently material, defiantly vulgar, corporeal" and some porn texts like *Hustler* magazine play up the art/porn distinction even further in their fascination with a body which is "gaseous, fluid-emitting, embarrassing ... continually defying the strictures of social manners and mores and instead governed by its lower intestinal tract: a body threatening to erupt at any moment" (1996, p. 132). This emphasis is strikingly apparent in behind-the-scenes material that relies particularly heavily on bodily fluids and on toilet humor.

There is a strong connection between filth and comedy; farting, for example, is recognizable as standard comedy fodder. Despite being quite a common occurrence during porn shoots, farts (vaginal, anal, or otherwise) are almost always masked, edited out, or simply ignored. However, behind-the-scenes materials rely heavily on the humor derived from "sexiness" being undercut by the noisy expulsion of gas. Since anal penetration has become commonplace in porn, a "Platinum X" requirement, as one makeup artist on the set of *Sex Fest* (2006) puts it, the enema box has also become a mainstay of behind-the-scenes comedy. It is amazing how many stories and scenes a simple plastic box filled with water can give rise to. While movies and TV shows such as *Jackass* (2000–2002) have featured enemas for their shock value, porn behind-the-scenes sequences tend either to trivialize it—"it's just water" (*Sex Fest*, 2006) or to sexualize it—"We could bottle it and sell it" (*Squirt Factor*, 2005).

The bathroom is one of the most common settings for behind-the-scenes action and interviews are often conducted in and on the toilet, partly out of necessity, as there is often very little or no private space for the actors, but also because it offers opportunities for comedy and for shock value, which some actors exploit to the full by doing their interviews while urinating or demonstrating how to use the enema box. Other kinds of "filthiness" that are referenced in behind-the-scenes scenarios include the use of drugs and unhygienic habits such as eating community cold cuts before washing hands or using secondhand mouth tape, while the stars of *Whale Tail 3* (2006) spend their break between acts playing a game of "touch your pussy, touch your nose."

All of this suggests that sex and dirtiness go hand in hand, and "nastiness" has become an important characterization of much porn. A "nasty" form of presentation is exemplified by Kylie Ireland, the director and star of *The Whore Next Door* (2008), who tells her coperformers to "stretch me open, the worse the better, call me all kind of names. Slap me in the face, but not one of those pussy slaps" and in *Sex Fest* (2006) where a new starlet is introduced like this: "I've only heard good things about her, she's supposed to be a dirty filthy little whore."

However, the mainstay of on-set comedy revolves around misplaced semen, which is routinely presented as both gross and funny. A variant of this is found in *Squirt Factor* (2005), which features Cytherea, the "Queen of Squirting." Cytheria presents female squirting as an acquired skill requiring training, but as they set up her scene, the crew are shown discussing the likelihood of being sprayed on during filming. As they joke about the similarities between semen, urine, and vaginal juices, they decide that it would be gross to be "pissed on" by Cytherea.

The inability to produce the appropriate bodily fluids is also a source of humour. A blooper available on the site YouPorn, labeled simply 'Porn Blooper' and boasting around half a million views, shows a man frantically masturbating over a woman's calm face. His inability to produce the goods has made the director unhappy and his continued harassment of the male actor is not helping the cause. Even when—four hours later—he manages to produce some neat drops of fluid, the director continues to harass him and questions the actor's heterosexuality. The scene ends with a punch rapidly approaching the director and the camera crashes to the floor, accompanied by the director's moans. Two types of bodily fluids mishap are shown in the behind-the-scenes of the film *Squirt Factor* (2005), in which actress Flower Tissue combines her failure to squirt vaginally with the accidental squirting out of some leftover enema fluid, thus becoming the butt of many on-set jokes.

There are a variety of theoretical accounts for making sense of the way filth is dealt with in culture. Mary Douglas' study, *Purity and Danger* (1966), describes how pollution taboos and rituals are constructed to deal with issues of dirt, order, and hygiene. In *The Civilizing Process*, Norbert Elias (1969) shows how processes of bodily management and the production of shame and disgust have historically come to mark social distinctions between classes, and become a means of internalized, individualized regulation. Michel Foucault (1979) has also discussed the ways in which bodily and sexual functions have been constructed in the West as shameful or even disgusting, demarcating what is "normal" and constructing the body as a site of regulation. For instance, the "hysterization of women's bodies" from the 19th century onward constructed the female body as highly sexual, as an object of medical knowledge, as a matter of public interest and, indeed, in need of public control. In the same way, the psychiatrization of perverse pleasures highlights divergences from normal sexual behavior and identifies them as pathologies that need treatment. Foucault (1976) emphasizes that this does not repress sexuality but, rather, produces it. The concept of "normal" sexuality is produced and framed within its discourses of disgusting and abjected sexual practices.

According to Julia Kristeva (1982), abjection is the act of primal repression that founds subjectivity and begins a sedimentation of identity around the newly forming self through an expulsion of our bodily selves as "not-self." This becomes an important part of learning the boundaries between oneself, others, and the world, and part of the way that gender and sexuality are constructed. Often central to this process is a concern with what Douglas calls "matter out of place" (1966, p. 35), those things that threaten the boundaries of bodies or bodily norms. As Creed notes (1992), these are frequently also those things that are threatening in terms of sexual difference and desire. They become objects of horror and fascination in cultural rituals and in forms of representation, particularly in horror and porn texts where images that play with the body and its borders take up the burden of representing the significance of the body, sex, and gender for the culture at large. The idea of abject matter out of place has been a particular source of fascination and pleasure in much contemporary porn in various forms of cum-play, the spectacle of money shots, facials, pearl necklaces, and the ass-to-mouth scenes increasingly mainstreamed in many straight porn films.

Whereas semen out of place is a common motif in behind-the-scenes, as is humor deriving from other bodily fluids, a less popular representation is the advent of the talking rectum, which appears to comment on the discomfort and potential damage caused by repeated anal sex. Although this receives much less attention in behind-the-scenes material than other forms of "filth," female performers do make jokes about this amongst themselves. A performer in *Who Let the Whores Out* (2005), for example, gapes it wide open, while exclaiming "look it's the Grand Canyon"; another makes fun of her "hungry anus" in *Sex Fest* (2006), exclaiming "Feed Me." Here, play with the abject and the uncivilized becomes a way of making fun of the realities of the world that performers inhabit on set and at work and implies that they are aware of the physical limits of the fantasies and roles they are expected to fulfill.

Laura Kipnis has proposed that porn is a form of political theater (1996, p. 164), a transgressional space, which constantly traces the borders of mainstream culture and acceptable public speech. While behind-the-scenes revels in the pleasures of penetrating the body's borders and in matter out of place, it also traces and caricatures the limits of "sexiness" connected with pornography as an industry and with the porn set as a workplace. By sharing a laugh at the expense of the "messy" and "uncomfortable," behind-the-scenes footage exists in a strange tension with other porn representations, undermining audience expectations of pornographic imagery and the role of the porn star. The work of transgressing the boundaries and expectations connected with the porn industry is at the same time both gratifying and distasteful, dealing with issues that are usually the source of shame and embarrassment. It mocks the boundaries of privacy, personal space, bodily aesthetics, and conventions about appropriate topics for representation.

The Straight Face

Yet there are limits to what is represented in porn. Even in behind-the-scenes materials that are fascinated with bodily fluids, there is no menstrual blood, for example. The limits of behind-the-scenes materials can also be traced in the representation of nonstraight sexuality. One of the staples of mainstream porn representation is the oft-professed bisexuality of female porn actors. Behind-the-scenes interviews often explore this further, asking performers, "What is your favorite position?," "Do you like anal?," "Do you like to fuck girls?" But these questions are generally addressed only to female performers; men are never asked whether they "like to fuck men." The "heteroflexibility" in which apparently straight women experiment with same-sex activity (Diamond, 2005) extends only to female performers in on-set discourse.

Female performers are assumed to be almost as "into women" as they are "into men," and it is hard to find a female porn star who has not performed in a scene with another woman. In the behind-the-scenes of *Contract Killers* (2005), when an actress says she won't participate in a lesbian scene, she is greeted with disbelief and the director tells her, "you're doing girls today." Later, when we see her prepare for a two-girls-one-guy threesome, her male coperformer tells her, "I know you don't fuck chicks, but you're gonna fuck me and my girlfriend today." However, this form of bisexuality is often trivialized. In *Skeeter's Fresh Asses* (2006), an actress informs the viewer that "girls don't count." Indeed, the professed and displayed bisexuality of most female performers is simply an extension of the free-from-inhibitions porn star persona. This is reflected in the list that an actress in the behind-the-scenes of *Contract Killers* recites when asked what she likes: "Cock, strap-ons and anal. Oh, and eating pussy," the final item appearing as an afterthought. It is also the only part of the list mocked by her male costar who we see making a hand gesture imitating her "blabbing on" as she goes on to complain about not getting any pussy for a long time. The implication is that it is only sexy when girls have sex with girls to entertain others, not when it is for their own pleasure.

Many performers, as well as viewers, directors, producers and camera operators consider on-screen action as "proof" of porn stars' authentic (hetero)sexuality. Behind-the-scenes almost always include some footage of off-camera sex, usually accompanied by comments about the horniness or virility of the actors. Performers often speak of themselves as having a dream job as they get to live out their sexual fantasies. Kylie Ireland, director and star of *Sex Fest* (2006), reassures the viewer that she is "like this in my private life too," so we are not to be alarmed when we see her engaging in (what at least is meant to look like) quite violent activities. And yet, behind-the-scenes materials also clearly and literally show the construction of porn heterosexuality. In particular, we see male directors and crew members acting as experts, often instructing their charges on how to pose and behave for the camera; Skeeter Kerkove contorts himself to demonstrate the best position for anal intercourse, while a confident crewmember on *Getting Stoned* (2007) tells the performers, "I'll show you how it's done."

Shared laughter on set works to mark transgressions of pornonormativity and functions as an affirmation of shared sexuality, or what might be called the "straight face." In *Skeeter's Fresh Asses* (2006), we see Skeeter and his friend hugging and giving each other a little peck on the cheek as they dance to their own rendition of Duran Duran's "Rio," and in *Justine's Red Letters* (2005), crewmembers demonstrate sexual positions with each other. Here, the limits of what is acceptable are made visible. However, there are voices of dissonance. In the behind-the-scenes segment of *Narcassist* (2004), a challenge to the mainstream porn repertoire takes the form of a discussion of heterosexual male anal penetration, when the producer, Vin Owen, tells a performer and some of the crew members, "If you tongue my ass first, sure, you can stick a pinkie size dildo up there, I'll stick my finger up there in the shower, no problem." Although the crewmembers are quick to point out that their assholes are marked "No Entrance," Vin Owen's composure and the nervous fidgeting of the crew works as an invitation to laugh at the limits that heteronormativity imposes.

Similarly, in *Riot Sluts* (2004), the female director, Mason, lauds the porn performer, Katrina, during and after shooting:

"I dreamt of making a movie with you"
"I've abandoned Julie Knight for you"
"I get it now, why boys like girls so much"

This flirting mediates the traditional pleasures of watching porn and the viewer's relation to porn stars, placing the director and performer as female workers involved in representing straight desire. Among other things, the director films Katrina discussing where their relationship is going with one of the makeup people, and she spends the entire photo shoot giving a talk on the topic of Katrina's voluptuous behind. In these moments their lives outside of the shoots are brought into focus, and audiences might even find some of these more erotic than the outright displays of sexual activity they are sandwiched between. Indeed, one of the more erotic moments of the behind-the-scenes shows actress and director tasting each other's fingers inside the private changing room, a moment that seems designed, not only to titillate imagined viewers but as a record of a moment of shared affection between these two coworkers.

Behind the Scenes of Straight Pleasure

If one has not spent the last decade in the proverbial cave, then the structure of behind-the-scenes will be entirely familiar. Reality shows dominate contemporary mainstream media of all kinds, and in particular it is "celebreality" that has become the focus of fascination—mixing up the ordinary and the spectacular, the real person and the performer, and seeking out the slippage between public and private, front and behind. In this chapter, we have tried to show how this fascination plays out in pornography, in the behind-the-scenes stories of porn production that also work as commentaries about pornography, gender, sex, and sexuality.

Although hardcore porn is often seen as highly conventional in terms of its representation of gender and sexuality, because it has so long existed in determined opposition to other forms of mainstream culture, it has also been viewed as offering possibilities for social transgression. Porn has widened the visibility of sexual subcultures in the mainstream and provided spaces for different subjectivities, pleasures, and desires. Indeed, pornography's constant willingness to transgress the borders of "good taste," hierarchies, and the public/private divide has given it a unique vantage point from which to queer the alleged monolith of heterosexuality.

Behind-the-scenes material allows us to see porn as we have never seen it before and to see aspects of porn production that we would otherwise never see. It also facilitates different ways of viewing the sexual personae and practices on display, showing how "front of house" is constructed from a backstage view and from the viewpoints of porn practitioners we don't often get to hear—directors, performers, and crewmembers. It both affirms and undermines the notion that straight sexuality is a stable and unwavering monolith, presenting a "straight face" but frequently losing it—in the process revealing porn heterosexuality as a performance and a set of conventions.

The emphasis on the "reality" of behind-the-scenes material, coupled with its "dirtiness" and "nastiness," sets it in clear contrast to the monogamous straight sexuality found in more mainstream representations of vanilla sex, the "side-by-side, no one on top or bottom, altogether pretty sex" (Tong, 1992, p. 121) that characterizes more socially acceptable representations of heterosexuality. Porn sex is sex that is entirely focused on the pursuit of pleasure, even, potentially at least, at the expense of heteronormativity and the ideals of complementary bodies and desires, in this sense transgressing the very lines that it patrols. By showing what is also at stake in performing sex as a form of labor and for money, behind-the-scenes views make the economies of porn and the conditions and experiences of those who work within it visible in new ways, queering porn's realities further.

Chapter 7
Horrorporn/Pornhorror: The Problematic Communities and Contexts of Online Shock Imagery
Steven Jones

Making an assessment of pornography and horror genres is problematic, not only because judgments of these have frequently been based on moral or ideological beliefs about what constitutes obscenity, but also because the viewing context impacts so significantly on their meaning. Obscene images are offensive because they contravene moral principles or because they portray what is considered to be indecent or repugnant. They are not necessarily sexual, although sexual behaviors are typically positioned as hidden or shameful in many societies. The conjunction of sex and other taboos such as defecation increases a depiction's propensity to offend. The body's uncivil nature—its sexual urges and the production of waste—may be inextricable from the self, but we are required to denounce those aspects of being, even though they can never be banished altogether (McAfee, 2004, p. 46). For Kristeva, this attempt at exclusion is a defining feature of subjectivity; "'I' expel it ... I abject *myself* within the same motion through which 'I' claim to establish *myself*" (Kristeva, 1982, p. 3). In this violent process of abjection the "Other" comes to stand in for "repressed ... pathological violence and sexual perversion" (Bogue & Conis-Pope, 1996, p. 11).

Horror subgenres such as the rape-revenge film and the more recent "torture-porn" cycle revel in such juxtapositions, combining sex with violence and injury in a fictional context.[1] Online shock pornography, a form that also combines sex with violence, has been largely overlooked, perhaps because shock sites are such a recent phenomenon and because porn film is more readily suited to established interpretive models such as Mulvey's theory of the "male gaze" (1975), and viewer-response paradigms (see Barker & Petley, 2001) that remain at the forefront of horror studies, as well as underpinning the popular press' responses to online imagery.[2] The combination of violence and sex has been largely discussed from the viewpoint of 1970s feminist pornography studies (see Cornell, 2000, pp. 19–165), which is not so readily applicable to the static images, animated .gifs and community contexts of online shock imagery. However, according to Jensen, extreme imagery of this kind is on the increase (2007, pp. 16, 70) and needs addressing; a point that is underscored by the British government's move to make it illegal to possess such imagery.[3]

In this chapter, I focus on internet shock sites, which consist of a single image, or video-loop that straddles the ambivalent boundaries between sex and abjection, porn and horror, not least because the image has been extracted from its original intended context. The imagery that is used in shock sites differs from mainstream pornography because it revels in the physicality of the body, destabilizing the ideological imperatives that underscore heteronormative representations of sex. Shock sites also exhibit bodies that are pushed beyond expected corporeal limits. Most images and videos found on shock sites have been culled from pornography (especially porn involving urolagnia, coprophilia, or graphic homosexual imagery) or from medical contexts (pictures of bodily abnormalities, severe injuries, and corpses). Where the erotic and the abject are juxtaposed, the obscenity-effect deepens. Shock sites valorize such combinations, framing representations of the exposed body in terms of repulsion and amusement.

Shock sites should be differentiated from "sites with shock content," even if the material on offer is remarkably similar. In the case of the latter, the host site is searchable—for example, Rotten features obscene videos and images, but these have to be sought via an in-site search engine or by browsing archives. Shock sites, on the other hand, are comprised solely by the image/video itself, the instantaneous revelation of which partially constitutes the affront to the viewer. In both cases, the object is assumed to be "real" rather than contrived, the viewer's pleasure or disgust arising from the "unseen" being put on display. Communities that seek out extreme online imagery may do so from sexual motives, out of morbid curiosity, or for more malevolent reasons, such as its transmission to unsuspecting users, especially in an inappropriate context such as an unrelated chat room. A viewer's potentially appalled response negates the subjectivity of the individuals depicted, reducing them to an anonymous object, pushed to, and beyond, expected corporeal limits. It is vital to understand the interplay between users in examining such imagery—not only because an appreciation of context is required in order to construe its significance but also because the image only comes into meaning in conjunction with a viewer; a point that has been convincingly argued in relation to pornography, and especially the Dworkin/MacKinnon school of anti-pornography feminism (Parent, 1990).

In this chapter, I examine the moral and philosophical implications of representations that place the body in extreme states of sexualized deconstruction—both real and faked—and how these apply to images and communities in cyberspace. My attention is primarily focused on shock sites, the collectives that use them, and their potentially problematic negotiations of viewer consent. However, we must begin with a dissection of what constitutes the "extreme" imagery of shock sites and the socio-political implications of its definition.

The Pornography Problem

Pornography is taboo by definition, but its characteristic elements are continually shifting; as Alan Sinfield proposes, "labeling a practice pornographic reflects a decision to regard it as bad. Pornography is not the opposite of worthwhile sexuality, but a way of asserting which sexualities are worthwhile and which are not" (2004, p. 64). Pornographies are deemed extreme only in relation to what is considered ideologically "normal" at any given time, just as the "abnormal" may become mainstream, as the increased prevalence of anal sex in heterosexual porn during the past 20 years indicates (O'Toole, 1999, p. 357). "Extreme" porn images can therefore be seen as those that, in their presented context, gratuitously contravene dominant ideological discourses of sexuality at a given moment in time.

"Extreme images" depict that which falls outside the parameters of ideologically normalized sexual behavior, even that shown in graphic hardcore pornography. They are obscene because their representations of "the body, violence, or sex … exceed the bounds of propriety that a significant part of the public finds appropriate for the context and requirements of the situation in which they are used" (Gastil, 1976, p. 231). In the current climate, images concerned with bodily waste (urine, vomit, feces, menstrual blood, or cadavers) are considered "extreme," as are those that problematize the line of consent—hard sadomasochistic imagery (especially when featuring injured genitalia or rape), bestial/ crush/squish films in which stiletto-wearing dominatrixes kill animals ranging from insects to kittens, while directly addressing the viewer,[4] necrophilia, and pedophilia—whether real or faked. Pornographic imagery featuring fixations such as shoe fetishes or clown porn may be considered abnormal, but are not necessarily deemed extreme or shocking because they do not problematize the sex/horror division, and because the object of desire is non-bodily.

Sexual behaviors like these that are deemed to be or are coded as obscene and Other are relegated to less public locales marking their ideological segregation. Those failing to observe that they have been categorized as extreme may be forced to recognize that the moral majority does not concur. Ultimately, the law enforces dominant ideological/ moral principles, as demonstrated by the British government's legislation against "extreme" pornographies.[5] Yet the authorities face a daunting task in attempting to police cyberspace (see Akdeniz, 2002) because it defies geography; Gossett and Byrne question "the feasibility and legality of regulating personal computer access to a worldwide market of pornography … since there is no legal [thus, ideological] global community standard by which to regulate pornography" (2002, p. 704).

The internet has created new opportunities to market to all tastes with relative ease; as Feona Attwood observes, "[t]he last 20 years have seen the appearance of a much greater variety of porn … taking as its starting point the desire to reconcile the sexually explicit with radical politics" (2002, p. 94). But even given the pervasiveness of the internet, and the degree of anonymity available to the consumer of extreme pornographies, users of such networks are still wary of legal prohibition. Their abnormality is consolidated by their relegation to taboo locales as more mainstream pornographic representations become increasingly acceptable (see Levy, 2005, and Nikunen & Paasonen, 2007, p. 30).

Lemon Parties and Last Measures—Shock Sites

The availability of obscene and often illegal material is commonly centered around communities and facilitated by word-of-mouth, not least through forums, newsgroups,[6] P2P networks,[7] and private/instant messaging. The existence of such networks was infamously highlighted when it was discovered that American troops in Iraq were trading real-life horror (images of dead Iraqis) for pornography (pictures of nude women) through the site, Nowthatsfuckedup.[8] This site appears to have been removed from circulation since the media furore—demonstrating the consequences of compromising anonymity in relation to shock material. The now defunct Ogrish, a site specializing in horror photographs and footage such as the beheading of Kenneth Bigley[9] has been transformed into the much "safer" Liveleak, a site that filters its submissions so as to avoid the more dubious content hosted by its former incarnation. Ero-Guro (erotic-grotesque) sites such as Gurochan also explicitly combine sex and horror (including amputee sex, blood, scatological, and hentai imagery), although a number of the representations are clearly digitally manipulated or fictional.

Shock sites unabashedly work against an axis of normality. This is clearly illustrated by their persistent reliance on Othering to instigate a shock-response. Shock imagery features nudity, genitals, or sexual fluids that are contextualized, or have been recontextualized, to cause offence or become the object of comic distaste, especially through the use of music and captioning. For instance, the shock site video-loop known as

"Meatspin," which focuses on the rotating penis of a man engaging in anal intercourse, is extracted from an anonymous gay porn context and framed as an instance of comic disgust. It is used to "shock" or offend inasmuch as the graphic display of the homosexualized male body is considered taboo in a society that regards the exposed female body as the epitome of normative pleasure. Infamous shock site images such as "Lemon Party" equally typify this trend by rendering the (homo)sexualized, elderly, or overweight body in terms of disgust or amusement. That the body in question is typically male reveals that such sites implicitly address their target viewer as young, heterosexual men ("normal"). They transgress normative boundaries—female bodies are accepted as a locus of sexual attraction, while naked male bodies (especially when homosexualized) are designated as taboo/Other.[10] Here, the abnormal Other is used to provoke, and can only do so if the receiver is positioned in accordance with such ideological value systems. Not all shock site imagery works against sexuality, age, or weight taboos so explicitly; "Tubgirl," and the "Hello.jpg" of the defunct Goatse may be partially informed by these discourses, but their ability to shock arises primarily from pushing the body beyond its expected limits (in the case of the latter, by stretching a distended anus to a remarkable degree). However, both use the same normative body-conception to Other bodies whose integrity has been compromised.

The age of digital video streaming has made it possible to easily obtain pornographies previously only available "under the counter" in backstreet sex shops. These range from the simply hardcore (XTube and PornoTube host free graphic sex videos), to more "specialist" imagery (the now defunct BeastTube, for instance, hosted amateur zoophilic video-clips). In the case of newsgroups and forums, the presumed anonymity of the internet is a means of protection, enhancing the communal aspects of file-share fantasy, via, for example, the bondage-degradation forums of Extreme-board. However, the internet can also be a dangerous place where "the gullible are vulnerable to being taken for a ride" (O'Toole, 1999, p. 278). The distribution of uncertificated extreme horror or pornography is usually conducted anonymously—the individual is rendered as username and avatar and the material must be actively sought.

Although their content may be comparable, shock sites and sites with shock content differ in terms of context. Most original shock sites are now affiliated with more general purveyors of extreme material such as Consumption-junction or Brooklynbizarro, the images having become part of community networks.[11] Online interactions are easily misread by those unfamiliar with the mores of such communities. Flaming (hostility between users during online discussions) can be playful and consensual (Kuntsman, 2007), much like sadomasochistic activity. These communities are characteristically formed on playful one-upmanship, using shock imagery in an attempt to astound other willing participants with new images and videos. They gather around specific webrings, or instigate their own closed forums to harvest dubious objects privately.[12] In contrast, shock sites have a wider proliferation, as they straddle the line between communities in a particularly problematic way. They usually consist of a single extreme image or animated .gif file, sometimes leading to an additional forum. "Tubgirl" is one of the more famous examples, and is typical of the material found on such sites.[13]

Shock sites have two primary functions—their raison d'etre is to amuse, or to offend. The two are not wholly incompatible as the amusement can arise from being affronted or from *causing* offence to others. Because of their similarity to some types of pornography, it may be inferred that these images are meant to sexually arouse the viewer. However, while the images themselves are not incompatible with this reading, the context of distribution is. For example, the front page of Cupchicks contains video responses of viewers watching the shock material, not only to provoke the user into clicking the "view now" link[14] but also to frame the experience in terms of gross laughter. Similarly, the animated .gif of Blink-182 has been placed alongside a previously unrelated pop music sample,[15] a juxtaposition that renders the image amusing because of the unexpected relevance of the lyric to the sexual act portrayed. Thus, the imagery may be erotic in some sense, its context is crucial in determining its interpretation.

The fairly innocuous site name in this instance was designed to mislead fans of the popular American band, Blink-182, into accidentally encountering the video. This kind of naming is commonplace and is not simply to preserve the "anonymity" of the site. Shock sites are frequently linked, especially on open forums and chatrooms, by users known as trolls who are often malevolent in intent. Being tricked into visiting a shock site, believing it to lead to something useful or advantageous, is potentially distressing for the unsuspecting user. Moreover, being directed to such a site by an anonymous stranger differs greatly from receiving the link from a user with whom the sender is acquainted (accompanied by a jovial message). If directed to a shock site by a friend, the image can be decoded as morbidly amusing, but not personally offensive. Yet such images can also be intended to disturb—and modes of dissemination which involve trickery are especially effective because "some of the main pleasures of computing include those of mastery and control" (Sofia, 1999, p. 61).

VirtualRape—The Issue of Consent

Thomas Craig and Julian Petley observe that "there are very few porn sites today which, apart from a few soft tempter images at the front end, are anything other than pay-per-view, thus necessitating a credit card transaction before anything remotely pornographic can actually be seen" (1998, p. 193). Even given a change in climate over the last decade which has meant that hardcore sexual imagery is now much more freely available, the viewer is still required to actively search for it. Shock sites differ inasmuch as they shift agency away from the recipient. The line between amusement and offence largely hinges on the viewer's assent; if one allows oneself to be exposed to an image willingly then it may be perceived as obscene, but permissible. Where the viewer is forced to see something beyond their consent to witness it, that image is recontextualized as horrific, and may become the site of disgust. Thus, the image may cause offence not only because of its content but also because it defiles the viewer's control over their networking.

In shock porn, the content—often depicting genuine medical injuries, anomalies and authentic feats of the body exceeding its expected genitosexual limits—is assumed, correctly or not, to be real. This is part of a more general cultural trend—as Shauna Swartz observes, "[f]aux reality has become the norm in pop culture" (2006, p. 318), and this is also true of mainstream pornography where faked amateur porn and the XTube phenomenon have become a prevalent "pornosthetic." As Swartz notes, "[s]urrounded by convincing fakery, perhaps we're so hungry for something genuine that we're willing to suspend disbelief, ingesting even sham authenticity to sate our voyeuristic appetites" (2006, p. 320). In the same way that the myth of the snuff film persists despite a lack of evidence to support its existence,[16] extreme images that are contextualized as genuine are often treated as if they are authentic, both by viewers and by the law.[17] It matters little if the image *is* real, as long as it appears to be legitimate in context.

Also affecting the viewer's belief in horrific porn imagery is the acquiescence of the person portrayed; here the moral issues raised by reality porn (a vérité style of pornography that seeks to depict the sexual act in terms of authenticity, sometimes utilizing or depending on tropes of nonconsensuality) are a useful point of comparison. These include a concern with "effects," based on the notion that a confusion between fantasy and reality will lead to the enactment of violence in real life (Labelle, 1992),[18] and the contention that new reality porn genres are intertwined with and encourage misogyny and humiliation (Jensen, 2007, pp. 57–64). Swartz notes that while "'Real' sex has always been valued in porn ... what distinguishes this new smut from its predecessors isn't whether the action is scripted, but whether it's portrayed as nonconsensual" (2006, p. 318).

As Gossett and Byrne also contend of rape films, victimization *is* the selling point; the source of pleasure is the immoral, hyperbolic indulgence in the transgression of another's compliance. The omnipotence and dominance of the perpetrator, and the depiction of the victim as small and physically restricted are emphasized (Gossett & Byrne, 2002, pp. 703–705). Because the victimizer is usually anonymous in this type of film (the footage being filmed from a first-person perspective, leaving the perpetrator unseen), the act also situates the viewer as passive. The viewer is positioned as lacking control; only *vicariously* involved in the action, in contrast to the *real* pleasure of the victimizer and the *real* pain of the victim. The first-person perspective on the action denotes a private intimacy/violation made public, further emphasizing the viewer's absence from the act itself and its "reality." An additional appeal to reality is made through the moral context of the image which refuses to explicitly frame the footage as a performance. The pleasures of "mastery and control," which are inherent to computer use (Sofia, 1999, p. 61), take on rather more sinister overtones here, becoming intertwined with imagery that specifically deals in the violation of another person's rights.

In the case of shock sites, the subject of the image is thus always-already victim of a double denigration; first, in the misappropriation of their image as an object of pleasure/repulsion and, second, by being positioned as subservient to the viewer's self-interests. Even if the image was originally captured with the subject's consent, its recontextualization in a shock site and its anonymous and virtual redistribution further distances the viewer from the depicted party. Although pornography more generally is charged with objectifying bodies, shock porn intensifies this process because of its means of deployment, which renders the depicted party's body as abnormal. Moreover, the dissemination of the shock image may transgress the viewer's willingness to view the image, meaning that both the subject and consumer of the image are potentially violated by the user who circulates the image-link.

Cyberspace is the unique catalyst for this dichotomy. It appears to be an unreal nonbodily space of potentially infinite proportions; it is *known* and exists, yet always *is not*. As Sofia contends, "[c]yberspace forms an irreal technological cocoon with no necessary external referents" (1999, p.

63). The fact that the behaviors and bodies of shock porn are *represented* through this medium renders them "safe" for viewer consumption, even if they are horrific or disturbing. The fictional networks through which these images are disseminated also mask the reality of the viewer during their encounter with the image; the viewer is reduced to an avatar/ username, and profiles are often faked and accompanied by faux contact e-mail addresses, locations, ages or genders. In this sense, for the duration of the interaction, the *user* becomes potentially two-dimensionally objectified; as deconstructed as the object-body of the shock image. As O'Toole suggests, cyberspace "seem[s] like a place where corporeality no longer has such a central role" (1999, p. 295). However, the shock image is designed to evoke a specifically bodily response; just as porn aims to sexually entice, the shock image may provoke physical revulsion or laughter, possibly in combination with, or repression, of sexual arousal. These are not simply images of disgust, even if their aim is to repel; they are situated between horror, amusement, desire, and morbid curiosity. Perhaps it is because of the mutability of what they signify—a propensity echoed in their contextual adaptability—that they are sought.

Even if it is only fleeting, belief in the reality of the image is necessary if the image is to shock the viewer. The perceived authenticity of the image, coupled with the sudden affront to normalized expectation, results in a shock that may momentarily displace the viewer's self-awareness; so strong is the impelling of attention toward the unexpected image of an Other, recognizably like, yet unlike, the self. This is why the viewer reconstitutes self as different to the represented Other with such violence, through the physical reaction of a full-body jolt of surprise, or nauseous revulsion. Such a response may reaffirm the bio-logic of the viewer's body, rejecting the image as virtual. This acts to rebalance the initial perception of the depicted party's body as real and of the viewer's status as a virtual presence while online.

As Gloria Steinem writes, the affix "graphos" in pornography, meaning "description of," implies that there is a "distance between subject and object ... replac[ing] a spontaneous yearning for closeness with objectification and voyeurism" (Carter & Weaver, 2003, p. 97). The impossibility of closeness always dominates the experience of engaging with pornography. Engaging with online shock imagery is different. The viewer is potentially rendered powerless, forced into interaction with an image, and reminded that cyberspace can be an unstable place of instantaneous, malicious, and random violence. The viewer's belief in and objectification of the abnormal appear to collapse rather than accentuate the space between viewer and object, emphasizing that the online user is as virtual as the subject of the shock image—at least until the viewer's body reacts to reassert their physicality, reality, normality and the distance between viewer and object. The shock bodily reflex, stemming from the twin responses of sexual arousal and horror—and made possible by the portrayal of the depicted body as abnormal and Other—reminds the viewer of a physical reality that online identity threatens to negate. The return to physically sensate reality reasserts and reestablishes ideological binaries, including the supremacy of the physical, evinced by corporeal response to the image.

Affrontiers—Shocking Conclusions

As Carter and Weaver observe, since the 1980s we have seen a general increase in "highly graphic depictions ... devoid of meaning beyond the sheer delight of their (intentionally) shocking cinematic spectacle" (2003, p. 65). This is true of torture-porn and of obscene online imagery, both of which continually seek to "push the envelope as far as it will go" (O'Toole, 1999, p. 357). In both cases, the driving of the body to extremes may provide an opportunity for the viewer to redefine their relationship with their own body's limits. As Angela Carter notes, while "the pornographer's more usual business is to assert that the function of flesh is pure pleasure," impelling the body beyond typical frames of reference leads us to "question ... the nature of pleasure itself" (1979, p. 22). This is all the more true when pornography problematizes civility—

the "critical difference between man and animal" (Gastil, 1976, p. 239)—
by literalizing the failure of the body to suppress physical requirements
such as defecation, urination, and sexual fulfillment of a non-reproductive
kind, or when it radically asserts the biological tenuousness of the body
by combining Eros (desire) with Thanatos (finitude).

Engaging with shock imagery may be included in C. R. Williams'
list of "urban leisure activit[ies]" that "provide a license for temporary
transgressions from normativity, for participation in playful deviance,
and for the unbounded expression of subjectivity." Such activities typify
our "transition to aesthetic modernity," which has "ushered in a new
image of being human; one in which creativity and expression are linked
to the ontology of human existence" (2004, pp. 240–243). In the digital
age, pornography has moved from the backstreet sex shop to the home,
just as reality culture has blurred the line between fantasy and our daily
lived reality.

The diffusion of the kinds of unsolicited sexual imagery that I have
described represents a more shocking interruption of the construction
of civility by reminding us of the "obscenity" of our own beings—the
bodily urges and gratifications that are constructed as obscene, yet are
inescapably part of our lived experiences. This disruption is much more
extreme when the images that are featured are neither clearly of horror
or of porn, but a hybrid of the two. However, while this combination
appears to destabilize the ideological imperatives that underscore
hegemonic representations of sex, the more dramatically it shows the
body pushed beyond its normalized or expected limitations, the easier it
becomes for the viewer to Other what is portrayed.

Shocking images are no more dangerous than the recognition that
the most normal of us are only as genuinely "normal," or real, as any
of the bodies depicted in them. A consideration of shock pornography
should lead us to reevaluate how we respond to horror and porn more
generally. It is too often taken for granted that horror disgusts and porn
attracts. The combined and confused lines between arousal and nausea,
offence and pleasure, should make us question what body-genres seek

to achieve, and how they permit us to reconsider our notions of beauty, pleasure, and visual gratification. This is increasingly important as the accessibility of internet pornography allows taboos to be more easily broken, and makes those hidden spaces of obscenity increasingly more visible. It is time to look for ways of accounting for the presence and appeal of such imagery, rather than simply trying to obscure, deny, or legislate against it.

Notes

1. For more on the history of rape in film and the rape revenge cycle, see Read, 2000; Projansky, 2001; and Horeck, 2004. For an overview of the torture porn cycle and its alleged celebration of sexualized, misogynistic violence, see Cochrane, 2007, and Queenan, 2007.

2. Recent examples in the British press making this connection include; "MPs Attack 'Dark Side' of YouTube" (Kirkup & Martin, 2008); "Police Target YouTube Over Copycat Crimes" (MacLeod, 2007); "Gangs and Gun Crime Rekindle the Debate on Tighter Internet Regulation" (Sabbagh, 2007); "REVEALED: The British Links to Internet Rape Site Viewed by this Girl's Sex Attacker" (Nicol, 2007).

3. http://www.opsi.gov.uk/acts/acts2008/ukpga_20080004_en_9#pt5-pb1. Accessed 30 March 2009.

4. See Thompson, 2002; and McGavin, 2002.

5. http://www.opsi.gov.uk/acts/acts2008/ukpga_20080004_en_9#pt5-pb1. Accessed 30 March 2009.

6. See Akdeniz, 1999, pp. 22–26 for a discussion of police shutting down Usenet discussion boards and newsgroups over alleged child porn content.

7. Peer-to-peer fileshare networks allow content to be distributed between users as files rather than streamed as motion video.

8. See Harkin, 2006, for more detail of this incident. This follows from allegations that inappropriate modes of torture were being employed by the U.S. Army in Iraq. Leigh Gilmore (2005) observes that "images of torture at Abu Ghraib ... resembled pornographic tableaux vivants with prisoners stripped naked and placed in sexual positions."

9. Similar shock-content site Gorezone also appears to have disbanded, although Rotten is still up and running at the time of writing.

10. Where female bodies are utilized, they are portrayed as grotesque; obese, anorexic, aged, menstrual, fecal, and so forth.

11. Sometimes communities are founded specifically around the images—Facebook has a Goatse appreciation group at the time of writing (http://www.facebook.

com/group.php?gid=2207245174). I wish to thank the members of the "Off Topic Guys Forum" and "Inner Sanctum" for their help and primary material suggestions.

12. Sites such as Lastmeasure and Gnaa are of a wholly different order, containing embedded malware that opens an endless cascade of pop-up windows displaying pornography or horrific medical pictures.

13. My decision not to describe the image content is conscious, as the perpetuation of these images relies on viewer intrigue, and an ability to shock, which may be diminished with forewarning.

14. Although this may make it seem as if it is a "shock content" site, it may be distributed as an instant-play video via this link from the hub site; such dissemination thus alters the meaning of the image received, and testifies to its ambivalence.

15. The music accompanying the imagery is a looped sample taken from Gwen Stefani's song "Hollaback Girl", which chants "this shit is bananas."

16. For a history of the myth, see Kerekes and Slater, 1995. The line between fiction and fact has been overlooked by many of the most irate proponents of these debates; see Labelle, 1992, p. 189.

17. A specific point of contention raised during the House of Lords proposals to amend Clause 113 of the Criminal Justice and Immigration Bill, which contained the phrase "is or appears to be," meaning fictional material may also fall within its jurisdiction. See http://www.publications.parliament.uk/pa/cm200607/cmbills/130/07130.43-46.html#j400. Accessed 8 October 2007.

18. Numerous feminists have argued against such a stance, including Cameron and Frazer, 2000, and Segal, 1993.

Chapter 8
Good Amateurs:
Erotica Writing and Notions of Quality
Susanna Paasonen

Distinction and categorization are central to pornography, as is evident when browsing—now matter how randomly—through pornography link sites or metasites, online adult DVD stores, or porn portals. The genre is marked by endless categorization, from the broad markers of hardcore and softcore to the myriad subcategories divided by orientations, tastes, preferences, and body aesthetics. In addition to marking the specificity of sexual fantasies, porn distinctions are central in marketing and branding texts in order to attract new users and consumers (Bennett, 2001, p. 384). The diversity of pornography and the importance of marking choices and preferences as distinct from one another have become even more pronounced with the increased accessibility of online content and novel ways of displaying it in menus, links, and listings (Chun, 2006, p. 106).

The centrality of categorization and the diversity of pornographic texts are equally evident in the numerous online sites dedicated to amateur erotica writing. In what follows, I examine the construction and definition of quality in one such site, namely Literotica, a massive erotic story archive established in 1998. Addressing its author guidelines, top-rated stories, and user comments, I investigate the aesthetic and affective criteria of a "good story," and the ways in which these are connected to the dynamics of amateurism and professionalism, porn and erotica. My aim is to examine both the collective creation of value within Literotica and the ways in which this connects to the traditions of literary pornography, and hence to bridge something of the current knowledge gap around erotica writing, criteria of quality, and amateur production. Addressing the rise of amateur online content production, the chapter develops an understanding of sexual stories, their narrative dynamics, and affective power through an analysis of amateur erotica texts as well as the ways in which readers experience, evaluate, and value them.

The chapter is partly motivated by the fact that public debates, moral panics, articulations of offence, and studies of online pornography have tended to focus on visual and audiovisual examples. The tendency to understand porn in terms of the visual is common, yet this ignores the fact that the history of pornography has largely been one concerning the written word. It also fails to account for the diversity of contemporary practices. While erotica writing has proliferated online since the mid-1990s, it has failed to evoke any significant public uproar. On the contrary, there has been some enthusiasm about the possibilities for exploring sexual expression and fantasy in "safe," anonymous, and textual online spaces—particularly for women (Leiblum, 2001, p. 398; Cumberland, 2004). In contrast to audiovisual pornography that is, at least to a degree, anchored in an indexical relationship to that which has been acted out in front of the camera, erotica—often authored by women—has been understood more as a realm of fantasy, play, and experimentation and linked to aesthetic notions of quality (Juffer, 1998, p. 7; Kibby, 2001). Definitions of erotica and pornography are often political, aesthetic, and strategic, but here I consider them as categories with particular kinds of dynamics and affective power, and ones that invite and receive particular kinds of reader responses.

For the Love of It

Amateur porn has become increasingly accessible because of its online distribution in a variety of sites from Bulletin Board Systems (BBS) to Usenet newsgroups, peer-to-peer (P2P) networks, and the World Wide Web. Creating porn for their own pleasure and sharing it for no profit, amateurs have been seen as circumventing the operating principles and commodity logic of the porn industry (Tola, 2005). In a sense, amateur films, texts, and images have come to connote a "better kind of porn" that is ethical in its principles of production, and somehow more real, raw, and innovative than the products of the mainstream porn industry (Dery,

2007). Amateur productions are caught in a web of conceptual divisions that mark amateurs apart from the professionals, the non-commercial from the commercial, and the independent from the mainstream. As Patricia Zimmermann (1995, p. 1) points out in her social history of amateur film, professionals are assumed to work for financial gain, but amateurs work for pleasure, for "the sheer love of it, as its Latin root—*amare*—denotes." Amateurs do what they do for the love of the activity itself, independent of ulterior motives such as financial compensation. In practice, the divisions between amateurs and professionals are far from being this clear: amateurs aspire to professional standards, professionals do things out of pleasure, and the categories themselves are contingent to start with.

The term, "professional amateur" (ProAm), has been coined to describe the blurring of such divisions, as well as a shift in the production of culture: networked amateurs with professional skills participate in software development, design, and knowledge production without identifying their activity as work, thereby challenging the traditional hierarchies of experts and laymen, or professionals and amateurs (Leadbeater & Miller, 2004; Bruns, 2008, pp. 202, 234). ProAms do their thing—be it writing, computer programming, sports, video editing, or pornography—"on the side." They may be paid for their efforts but this is by no means their primary source of income. Describing the rise and significance of ProAms, Charles Leadbeater and Paul Miller (2004) argue that they are transforming the innovation and development of cultural artefacts, and also their distribution.

Within pornography, ProAm is used to refer to performers working in reality and gonzo genres, perhaps trying to break into the industry as full-time professionals (Esch & Mayer, 2007, p. 102). During the 2000s, online publishing platforms for amateur porn videos, such as the popular YouPorn and seemingly endless amateur image galleries, have come to challenge commercial porn enterprises featuring professional performers. Such developments point to a need to rethink the categories of amateur and professional, and of porn consumer and performer, as well as the general notion of pornographic practice.

In the context of erotica writing, the division of amateurism and professionalism is linked to publication (published versus unpublished authors) and formal skills such as the mastery of grammar and vocabulary. As an open and free publishing platform enabling collaborative authorship and feedback, Literotica can be seen as exemplifying the means of cultural production and distribution that Leadbeater and Miller identify as ProAm and Axel Bruns (2008) terms "produsage." Literotica provides a creative community detached from the institutions of publishing and literary critique—even if it remains implicated by them. This community is inhabited by networked, dedicated, and enthusiastic contributors who work, not for monetary compensation, but for "the love of it" (cf. Leadbeater & Miller, 2004, p. 20). On both individual and collective levels, ProAm involves a redefinition of skill and expertise across the divisions of work and play, and consequently, of creative work, authorship, and the meaning of cultural products.

Of all forums for amateur writing, fan fiction—and slash fiction in particular—has gained by far the most scholarly attention to date (see Penley, 1997; Cumberland, 2004; Driscoll, 2006; Bruns, 2008). Slash authors write stories which narrate homoerotic tension and encounters between characters familiar from TV shows, literary fictions, and films such as *Star Trek, Xena, Harry Potter,* or *Lord of the Rings.* Slash is illustrative of new kinds of creative communities of interest, as well as of the blurred boundaries between the consumption and production of culture. It involves elements of erotica and porn (Cumberland, 2004; Driscoll, 2006), yet tends to be circulated in specific slash communities and platforms, rather than in general erotica or porn story archives.

One of the numerous sites dedicated to erotica (in different languages, with varying subcultural emphases and levels of activity), Literotica is a large amateur story archive accumulated over a decade, with over 150,000 individual submissions to date. Literotica stories are divided into 32 categories or subgenres, the most popular of which are "Erotic Couplings" (depicting one-on-one consensual sex), "Incest/ Taboo," "BDSM," "Loving Wives" (stories about married women), and "Group Sex." Other sub-categories include "Fetish," "Celebrities," "Mind Control" (involving "erotic hypnosis and mind control"), "NonHuman" (stories with "aliens, ghosts, androids, and more"), and "Erotic Horror."

Readers have the opportunity to rate and give feedback on the submissions and the top stories are presented in separate listings. Stories are also rated in numerous competitions such as a Valentine's Day contest and monthly and annual author awards, and are ranked according to their number of downloads. Literotica is very much concerned with definitions of a good story. Aspiring authors have access to numerous guides and how-to essays on erotica writing and, if they so desire, they can use the services of volunteer editors before submitting their stories. Authors and readers can also interact on a bulletin board and chat forum, as well as through personals, all indicative of Literotica's status as "free adult community." Out of the numerous possible directions offered by the peer practices of Literotica, I focus here on the definition of erotica and pornography, and its relation to definitions of quality.

Skill and Genre

Writing on *Star Trek* fiction, Constance Penley (1997, p. 111) argues that slash authors "feel free to express themselves as writers only insofar as they can conceive of their writing as a hobby and nothing more." Taking writing too seriously or being too concerned with technique is seen to diminish inspiration and the "magic" of writing as the central pleasure and motivation of amateur activity (Penley, 1997, p. 112). But the longer authors write, the more they occupy themselves with its craft, and the boundaries of "serious" and "hobbyist" writing become more elastic. The boundary between professional and amateur writing is equally porous, because skilled authors may "go pro" and publish their texts commercially. Such aspirations are supported by the contests and top listings of Literotica. The story archive has also given rise to one volume of erotica to date—*The Very Best of Literotica.com*, edited by Lori Selke in 2001—in which most stories are published with full author names rather than the usernames employed on the site. In the shift from amateur to published author, the writers "come out" from behind their aliases. However, on the site, writers are assumed to be amateurs by default, as is evident in the guide for erotica authors:

> This guide is not intended for those with a professional interest. ... Rather, this is for the use of the amateur, who likely has little interest in being professionally published, but who wishes to contribute to the body of work available in his or her particular genre.[1]

Addressing "novices" rather than more seasoned writers, the author of the guide self-identifies as professional. The guidelines—along with numerous other advice pieces listed on the site—are offered as tools for the novice to develop his or her craft, while also establishing and maintaining a boundary separating those "in the know" from those in need of guidance. In addition to the categories of amateurs/novices and professionals/experienced authors, the guide marks erotica apart from porn:

> Erotica is not pornography, though it can contain pornography. The primary difference is that the single purpose of pornography is to sexually arouse the reader, period. There is not much of a plotline, if any, and there is no character development. Erotica, on the other hand, tends to have a genuine story, which helps to emphasize the erotic elements.

The basic idea is familiar enough; erotica is about more than sexual acts and arousal and it involves the inner lives of characters (see Juffer, 1998, p. 114). More confusingly, erotica may "contain" pornography without becoming pornography, and sexual depiction in erotica is defined as "erotic," whereas pornography is denied any orientation or purpose other than arousal. Literotica stories themselves resist such categorical divisions as they cross genres and styles of writing—from pornography to romance, sci-fi, and suspense.[2] Although erotica is sometimes used as a euphemism for pornography, it also represents a normative model of a "good story" as one involving plot and character development, complexity, and nonexplicit elements. This model is actively employed not only in author guidelines but also in the story ratings and feedback.

The stories with top ratings on Literotica are notably often parts of a larger evolving narrative: out of the top ten stories in the categories "Erotic Couplings," "Interracial Love," and "Non-Consent/Reluctance," for example, nine are follow-up chapters or sequels. The same goes for all of the "Incest/Taboo" top stories, as well as seven of the top ten "Gay Male," "Transsexuals and Crossdressers," and—perhaps paradoxically— "First Time" stories. These narratives tend to be long and involve the development of plot and characters alike. *All that I am*, a story in eight chapters, three of which dominate the top of the "Gay Male" category (with ratings varying from 4.90 to 4.93/5, the last chapter topping the chart), is titled *Finding a Lifetime Love*. Similarly, *A Good Student*, a story in seven chapters, two of which top the "BDSM" category, details the development of a relationship between student and teacher and ends with the words, "Emma. Come on, precious, let's go. We're here, baby. We're home." These somewhat long narratives not only focus on the development of relationships that are emotional as well as sexual but, following the conventions of romance, culminate in happy endings, leaving the lovers on the threshold of their future life together.

Out of the 16 stories with the perfect rating of 5/5, all but three are sequels or further chapters. The stories with top ratings are also predominantly found under "SciFi/Fantasy" and "Novels and Novellas"; categories that are less explicitly tied to particular sex acts, preferences, or paraphilias, and more "literary" in orientation. The "best" stories, then, involve evolving—often very romantic—relationships as well as explicit sexual action. The stories with lower ratings tend to be short and these are accused of poor execution and overall unpleasantness. Several readers identify *Backstabbing Bride* (rating 2.16, and sporting several 0 ratings) as the worst Literotica story ever. It depicts a wedding night where the best man turns a virgin bride into the "nastiest, sluttiest whore" with a fondness for rectum licking. The readers define the story as "putrid scum" and "sick shit" and the author is encouraged to learn how to write or stop writing, and even advised to check into an institution. There is a sense of a genre agreement being violated since stories in the "Loving Wives" category do not generally include violence or coprophilic play. The readers are not concerned that the story is pornographic per se, but that it is unsatisfactory and poorly executed in terms of style and content alike.

For the Ladies?

The low cultural status of pornography has been associated with its preoccupation with sexual acts, genitalia, and bodily fluids that are deemed obscene. From a literary point of view, pornographic stories are representative of genre fiction—formulaic, repetitive, making use of stock characters, mass-produced, and generally lacking in stylistic experimentation. As Jane Juffer (1998, pp. 104–105) points out in her consideration of erotica and aesthetic value, the cultural status of literature works both to render erotica "respectable" and to mark it apart from pornography. The pornography/erotica division is, then, based on aesthetic value—separating "quick masturbatory fix" from depictions of "the complex nature" of desire (Juffer, 1998, p. 106).

Writing about online fan fiction, Catherine Driscoll analyzes the similarities and differences of romance and pornography in amateur stories. As she points out, both genres developed during the 18th century and were seen as "matters of social concern" (Driscoll, 2006, p. 79). The novel in general was seen as "providing immoral and unhealthy stimulation and encouraging improper fantasies" (Driscoll, 2006, p. 80), and romance, in particular, as something like "women's pornography" (Williams, 1989, p. 12). Literary fiction was read in solitude and these solitary uses gave rise to concerns about masturbation, which was seen as an extreme form of self-absorption and implying a lack of restraint and a retreat from reason (Laqueur, 2003, pp. 62, 203–204). Women were viewed as particularly susceptible to such excessive solitary pleasures capable of threatening social norms and modern ideals of the self. Dwelling in the pleasures of sensuous reading, readers were lost to the world, turned inwards toward their desires and imagination and into immoderate pleasures. Hence it was not only the literary content but the intimate act of reading that was seen as a social peril (Laqueur, 2003, pp. 21, 308–309; see also Schindler, 1996).

Caught in the fervor of "reading mania," women and girls—much like the lamented internet porn addicts of today—were seen as seduced by novels and, incapable of telling fiction apart from reality, impressed by their "untruthful, exaggerated, or bizarre depictions" of love and romance (Schindler, 1996, p. 67). The world of fiction was thought to affect the readers in profound ways, corrupting their imaginations as they imitated the sexual "dreams and passions of others" (Schindler, 1996, p. 68).

As Stephan Schindler shows, 18th-century German literary debates gave rise to later divisions between "high" and "low" literature, their labeling as "useful" versus "entertaining," and the gendering of their readers as male versus female. These divisions paved the way for dismissals of popular genres, particularly ones aiming at affective and sensuous responses, such as romance, pornography, and horror. In the realm of pornography, the literary has become coded as feminine, partly due to the intertwining of romantic fiction and sexually explicit depiction in mass-market paperbacks, and perhaps also to antipornography feminists' embrace of the erotic (as opposed to the pornographic) since the 1970s. The label of erotica has also enabled sexual fiction to be sold in "respectable" locations and to be openly purchased by women (Juffer, 1998, p. 107).

This, however, is not to say that erotica is a uniquely or predominantly female preoccupation. The Literotica archive, for its part, is nothing if not diverse. Although usernames do not necessarily convey the gender of the author, biographical information is accessible in the member pages if the author wishes to disclose it. Reader feedback suggests that both women and men write and read erotica with considerable zest, making the idea that there are characteristically "female" or "male" modes of sexually explicit writing unconvincing. Instead, women, men, the intersexed, straight, queer, and undecided express pleasure in pornographic explicitness, romance, emotional intimacy, and experiments in domination and submission.

Realism and Bodily Appreciation

Recent feminist critiques of textual analysis have pointed out a general scholarly unwillingness to address bodily reactions to texts. Cinema scholar Vivian Sobchack (2005, pp. 53–57) argues that while sensory reactions—sides aching from laughter, tears evoked by melodrama, or shivers of horror—are at the very core of cinematic pleasures, academics seem embarrassed by them and tend to ignore the question of sensory engagement as anything other than visual and occasionally auditory stimulation. Isobel Armstrong (2000, p. 95) argues that close readings of literary fiction have never been close enough, instead guarding the reader/scholar from the power of texts to move her.

In sum, vulnerability to texts (Williams, 2004c, p. 172) has played a marginal role in considerations of meaning or aesthetics. This has posed interesting challenges for considerations of pornography and erotica. If acknowledged and addressed at all, their sensual dynamics have, for the most part, been analyzed on the general level of "experience" detached from actual reading bodies, even though these sensations are the obvious motivation for reading such texts. However, the sensations and experiences conveyed in Literotica feedback and reviews are decidedly personal and intimate. The pleasures of Literotica are not exclusively solitary but involve multi-layered interaction with other community members and casual visitors. The stories themselves have an extensive "social life" (Klastrup, 2007) following their initial submission as they are accessed, recommended, rated, receive feedback, and perhaps even republished at a later occasion. The author herself may have long left the community while her stories linger on and enter various kinds of exchanges.

In addition to thanks addressed to the author and encouragements to keep up the good work, the feedback can be, with some analytical violence, divided into two main strands: one focusing on the formal and stylistic aspects of the text (grammar, credibility, vocabulary) and the other addressing the affective appeal and carnal effects of the text (sexual arousal and pleasure). The two strands involve different criteria of a good story: for the former, a good story is good literature, skillfully composed and original, whereas for the latter, it is one inviting a certain intimacy, appealing to and arousing the senses, turning the reader on. The two styles of commentary may be presented jointly—for example, by pointing out stylistic issues that prevented the reader from getting "into it"—and they are often points of some debate among readers. What is poetic to one reader is pretentious to another, and scenarios driving one to masturbate turn another one off. As responses (125 in total by March 2008) to the story *Service*—the second most popular of all Literotica stories with more than 3.5 million reads—show, the fleshy appreciation of texts is expressed in clear terms:

> Excellent work. I had to read it in 2 sessions, not only was it long but I had to have time to clean myself up I haven't come so many times and so hard just by reading. The writing was OK but the horny factor was fantastic! I will be looking out for your work in the future!!

> each and every page was hotter than the last. i got harder while reading this than ever before. im normally 6″, but when i was reading this, i got up to about 7 1/2″. i really hope you come out with something else like this! :)

> i cummed once per chapter … amazing!

> What a dynamite story! Just thinking about it is going to have me damp for days to come. Big extra points for good spelling and grammar—I always find poor writing in erotic tales pulls me out of being able to fully enjoy the experience of reading them. Fine, stimulation scenarios are marred by dreadful prose. Please, oh please, write volume two of this tale!

Divided into 19 parts, each seven to eight pages long, *Service* is one of the longer stories on Literotica and the length of a novella. It is praised as "beautifully written, great prose" and even as a "msaterpiece" [*sic*], yet not all feedback is equally appreciative. The story is also criticized for its extensive length, repetition (in terms of scenes, details, and word choice), for rushing the action, poor language, and general lack of realism ("your characters are not realistic"; "needs some grammer [*sic*] work").

Both positive and critical feedback revolves around notions of realism—the plausibility of the characters and actions. I found this somewhat surprising, given that *Service* is quite a fantastic narrative. The story describes the adventures of 18-year-old twins, John and Kelly, and their sexual adventures with each other, their parents, friends, and friends' parents. The twins set up a "service" as John starts procuring Kelly for profit to their parents' friends. Kelly, for her part, simply loves sex as well as the money. Set in a suburb, *Service* is an epic narrative of sexual taboos transgressed (sister with brother; son with mother; daughter with mother; daughter with father all engage in anal, vaginal, and oral sex, and multiple variations thereof) and teenagers testing their sexual desirability in exchange for money.

The epic transgression of sexual taboos and the hyperbolic display of endless sexual pleasures and climaxes in *Service* render character development and motivation secondary concerns. Consider, for example, a scene where Karin, the mother of the twins, discovers that she has not been penetrated and gratified by her lover, Tom, but by her son, John: "I'm your mother, damnit. Doesn't that mean anything to you?" she exclaims, to which John replies, "Sure it does, just like you being dad's wife and all that … Your pussy feels great." The couple then engage in elaborate oral and vaginal sex while Kelly and her friend Becky, both of whom John has had oral sex with some moments earlier, watch. The scene culminates in motherly concern: having sucked John "clean," Karin states, "Now, off to school with you and we'll talk later." Kelly congratulates John ("You fucked mom so good") and later the same day has sex with Becky's father, Tom, who is also her mother's lover, while

John watches. Karin has "mixed feelings" about having had sex with her child, resorts to having sex with her husband, and falls asleep "thinking of her son's cock."

The marking of a division between erotica and pornography has frequently been criticized because of its assumption and reproduction of cultural hierarchies and its strategic drawing of boundaries between the more and the less acceptable. When browsing and reading through the different story categories of Literotica—and I have been a reader for a decade—I have, however, come to think that the notions of pornography and erotica may indeed be useful in describing the different interests of texts. Pornography need not be interested in character development or motivation, or the building up of sexual tension: it is not necessary to ask why the characters want to perform the given acts—they just do. Porn is about showing and telling the details of sexual acts and bodily sensations and the events leading up to them are ultimately of secondary importance (Borenstein, 2008, p. 98). Although it may be tempting to see erotica as a mere euphemism for pornography, I argue that there is something specific to the genre of porn; namely its explicit carnality, its unabashed commitment to the sexual, and its power to move and arouse its readers in and through fleshy stories. Differences between textual modalities matter: the point is not to make them questions of value. Differences between textual modalities such as porn and erotica are matters of degree rather than matters of kind. In other words, they are not "poles at either end of a scale but axes between which every story can be plotted" (Driscoll, 2006, p. 91) and which give rise to different kinds of reader sensations.

In *Service*, the modality is one of sexual abundance and excess: sexual desire knows no limits or boundaries, or better, while it recognizes taboos and prohibitions, it is only fuelled by them. Male genitalia are enormous and the women insatiable; sexual acts never fail to satisfy and orgasms know no end. Steven Marcus has argued that 19th-century literary pornography eliminates external reality and social actuality, "concerned as it is with organs, positions, events," pornography is "in reality very abstract" (1964, pp. 44–45). Similar remarks have been made of the visual pornography exchanged in IRC well over a century later:

> there are no material cares or dangers (including disease); no enduring commitments; performance is unproblematic; desire is inexhaustible, as is desirability (everyone is desired and included). Bodies neither fail, nor make non-sexual demands. Nothing external challenges the integrity of "the sexual."
> (Rival et al., 1999, p. 301)

In its displays of insatiable sexual desire attached to virtually any human object—sibling, friend, or elder—and its plethora of sexual acts, *Service* can clearly be categorized as pornographic. In erotica, character motivation, desire, and sexual buildup are central, and characters may have insecurities or traumas. In *Service*, scenes leading to taboo sexual acts involve anticipation and build up, but the story is otherwise notably free of character motivation. Although "the sexual" is still firmly at the centre in erotica, it is more embedded in relationships and histories (Juffer, 1998, pp. 107–108). For me, this working definition between porn and erotica is not a means to evaluate the value of individual texts, but a way of describing their different narrative dynamics, no matter how overlapping and leaky their boundaries may be.

In the same way, when readers discuss *Service* in terms of its realism they are referring to particular *kinds* of realism. The realism of porn is achieved through a dedication to recording the details of bodies and acts, while erotica is characterized by a certain kind of emotional and sensual realism. As Catherine Driscoll (2006, p. 87) points out, the realism of porn is evaluated by affect: "does it get you off? do you believe in it?" As with the fan fiction studied by Driscoll, the reviews of Literotica stories that attract the highest praise show that "the reader was really moved or the story was really convincing." In sum, realism is a question of registering the *affective power* of texts (Driscoll, 2006, pp. 88–89). The affective power of pornography depends on the detailed yet hyperbolic depictions of sexual arousal, scenarios, acts, and sensations aiming to turn the reader on, whereas the affective power of erotica revolves around desire and emotional realism. In both instances, affect both results from and structures the dynamics of reading: as Isobel Armstrong (2000, p. 124) argues, texts generate affect patterns, sensations, and structures of thought. As I see it, pornographic and erotic texts involve different narrative dynamics and their affective patterns vary accordingly. Stories need to be believable in their own register, be it the hyperbolic carnality of porn or the relationship scenarios of romantic erotica. Consequently, ways of registering affective power vary between different kinds of texts. In comparison to the explicitly sexual and genital pleasures derived from *Service*, the feedback on the short story, *Little Love Song*—ranked third in the 2008 Valentine's Day contest with an overall rating of 4.73/5— focuses almost solely on the skill of writing with no explicit references to physical reader responses:

> Simply and purely beautiful, Millie :) It's good to see that your characters weren't all perfect 10, with perfect bodies and perfect lives. You've captured the essence of a woman left for another woman and her insecurities. Bravo!

> I loved the slow build up, the building of tension—it made it so much more believable that something like that could really happen. I've never read anything of yours before—and now I'm wondering why! I'm off to find more... :)

> Your writing is so articulate and you made both characters believable. I especially like the way you handled the erotic elements: great build-up and a great mix of graphic and poetic description. Thanks for the read. :-)

In these examples, emoticons (smileys) come to stand for reader satisfaction that is articulated in terms of realism, credibility, and skilled narration. The romantic and partly melancholic tone of *Little Love Song*, a story about the budding affair between a divorced woman in her 40s and a younger pianist, evokes a less sexually explicit range of responses that acknowledge the quality of sexual depiction without becoming detailed accounts of readerly arousal. In other words, the feedback resonates with the style and feel of the story itself.

Blurred Boundaries

As Driscoll argues, the boundaries of popular genres are leaky and blurred to the degree of making categorical distinctions questionable. Romance, erotica, and pornography all depict the coming together of partners and bodies. Once the climax is achieved, the narrative generally ends or starts again with a slightly altered focus, possibly involving different sets of acts, settings, or partners. Arousal, pleasure, and desire are intertwined in particular textual dynamics that refuse to be resolved in one point of climax. I believe that it is such affective movement, rather than any particular text or label given to it, that drives and touches the authors and readers of Literotica stories.

The division of pornography and erotica is in active use as a system of value, as manifested in Literotica author guidelines. It should, however, be noted that, given the massive volume of stories, the margins between ratings are extremely small; that stories of straightforward sexual action do get high ratings; and that the criteria of "literary value" are by no means uncontested. The value of the story is not necessarily tied to its literary merits but to its affective power, its capacity to grasp the reader's attention while arousing her senses. The sexual arousal and masturbation involved in reading become framed, not as secrets of any kind, but as proofs of the text's quality that are shared with fellow readers and offered to authors in the form of compliments. Rather than seeing the pornographic and the erotic as somehow opposite or even mutually exclusive categories—or seeing the erotic as porn that does not dare to speak its name—they should be understood as story dynamics giving rise to different kinds of affective encounters. While notions of literary value continue to be central to identifying stories as erotic rather than pornographic, I see such distinctions as inseparable from their affective registers.

All in all, the erotic fiction available on Literotica, along with the feedback, interaction possibilities, and contests, provide a distinctive space for negotiations over value that are not in any direct way conditioned either by the principles of commercial publishing or by the value and genre norms of literary critique. Carnal proximities with, and sensuous pleasures derived from the stories are central criteria of value that do not foreclose considerations of language, style, or grammar, but are intrinsically bound to them. Rather than debilitating their value, the power of texts to move the reading bodies is an end in itself. In this framework, the divisions of erotica and pornography are ultimately blurred, and to a degree even irrelevant when defining a "good story": readers may be moved by the sexual tension gradually building up between the protagonists; by the detailed depiction of sexual acts between characters who are only sketchily drawn; by gestures of tenderness and affection; or by elaborate scenes of theatrical BDSM performance. In all these cases, the affective dynamics involve experiences of arousal, fleshy pulsations, and movements of desire as some of the intensity of the text attaches itself to the reading body. As a community platform, Literotica renders such movements of desire articulate, broadening the experience of reading into social negotiations over the meaning and value of texts. These kinds of platforms open novel spaces for addressing the appeal and experience of the erotic and the pornographic—ones based on affective movement rather than hierarchical judgment.

Notes

1. http://www.literotica.com/storyxs/stories/guide.shtml. Accessed 30 March 2009.
2. Interestingly, contrasting Literotica stories with fan fiction porn, Catherine Driscoll (2006, p. 91) argues that "characterization is necessary to fan fiction in a way that is foreign to most porn." For Driscoll, Literotica represents the generically pornographic, while the category of "erotica" has lost its specificity due to the convergence of popular literary genres (such as romance, sci-fi, and erotica), and become more of a story dynamic identifiable in a range of different fictions.

Chapter 9
Gay for Pay, Gay For(e)play: The Politics of Taxonomy and Authenticity in LGBTQ Online Porn
Jennifer Moorman

As Dennis D. Waskul suggests (2004, pp. 4–5):

> sex on the Internet ... displays a diversity that has historically eluded the pornography industry. ... Gays, lesbians, bisexuals, and transsexuals can gain access to materials and support networks specifically designed for them. ... On the Internet the voices, interests, and desires of women—long disregarded by the pornography industry—prove to play a significant role in Internet sex ...

Although most online porn retains a heterosexual address in its marketing rhetoric, visual style, and content, there is indeed a significant and increasing gay, lesbian/dyke, bisexual, trans, and queer presence online. This development has largely remained unexplored. In this chapter, I examine the diversity of sexual expression in online LGBTQ porn and the issues that emerge as important to the sites themselves and the communities they purport to represent, specifically those of taxonomy, community, and the evolving concept of "the real" in online porn production.

It is important to consider how online experiences are constructed and constrained, "the processes of watching and listening, identification with characters and images, the various values with which viewing is invested ..." (White, 2006, p. 6). Online architecture, visual language, and address often enforce a dominant view of sex and gender identity, producing particular positions from which to see and understand the online environment. Key to these processes are forms of categorization that fundamentally delimit the user's experiences, even as they promote what Zabet Patterson calls "the hallucinatory promise of fluidity" (2004, p. 107). For example, on popular mainstream porn sites, some kinds of "lesbian" and "bisexual" porn, typically focused on the display of women's bodies, are grouped with straight porn, while gay male porn and bisexual porn that includes guy-on-guy action are generally not included at all, or they are segregated from the other categories via a link to a separate page. Videos featuring two women and no men might be listed as "girl-on-girl" or categorized in relation to particular sex acts, such as "oral," but gay male porn is always "gay." Framed in this way, "lesbian" sex is incorporated as "girl-on-girl" action for a straight audience, gay male sex is presented as marginal and "Other," while queer sex is almost always absent. As Patterson (2004, p. 107) argues:

> The "click here if you're gay!" button, like the "S/M" button, indicates a technology of desire both productive and regulatory. These buttons do allow for a kind of limited role-playing, but it is one in which the "exploration" is always already constrained by a logic requiring instantly recognizable cues, cues frighteningly regularized under the dictates of maximum efficiency and maximum profit.

On the porn "tubes"—XTube, PornoTube, and YouPorn—quickly becoming major sites of porn distribution online, the user is often presented with the choice of filtering out the straight or the gay content, or of viewing all content. This latter option seems to offer the patently queer opportunity for straight-identified men and women to view gay or queer content—certainly a more comfortable option than doing so under the potentially judgmental eye of an adult video store clerk. Yet the fact that the viewer must remove themselves from the "main" site in order to look at gay male content reproduces the sense that to click the "gay button" is to somehow move away from the norm and become deviant, whether the idea of that is arousing, shame-inducing, or both.

Tube8, one of the most popular online porn sites to host free content, allows the viewer to filter out three of its categories—Fetish, Gay, or Shemale—from a possible 15—Amateur, Anal, Asian, Blowjob, Ebony, Erotic, Fetish, Gay, Hardcore, Latina, Lesbian, Mature, Shemale, Strip, and Teen. However, the viewer does not have the option of filtering out lesbian porn, and viewing it does not involve marking oneself as deviant. Thus, while the binary opposition of "gay" and "straight" may be disrupted by the indication of a preference for "all" porn, this method of categorization reinforces a particular conception of what it is to be gay. The category "lesbian" is made invisible as a marker of difference or identity, and as in most straight porn offline, lesbians are shown that "they don't really exist in the heterosexual cosmos as lesbians" (Butler, 2004, p. 191).

Lesbian and Dyke Porn Online

Communities based around sexual preferences and identities have proliferated and evolved online, and as with film and video porn, the notion of authenticity has emerged as an important means of distinction. Bound up with notions of "the real," authenticity is a treasured commodity in nearly all kinds of film, video, and online pornography, but it has been a particularly contentious issue with regard to lesbian porn. Porn marketed to straight men often involves women having sex with women, and is indeed sometimes entirely comprised of such scenes. As Linda Williams has noted, this kind of "lesbian number" has often been presented for the gaze of a male intruder in straight porn, so that it is "contained and consumed by masculine heterosexual frames" (1992, p. 253). Lesbian sex in straight porn is also frequently presented as a warm-up for sex between a man and a woman, or as "'lesbo-jelly' in the hetero-donut" (Butler, 2004, p. 168). Susanna Paasonen has documented how spam email often includes scenes that are labeled as "lesbian," but which reproduce these "girl-on-girl" conventions online, suggesting the possibility of men "joining in" (2006, p. 406).

On popular mainstream porn sites, "lesbian" porn is almost exclusively girl-on-girl and targeted at a straight male audience. At Megaporn, one of the first videos to appear in the "lesbian" category is titled "2 Bitches and a Man," while WeLiveTogether features "three hot babes [. . . who] live together" and who "pick up other hot girls off the street and bring them back to their apartment for a girl-on-girl-on-girl sex fest!" The women are described as having "juicy racks and fat asses" and lounging around in "sexy lingerie," and the images that accompany these descriptions depict conventionally attractive and feminine women in poses that are awkward and designed for maximum visibility of the women's "assets." There is little pretense to authenticity; the "lesbian roommates who LOVE to eat pussy!" are clearly not intended to be read as actual roommates or actual lesbians. Girl-on-girl conventions are also evident at RichSnob, "the personal lesbian porn blog of a rich snobby lesbian from Cali." One entry describes how she has found some "hot lesbian porn for you girls to check out"—a set that "made my pussy wet, and hopefully will do the same for you . . .". The porn site that this links to, however, leads to an image of three women performing oral sex on a man and the rhetoric itself seems calculated to appeal to a standard male fantasy about a "lesbian" sharing porn that makes her "pussy wet" with other "girls," for whom she hopes it will do the same.

In contrast, sites that purport to be run by and for lesbian, bisexual, and queer women consistently use phrases like "real women," "genuine arousal," and "authentic" in order to set themselves apart from these more mainstream sites, which trade in what the Cyber-Dyke site calls "silly, contrived plot-line[s] or artificial-looking women."[1] Julie Levin Russo identifies four ways in which pornography has been understood to have a privileged relationship with the real: with regard to production, representation, reception, and social context (2007, pp. 239–240). The porn at Cyber-Dyke is claimed as real on all counts—its models are "real people," it presents sex "the way people really have it," it is "aimed at real women and lesbians," and it is part of a broader political project to "redeem porn" by providing women with "a safe space" in which to produce and consume it.

This focus on authentic lesbianism draws on an aesthetic emerging in the mid-1980s, for example in the work of Fatale Video, which was "safe-sex savvy and not afraid to appropriate sex acts once considered definitive of heterosexual and gay male pornography, such as penetration, dirty talk, rough sex, and role-playing," and in which the dyke figure became "*the* visible marker of lesbian authenticity" (Butler, 2004, pp. 181–182,

169). The dildo also became important in establishing the notion that "the phallus is not the penis, but, rather, a detachable, performative, even phantasmatic object that nobody owns and that everybody can play with, wear, or discard" (Butler, 2004, p. 183). These themes have continued to be important, and contemporary dyke porn is still largely characterized by "the attempt to create a fantasy of authenticity—utopian in its scope, yet strangely admirable, always optimistic, and almost believable" (Butler, 2004, p. 189).

While some recent girl-on-girl porn produced by and for straight men includes markers of lesbian authenticity such as strap-ons, dirty talk, and rough sex, it does not appeal to a sense of community or shared experience through visual and verbal cues such as the figure of the butch, the word "dyke," or practices such as fisting. But lesbian/dyke-run sites are overwhelmingly concerned with authenticity, emphasizing that they depict "real sex" and "real dykes." In terms of representation, sex is presented as "real" in that the camera is often not acknowledged and the performers do not seem to be performing for the audience, but rather for themselves; there are no awkward positions and no posing or seductive looks into the camera.

The sites also make appeals to what we might call "lesbian community standards." These include the use of political language and references to community ties, for example, through links to other lesbian, queer, indie, or alternative sites. Crash Pad Series is one such site, run by lesbian adult video producer/director Shine Louise Houston, director of the film *The Crash Pad* (2005), of which the site is an offshoot. The home page describes the site as "Authentic Lesbian, Dyke, Trans, Queer Porn," and there is an endorsement by sex educator, Violet Blue, who praises the porn it presents as "incredible," featuring "Straight-up, hard-core authentic San Francisco lesbian sex." Houston lives and works in San Francisco, as do many of the performers featured on the site, and the mention of this here works as an appeal to the sense of queer community that the city has come to signify, and to earlier authentic lesbian porn film (Butler, 2004, pp. 185–188). Its authenticity is bound up with the fact that the site is run by lesbians, that the performers are lesbian, dyke, trans, or queer folk, that a variety of body shapes, sizes and gender expressions are featured, as well as with a notion of lesbian space, community, and tradition.

Cyber-Dyke, a joint venture by lesbian and bi webmistresses to "create a network of high-quality erotic sites for women," also offers authentic alternatives to girl-on-girl material: "if you've been in search of lesbian porn and erotica, you've finally found the real thing!" Joining the network allows access to a number of porn sites for lesbians, including Sappho's Girls and Playbutch, and thereby to imagery which includes SM and bondage, ultra-femmes and "rough and ready butches." Other links provide the broader setting for the Cyber-Dyke community; sites such as I Shot Myself and I Feel Myself, which focus on women's pleasure, DIY production, art photography, and erotica; lesbian/bi/trans personals; alternative sites such as Bella Vendetta; the sites and blogs of sex writers and educators such as Violet Blue,[2] Audacia Ray,[3] and Ducky DooLittle,[4] and All Lesbian Nation, a directory for lesbians online. Here, the authenticity of the porn is derived through its location within the context of the broader community of lesbians online; where producers and consumers are lesbian, bi or queer, and where porn is offered as an expression of lesbian, bi or queer sexuality for a community of like-minded women.

Gay Male Porn

As Linda Williams notes, gay male porn is "almost as prolific and as long-lived as its straight counterpart," and the two are alike in their devotion to "revealing visible evidence of phallic power and potency" through "frequent money shots" (1992, p. 244). Richard Dyer has criticized the tendency of much gay male porn for its adoption of a goal-directed narrative organized "around the desire to ejaculate" rather than to be fucked (1992, p. 128). As Mandy Merck notes, the extent to which gay male porn narratives approximate the "phallocentric, male-supremacist, sadistic, homophobic" conventions of straight male porn, or deviate from them to provide "crucial affirmation of homosexual identity, fluid role-reversals, multiple eroticism, subversive humour," becoming an "educational necessity in the age of AIDS" (1993, p. 217, see also Waugh, 1985) has become a key source of debate.

Yet gay male porn must be understood, not only in terms of its textual conventions, but its place within the context of gay men's cultural and social practices (Champagne, 1997). Gay porn has been culturally important for gay men, working to make them visible; as Cante and Restivo note, "gayness is unquestionably *much, much more* commonly represented than in any other category of U.S. moving-image product" (2004a, p. 147, original emphasis). Dyer has argued that gay porn is "analogous ... to aspects of gay male sexual practice ..." (1992, p. 121), not only in some instances of its consumption; for example, where porn viewing and public sex are combined in visits to gay porn movie houses, but in its visual embodiment of a utopian view of a gay sexual lifestyle which combines romanticism with promiscuity (1992, p. 130). More broadly, gay male porn has worked to represent a "world" of men and of homosexuality (Cante & Restivo, 2004a and 2004b), making gay culture visible while becoming an integral part of that culture (Watney, 1987; Burger, 1995; Waugh, 1996).

Some gay male porn films have attempted to marry porn with politics (Merck, 1993, p. 234), while others work self-reflexively to draw attention to their status as performances staged for the camera (Dyer, 2002). And, as Sharif Mowlabocus writes, even mainstream commercial "gay-porn" with its "toned, often hairless, well-endowed actors," "hammy narratives" and the promotion of an "'all-American' ideology of hegemonic masculinity" is important within gay culture (2007, p. 61), offering "a representation ... and ... validation—of the desires and experiences of this culture" (2007, p. 63). It has also worked to create a "pornographic typology" (2007, p. 67), which, combined with online technologies, has become a "shaping force within contemporary urban gay culture," providing a "cultural framework through which sexual identity is produced, negotiated and maintained" (2007, p. 64). For example, in gay online communities such as Gaydar, users draw on a range of categories established in gay-porn which are related to clothing such as "leather" or "sports gear," age such as "twinks," and body types such as "bears" or "skins."

As in girl-on-girl sites and much offline "gay-porn," gay male porn sites typically feature performers who are conventionally attractive and masculine, rather than androgynous or gender-ambiguous in appearance. Sites tend to be overwhelmingly white, and when men of color are featured, they are often fetishized, exoticized, or defined primarily by their race or ethnicity. Cante and Restivo suggest that unlike straight porn, in gay male porn there is "a supplemental question about what will happen when there are two bodies with two penises. Who will, and/ or who won't, get penetrated?" (2004, p. 162). But in some kinds of gay male porn there is never any question about this; as Richard Fung notes (2005), it is almost always Asian or Asian American men who are penetrated, and almost always by white men. As Daniel Bernardi puts it, "To be gay is to be white. To be a gay person of color is to be a source of white male desire and pleasure" (2006, p. 234).

As in straight mainstream porn sites, gay male sites are also relatively unconcerned with political issues, or with authenticity of identity and community. This may be because gay porn is already ghettoized within the porn industry in a way that girl-on-girl porn is not. For example, *Adult Video News* (AVN), the industry's primary trade publication, and AVN Online have a separate magazine and site for gay porn: *GayVN*. As a consequence, gay porn is always already authentic by virtue of its segregation from the mainstream. In contrast, lesbian porn struggles to distinguish itself from girl-on-girl action made for a straight male gaze, and, indeed, to be seen at all.

Instead, gay male porn is frequently more concerned with emphasizing the hotness of the scenes and the performers. At GayBlackHardcore, for instance, the emphasis is on "real live sex shows" rather than on the participants being really gay and the performers' blackness is fetishized as a sign of hypermasculinity and hypersexuality. Similarly, sites such as HisFirstGaySex celebrate "conning" straight men into having gay sex, and in this sense, their claim to the real is based on the "hotness" of fantasy. Elsewhere, gay porn is available in a wide variety of categories focused on race (Asian, Black guys, Latin, Interracial), age (Twinks, Mature), body types (Bears, Hunks, Hairy), sex acts (Gang bangs, Masturbation, Rimming, Anal), and so on,[5] but these are rarely framed in the same way as lesbian/dyke porn. The focus is on the imaginary, not on community building, except insofar as it creates a space for men to cruise one another online via the live chats or dating services that often accompany porn videos or photo sets.

Queer Porn

There are multiple uses of the term "queer"—to identify gay, lesbian, bisexual, transgender, and intersex communities; to denote non-mainstream sexual groups which might include both non-straight communities and straight transvestites, SM enthusiasts, and fetishists; to suggest an unsettling or deconstruction of fixed sexual identities and categories, or the celebration of differences; or simply to indicate resistance to sexual norms.

These uses can be detected in the various developments of queer porn that Katrien Jacobs (2004b) lists as a kind of "pride porn" and a key form of alternative pornographic production distributed amongst queer networks and increasingly more widely. The queer impetus has underpinned the recent creative and critical collaborations around porn at the C'lick Me netporn conferences in Amsterdam in 2005 and 2007[6] which drew together queer and net activists, theorists, performers and artists, and the postporn symposium in Berlin in 2006, which described itself as "a political intervention into both the heteronormative landscape of commercial porn production and the discourses of the mainstream public."[7] Artists and performers such as Bruce LaBruce, Del LaGrace Volcano, and Barbara deGenevieve have also been important in developing notions of queer porn,[8] and queer porn has been associated with a "postpornographic" challenging of distinct categories of art, porn, erotica, sex, education, and spirituality. For example, the porn performer/performance artist, Annie Sprinkle, has been described as exercising "a 'queer' ideology" and confounding "pornography's boundaries" (Straayer, 1993, p. 156). Similarly, the educational porn film, *Bend Over Boyfriend* (1998), has been seen as working to queer straight sex because of its focus on the "art of … sexual communication" and the "advantages of gender-play," and its promotion of "new and exciting ways to have sex" (Butler, 2004, p. 190, see also Carnes, 2007). More recently still, the success of FTM (Female-to-Male) porn performer, Buck Angel, "a real man with a real pussy," who merges the signs of hypermasculinity and hyperfemininity and denaturalizes binary gender roles (Jacobs, 2007, p. 228), suggests a growing visibility for queerer pornographies generally.[9]

Barbara deGenevieve whose site, Sssspread, operated from 2001 to 2004 as a "prime porn site for hot femmes, studly butches, and lots of gender-fuck" (deGenevieve, 2007, p. 233), has argued that queer porn portrays bodies which are "insubordinate, disobedient, unruly," creates a world where "everything is possible" (2007, p. 233), and makes "a world of difference" in the enactment of everything "from vanilla sex, to masculinity, to blood sports, to violence" (2007, p. 234). The coding of action as "play" and as part of a "scene" means that its mimicking of heteronormativity, for example in the fetishization of the penis or the hypersexualization of femme performers, works to queer them, while existing sexual categories are confounded; we may see "a male born person identifying as a pre-op female transsexual strap on a dildo and fuck a butch dyke identifying as a trannie-boy in his pussie," or "a trannie-boy who was a butch dyke get fucked in the ass by a gay man" (2007, p. 234). Either way, "power dynamics are subverted, inverted and perverted," and in the process the essence of "who we think we are as gendered beings is called into question and unmercifully interrogated"

(2007, p. 236).

No Fauxxx, launched in 2003 by Courtney Trouble, features "hot, radical porn made by ladies, artists, and queers," and embodies many of these queer characteristics. Its claim to authenticity is made primarily on the basis of its diversity in representing "normal people interested in expressing their sexualities ... all sizes, all genders, all sexual orientations, all races, and from all sorts of places, doing all sorts of things," expressed all kinds of subgenres; "Soft core, pin up girls, black and white erotica, sensual shots," and sexual practices, "masturbation, role-playing, kink, and fetish ... BDSM, bondage, SM." Thus, its claim to produce "porn that doesn't fake it!" rests on the replacement of a singular "fake" presentation of sex with a plurality of authentic expressions.

Sex and gender are also presented as plural categories. Trouble, its webmistress, insists that:

> [the site is] not split into groups based on gender, because there are many models on my site who could never pick just one. Same goes with size, race, orientation. Everything is so fluid, and it all gets lost in the creation-to-consumption translation anyhow—why label it? I also work under the understanding that people do not watch porn that matches their sexual orientation. (For example, dykes don't only watch "dyke porn," heterosexuals don't always watch heterosexual porn, etc.). I think my work is authentic because I give my models a chance to be themselves, which is something not many pornographers do. I think it's distinct because it's real, but artistic, and it's unassuming. I wouldn't call my site "alternative" but I would call it subversive. A piece of the underground community.[10]

Trouble argues that the porn at No Fauxxx is queer because it:

> represents a community of sexual exhibitionists, explorers, and outcasts. It's slightly political in a sex positive or feminist kind of way. The site has models who identify their gender & sexuality as "fag," "femme," "trannie," "grrrl," "boi," "butch," "girl fag," "whatever," "i don't know," "genderqueer," and "who cares?"[11]

Performers may choose to define themselves in any number of ways in their individual profiles, but the porn itself is not categorized. The performers remain unmarked racially—black performers are not defined by their blackness, and Asian-American performers are not exoticized. Indeed, there is no system of categorization whatsoever—one must sift through the thumbnails for the videos and photo sets in order to choose what to view.

No Fauxxx makes a claim to a comprehensive authenticity in its mission statement; "We are creative exhibitionists who want to recreate our roles in the porn industry. We are dirty and honest. We are an inclusive community. We are fucking hot."[12] Authenticity relates to production (it is made by "queers"), representation (the models are "exhibitionists"), reception (they are "hot"), and social context (the site offers an "inclusive community" and is engaged in recreating roles within porn). In this, it can be compared to lesbian/dyke sites such as Crash Pad Series, and in the same way differs from gay and straight mainstream sites in terms of its social and political sensibility. Despite the many overlaps in terms of content and mission, No Fauxxx differs from Crash Pad Series in its inclusion of (bio) men, and its refusal to define, organize or categorize its content according to gender or sexual identification. In this respect, No Fauxxx largely stands alone.

Although various commentators have suggested the radical political potential for gay, lesbian, and queer porn to transform the broader cultural landscape of sex and gender representation, many qualifications must be acknowledged. Lesbian/dyke sites online are vastly outnumbered by sites featuring girl-on-girl material, which, with its conventionally attractive, youthful, and often breast-implanted performers, and its address to heterosexual men, does little to challenge sexual or gender norms. Gay-porn challenges some taboos by virtue of its very existence and accessibility, but it is ghettoized and stigmatized on the larger porn sites such as YouPorn, and often does little to challenge gender norms, in that the performers tend to be as conventionally attractive as their girl-on-girl counterparts, and as traditionally masculine as these women are feminine. Queer porn is much more challenging, but little of it is readily accessible—a Google search for "queer porn" calls up mostly conventional gay-porn sites, along with Crash Pad Series and No Fauxxx.

Mainstream pay sites run by the major porn studios such as Vivid or Evil Angel continue to be as concerned as ever with the bottom line, and their assumptions about what online audiences seek from porn seem to be based on the view that those audiences are overwhelmingly straight and male. Free and independent subscription sites like Cyber-Dyke and No Fauxxx are able to fill a variety of niches without having to worry about corporate profit margins. This means that they can be infinitely more diverse, as well as more accessible to women and minority groups, than mainstream sites could ever be. While we may still be a long way from the vision of an all-inclusive pornotopia, the variety of LGBTQ porn available online offers, at the very least, a space for the expression and exploration of a multiplicity of desires for people of all genders and sexual orientations, and hopefully sends the message to mainstream porn providers that there is more than one pornographic "real," and that porn audiences are more diverse than they would have us believe.

Notes

1.   From the 'Cyber-Dyke FAQ,' http://www.cyber-dyke.net/faq.html. Accessed 10 September 2008.
2.   See http://www.tinynibbles.com/. Accessed 30 April 2009.
3.   See http://www.wakingvixen.com/. Accessed 30 April 2009.
4.   See http://www.duckydoolittle.com/. Accessed 30 April 2009.
5.   See http://www.freegaypornfinder.com/ and http://www.gaymoviedome.com/ for examples. Accessed 30 April 2009.
6.   See http://www.networkcultures.org/clickme/. Accessed 30 April 2009.
7.   http://www.postpornpolitics.com/. Accessed 30 April 2009.
8.   See LaBruce's book, *The Reluctant Pornographer* (1997) and films such as *Skin Flick* (1999), and Del LaGrace Volcano's publications such as *Sex Work* (2005) and film, *Pansexual Public Porn* (1997).
9.   Buck Angel was the first female-to-male performer to win the AVN Award for Transsexual Performer of the Year in 2007. See http://www.buckangel.com/. Accessed 30 April 2009.
10.   Interview with the author, 5 September 2008, via e-mail.
11.   Ibid.
12.   From the No Fauxxx home page, http://www.nofauxxx.com. Accessed 20 August 2008 and 15 December 2008.

Part Three: Porn Cultures

Chapter 10

Widening the Glory Hole:
The Discourse of Online Porn Fandom
Simon Lindgren

If one does not count the large number of lackluster "effects" or attitude surveys that have been carried out over the years, there is a conspicuous lack of studies of porn audiences. This is both surprising and problematic, given that porn debates frequently revolve around concerns about what pornography might do to the bodies and minds of its users. The need for audience studies has become all the more urgent now that the perception of porn use is shifting and that pornography has moved online.

The internet has brought pornography closer to mainstream popular culture, and in doing so has made it more generally available to audiences. Pornography still ranks among the most sought-after types of content on the Web (Lyman, 2006), though the numbers of searches have decreased recently (Miller, 2007). But porn does not need seeking out as it used to, and even audiences who previously had little access to it, especially women and young people, can now find it more easily. At the same time, an existing male heterosexual viewer base has expanded, numerically as well as demographically, with the removal of many of the practical obstacles related to discreetly obtaining and viewing porn. Elsewhere, digital cultures are increasingly conceptualized in terms of creativity and participation (Harris & Alexander, 1998; Baym, 2000; Gray et al., 2007), although this view has not been applied specifically to online porn audiences.

The aim of this chapter is to explore how porn fans collectively construct topics, actions and subject positions on a popular mainstream heterosexual pornography message board, which is a part of the Web site, Free Ones. The main focus of the site is to provide links to free pornographic content in the form of picture and video galleries. Much of the linked material consists of sample images or video clips that advertise the content of various pay sites. Free Ones includes a section of pay site reviews, an online DVD store and a blog advertising site updates, new DVDs, and so on. It also has a sister pay site—PayOnes—which, according to its own description, is "the largest adult video download site on the internet." The focus of this chapter, however, is the conversations held on the Free Ones message board, which is one of the most active porn fan communities on the internet with over 130,000 members— almost exclusively male. A post with the header "some questions for you girls" was answered by only one member with a female nickname ("Miss Brittany"). A number of men also replied to the post, with one typical answer being: "female members? there is like 5–10 on here if you're lucky ... and maybe 3 that post ...." My analysis examines how audience members consume and discuss pornography and how pornography is used in social interaction and identity construction.

From Shamed Masturbator to Creative Transgressor?

The stereotypical image of the porn consumer is that of a masturbating loner and it is still generally assumed that most porn consumption takes place in individualized and private settings. However, in academia a paradigm shift in perspectives on porn (Attwood, 2002; Williams, 2004a) has emphasized the need to contextualize sexual imagery and its use. The emergence of a range of feminisms has also illustrated the problem with orthodox understandings of gendered experiences, interests and desires (Butler, 1990 and 1993), highlighting the need to investigate the potential multitude of ways in which pornography is consumed, used, interpreted, and integrated into the everyday lives of different individuals and audiences.

As an early study of men's consumption of pornography, in Shere Hite's report on male sexuality (1981), showed, men tend to use porn both for promoting male bonding and for individual sexual stimulation. Studies such as those carried out by David Loftus (2002) and Simon Hardy (1998) since then have emphasized the need for closer examinations of the male mainstream porn audience. In Loftus' research, men appear to be rather critical of pornography, perceive it in a number of different ways, and display sensitivity when negotiating their porn fantasies with their girlfriends, wives, and lovers. Similarly, Hardy argues that men tend to have mixed feelings about pornography and that they make a great effort trying to reconcile their porn use with their real life relationships with women. Further, he discusses how porn is decoded in a variety of ways, ranging from preferred, via negotiated, to oppositional readings by different men in varying contexts (Hardy, 1998, pp. 133–155). Younger men and boys often tend to use porn consumption as a bonding exercise employed in ways that are "socio-political" rather than sexual, serving as part of a rite of passage into macho and sexist cultural domains (Hardy, 2004, p. 7). Porn may serve relations of domination that are very powerful. Susan Shaw (1999), for example, has shown that although some men's porn use may make their female partners feel self-conscious about their own bodies or worry about the negative impact on their relationships, women are often reluctant to speak out for fear of being seen as old-fashioned and antisex.

Today, the context of porn use is changing. Porn has moved out of a small number of segregated public spaces—shabby sex shops and triple-X theaters—to become ever present on cable, on the Web, and in new media. The development toward a "pornification" of the media, and of culture and society more generally, has been addressed by a number of authors (Paul, 2005; Nikunen & Paasonen, 2007; Mühleisen, 2007). The notion of the "pornographication of the mainstream" is, however, most closely associated with Brian McNair (1996, p. 23), who locates this development alongside an ever-expanding "pornosphere." Both of these tendencies are understood by McNair as part of a movement in the direction of a "striptease culture" in which digital technologies and the internet play a crucial role. According to McNair (2002, p. 88), this type of culture "frequently involves ordinary people talking about sex and their own sexualities, revealing intimate details of their feelings and their bodies in the public sphere." This is illustrated by the surfacing of popular cultural forms in which people are undressed and exposed—metaphorically as well as literally—in the public eye; from television shows such as *Big Brother*, to the mediatization of the Clinton-Lewinsky affair.

When porn goes online, a variety of new themes and issues for investigation come to light. As Zabet Patterson (2004, p. 106) puts it, we must consider "the ways in which the organization of on-line pornographic discourses function." The internet seems to offer "a sense of interactivity, which brings with it a sense of shared space and a collapse or disavowal of distance," and this can be seen most clearly in relation to online amateur porn (2004, p. 110). The relation of looking is produced, not as *watching*, but "being there"; there is a "sense of participation with that performer's life" and this "ever-elusive relationship ... becomes the obscure object of desire" (2004, p. 119).

The idea that the landscape of the pornosphere has changed in ways that call for a reconsideration of how its users think, feel, and operate, is further emphasized by the emerging literature dealing more generally with digital publics and fan cultures. In *Convergence Culture* (2006, p. 256), for example, Henry Jenkins writes that:

> Fans reject the idea of a definitive version produced, authorized, and regulated by some media conglomerate. Instead, fans envision a world where all of us can participate in the creation and circulation of central cultural myths. Media audiences will become more and more active, selective and conscious. This is an idea widely canonized within the rising tide of fan studies. (Gray et al., 2007; Harris & Alexander, 1998; Baym, 2000; Hills, 2002)

One common assertion in this line of research is summarized in Jenkins' writing when he argues, referring to Pierre Lévy (1999), that the "collective intelligence" of the members of the many active and dynamic fan cultures surfacing on the internet "will gradually alter the ways commodity culture operates."

> On the Internet ... people harness their individual expertise toward shared goals and objectives: [Lévy writes that] "No one knows everything, everyone knows something, all knowledge resides in humanity." Collective intelligence refers to this ability of virtual communities to leverage the combined expertise of their members. What we cannot know or do on our own, we may now be able to do collectively. (Jenkins, 2006, pp. 26–27)

In fact, both porn and fan studies need to be seen in the light of an emerging form of audience research which challenges a set of established ideas about media consumption. The shift is neatly expressed in David Gauntlett's (2007) concept of "Media Studies 2.0" marked by its "focus on the everyday meanings produced by the diverse array of audience members," and by a view that the internet and new digital media "have fundamentally changed the ways in which we engage with all media." Media Studies 2.0 distances itself from "[t]he patronising belief that students should be taught how to "read' the media [and replaces it with] the recognition that media audiences in general are already extremely capable interpreters of media content, with a critical eye and an understanding of contemporary media techniques ...."

This development, suggested by new porn research, writings on current fan cultures, and the emerging approach of Media Studies 2.0 raises the question of whether today's online porn audience is made up, not of isolated masturbating loners, but of an interactive and creative collective of critical audience members. This chapter analyzes how online discourse is produced in a porn fan forum on the internet, assessing what happens when a previously marginal behavior emerges as mainstream practice, and considering if and how the use of pornography changes once it is digitalized. In particular, the shifts associated with online consumption are used as a starting point for examining whether the image of porn consumers as isolated from one another needs to be revised.

The Discursive Space of Online Porn Fandom

The data on which this chapter is based has been gathered from the Free Ones discussion board. In March 2008 this consisted of more than 163,000 discussion threads; that is, topics initiated by any one of the forum's 42,000 active members. In total, these threads contained over 1.9 million individual posts. The board is divided into a number of themed subforums, of which the most popular is "Find your favourite babe" (700,000 posts in 42,000 threads). This, along with the third most active subforum—"Identify/name the babe," (250,000 posts in 65,000 threads)—is devoted to members helping each other to identify the female porn performers they have seen in images and video clips across the Web, and to find more material showing their favourite performers in action. The discourse of these two subforums consists of short single-sentence requests followed by many replies in the form of hyperlinks. The second largest subforum, "Freeones Talk" (425,000/18,000), is devoted to open discussion on any topic of interest to the members of the message board and it is this that I focus on here. The data I have used consists of all of the posts (a total number of 5,887) in 15 of the most active threads (with a total of 519,000 readers) within this subforum. Apart from the top three, the other sub forums are "Watch that Video" (106,000/14,000), "Funny Pictures" (62,000/7,000), "Adult Pay Sites Reviews" (5,000/3,500), "Celebrity News" (55,000/2,000), "Games and Stuff" (288,000/1,700), "Suggestions and Comments" (6,000/600), "Webmasters" (1,400/300), and "Register Problems?" (2,000/200).

According to Laclau and Mouffe (1985), the connections between meaningful elements in a discourse can be traced in terms of the way links between concepts are authorized and asserted, chains of signifiers are grouped, and certain arrangements of these cling together. I have combined bibliometric (see Borgman, 1990) and network analysis (see Nooy et al., 2005) to perform a quantitative analysis of the way concepts are related. This is graphically presented in Figure 1:

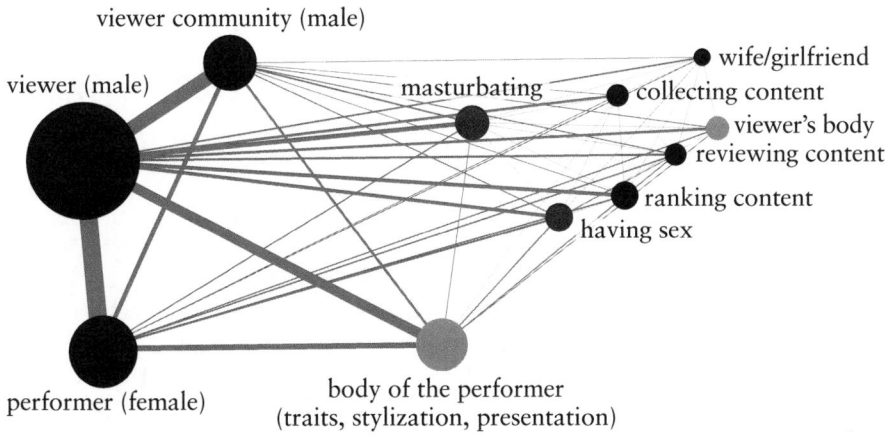

Figure 1. The discursive space of online porn fandom

My particular focus is on whether or not the patterns described elsewhere in internet fandom research are emerging among porn fans as well. To use a concept from Laclau and Mouffe (1985, p. 105), I am interested in how the viewer position is "articulated" on the Free Ones board. More concretely, I want to trace how specific signifiers are formulated and associated in an order of discourse where some identities and representations become dominant and legitimated while others are marginalized or invisible. This provides a way to map how the discourse of online porn fandom is actively articulated through linguistic and representational practice.

As can be seen, the most commonly occurring concepts within this discourse represent three subject positions or identities related to the context of porn consumption. These are the male viewer, the viewer community, and the female performer or "porn star." The sizes of these three vertices indicate the frequency with which words, concepts or formulations appear. Words and formulations referring to the male viewer as the "I" or the main protagonist of this discourse occur very frequently (with 3,800 appearances throughout the 5,887 posts under analysis). The male viewer (or rather, the assertion that the viewer is male) can therefore be seen as a "nodal point" in Laclau and Mouffe's terms (1985, p. 112) and a clearly dominant position.

A closer reading of individual posts also suggests that this viewer takes on the subject position of someone who can expect to get his needs fulfilled, and who is definitely in a position to make demands:

> When I visit a Black Girl site I don't want to see white girls. White guys on black chicks? Absolutely. Helps further my fantasy. When I visit a mature site I don't wanna see Gauge, Nikki Nova or NextDoorNikki. Get those babies off my screen and show me somethin' with wrinkles. When I visit an asian site I wanna see slim, tiny-titted chicks (with occasionally bad teeth) and a pubic bush that points straight OUT and UP. I don't wanna see the average American-Asian chick who happens to be corn-fed and loves McBig-Mc-f*cking-macs on her large American frame. When I want asian, I want petite chicks with dark nipples! I have spoken!

> A thing that turns me off is a fat girl. (No offense). It's just that it looks disgusting!

As Figure 1. also shows, there are strong discursive links (represented by the width of the lines measuring co-occurrences) between the viewer and the viewer community. It can be concluded that almost as much energy and space is devoted to cultivating the "We" of the viewer collective, as to discussing the female porn stars who are the main object of the viewers' attention. This impression does not go away after a closer reading of the material. The creation of homosocial bonds and a sense of unity among the viewers is without doubt a main concern within this discursive formation:

> If I post in all the "congrats" threads, it's because I want to show some love for my fellow Freeones members.

> Really enjoy the forums, girls are always nice but I find that I enjoy reading what the members have to say about so many different things that I would have never thought to discuss with anyone. I still look at the women, as I am not dead yet, but you can't beat the community here.

While much of the activity on the Free Ones board entails talking about porn stars and explicit visuals, it is striking that both the "I" and the "We" appear with so much force. One conclusion that can be drawn is that the discourse under study is just as much about presenting one's own needs and preferences in front of a homosocial peer group, as it is about individual onlookers in virtual porno booths drooling over pornographic images and videos.

A fourth subject position of note is that of the wife or girlfriend of the viewer. She is seldom invoked and when she is, she is ascribed a subject position that is somewhat hard to interpret. It is, however, noteworthy that she is not commonly referenced in relation or comparison to the performers or as the object of sexual activity; that is, the links between the subject position and "body of the performer," "having sex" and "masturbating" are weak. The strongest conceptual link is to the viewer. This may suggest that the wife or girlfriend mainly appears in this discourse as real-life sexual partner or viewing companion, rather than as the object of the same type of sexual desire as the porn performers. Such an interpretation is supported by a closer reading of the forum posts. It appears in many cases that the forum members' wives and girlfriends share their interest in porn, and acts such as hiding or suppressing porn use are rarely discussed.

> I'm married and I still wank. Usually wank 7–10 times a week and screw the wife about 5 times a week. One of my biggest turn-ons is for her to catch me wanking and that always ends up in great sex. I generally wank for 1–1.5 hours but once I was waiting for the wife to come home for a nooner and she was nearly two hours late and I ended up wanking for three hours: came once myself and then banged her for 30 min before I came again. Gotta say the best orgasms are wanking ones, although I'd give it up for more sex.

> I don't normally have any [porn] on my pc. Usually just a clip or 2 that I want to show my wife or something. Then it gets deleted. We are into DVDs and we just have them stacked on our entertainment unit. In the open. For everyone to see!

> I understand, porn is for women too, and I'm sure that women must like to look at some men ... but an extended close-up of a male pornstar's face is just disgusting (even my girlfriend agrees).

The posts suggest that the place of wives and girlfriends is closer to that of the viewer community than that of the female performer. Male forum members, to some extent, share their relationship to porn with their female partners.

The most prominent topic in the threads of the discussion board is that of the female performer's body and its stylization and visual presentation. Preferences, turn-ons, and fetishes seem to be the dominant theme throughout, and this is where it becomes most obvious that Free Ones is a mainstream heterosexual porn forum. Extreme or bizarre porn—or any sort of acquired taste—is virtually absent here. Instead, there is post after post after post about "big tits," "amazing asses," and "beautiful babes."

> Now I love tits obviously ... but I also like ass, however I only like ass when it's covered up (weird you might say but I think it just looks better with a nice pair of tight jeans for example).

> This was probably mentioned already, but I hate the macro-close-up shots of the dick in the pussy. I don't need to see every hair follicle on the guy's nuts for Christ's sake! When the woman has a hot body, then zoom the friggin' camera out so we can see her in all her glory while she is getting drilled.

> I'm a lot more cooler with more Romantic porn. For example, there doesn't have to be a lot of disgusting cum-play afterwards, with the blowing of cum bubbles, etc. "If you're gonna swallow that nasty shit, baby, then do it now" is what I wanna yell at the screen.

These three examples illustrate the articulation of a certain set of preferences which is in line with a rather straightforward and established heterosexual porn regime. It is rooted in a taste for somewhat soft-core imagery ("I only like ass when it's covered up"; "I hate the macro-close-up shots of the dick"; "I'm a lot more cooler with more Romantic porn'), and marked by a homophobically tinged "disgust" for the male genitalia and its "cum."

This last point is at odds with the patterns found within the recurring discursive topic of the viewer's body, or more precisely, his genitals. The strong emphasis on this theme can however be explained by the fact that the act of viewer masturbation is crucial to the discourse of porn fandom on the Free Ones site. As a matter of fact, talk about having sex, or watching other performers having sex with the female porn stars is of secondary importance in comparison with talk about "wanking," "jacking," and "jerking off" to the visuals in question. Here, once again, the construction of the "I" and the "We" is at the forefront. As Figure 1. shows, the lines (that is, the number of discursive co-occurrences) connecting the element of "masturbating" to the female performer and to her body are noticeably thinner than those connecting it to the viewer himself and to the viewer community. Masturbation is, in other words, constructed within this discourse as a primarily egocentric and, secondarily, homosocial, activity. This impression is further supported by a closer reading of the material. The topic of masturbation has a confessional and technical character, and the images and videos of female porn stars take on the role of mere props.

> I only jerk off twice in a row when I'm horny enough and/or there is good material for wanking available. Even then there is a break (sometimes shorter, sometimes longer) between the "sessions." But normally it's just once in the morning and once in the evening for me.

> I once ate a sandwich while wanking.

> What about you guys!? What/Who is your favorite "facilitator"? Where you do it? And how often? Any good technique or experience to share!

> Seriously, get off with yourself and feel good about it! Remember you're a man, and it's their loss. Unload and remind yourself that you're a man and you deserve to get off, and it's the loss of various women if they don't get to experience it.

These excerpts make it obvious that "wanking" is something completely different from the act of sexual intercourse. The act of "wanking" is incorporated into the daily routine ("once in the morning and once in the evening"; "I once ate a sandwich while wanking"), and it revolves around rather neutral technical aspects ("good material available"; "facilitators";

"techniques to share"). The final example, in particular, shows that "wanking" is understood as something that makes men into men, and for which the participation of women is of secondary importance.

At the right side of Figure 1., a cluster consisting of three dark gray vertices can be found. They represent the activities of "collecting," "reviewing," and "ranking" pornographic content, and this is where the similarities between porn fandom and other fan cultures become most clear. As the members of the message board discuss how they organize their collections, and how they rank and evaluate movies, genres or performers in relation to one another, one gets the impression that this could be about almost anything: *Star Wars*, heavy metal albums or sports collector's cards.

> I use to compile around 200.000 pics (not just babe pics) and then I begin to work on them. They should pass around 6 steps before rest safely in the hard disk or CD. It is a question of delete the pic who I think does not deserve to go to the next step. Finally the survivors go to different folders like, Best face, best body, best legs, best tits, hardcore, etc. Of course one folder is called "To be identified by the Freeones friends." Another folder tree belongs to the stars with a huge number of pics, like Anetta Keys, Sandy aka Vega Vixen, Tera Patrick etc. When all the process is finished I realise that during that time I also compiled more than 1.500.000 pics. The objective is a hot way to lose my priceless time and have a clear top 50 babes.

> I use csv files and software. A csv (comma separated value) file is simply a listing of images (a database) that may include names, size, crc value and location of a group of pictures. Their purpose is to organize your picture collections by allowing specific software to 1) scan your directories for pictures, 2) check for correct size, 3) validate the pics authenticity (crc check) 4) sort the pics into an organized collection, and 5) present you a report of what you may or may not need to complete the collection. A csv organizes a collection so that it will fit on a single CD, around 650—700 MB of data, amounting to anywhere between 1500 and 7000 pictures depending on the physical size of the pictures.

Although a more marginal aspect of the Free Ones discourse, comments like these further strengthen the impression that it has homosocial traits. The excerpts illustrate the technical pleasures of fandom as they have been lived by male members of "geek" or "nerd" culture for at least a century (Eglash, 2002). Ranging from the radio amateurs of the early 20th century, through the electronic hobbyists of the Cold War era and the Trekkies, *Star Wars* fans, and Dragons and Dungeons role players of the 1970s and 1980s, to the computer geeks (hackers, gamers, open source programmers) of "the information age," the world has seen a number of male subcultures based on the mastery of specific technological knowledge or skills. However, sorting, ranking, and ordering elements, are not only elements of a nerdy fan culture but are a continuation of a longstanding tradition within pornography to categorize and define (Shaw, 1999, p. 206). Digital technology simply aids the process of categorization: Big breasts, Small breasts, Asians, Euro sluts, Teens, MILFs, Hardcore, Softcore, Bizarre, and so on. Patterson (2004, p. 107) writes that:

> A subset of the cyberporn industry is devoted to the categorization and classification of these images and Web sites; these sites present categories of images, laid out in tables or allowing so-called key term searches. The "click here if you're gay!" button, like the "S/M" button, indicates a technology of desire both productive and regulatory. These buttons do allow for a kind of limited role-playing, but it is one in which the "exploration" is always already constrained by a logic requiring instantly recognizable cues ...

To summarize, the core theme in the discourse of online porn fandom revolves around the presentation and construction of the viewer's identity in front of a homosocial peer group. The wives and girlfriends of the viewers also have a place, however marginal, in this system of meaning. In addition, the act of viewer masturbation is not only of crucial importance but also interestingly constructed in egocentric and homosocial terms that actually downplay the female performer. Finally, online porn fandom seems to have similarities to other fan cultures—even if this element is of lesser importance than the other identified patterns.

A Widening of the "Glory Hole"?

The viewer position that has emerged from my analysis is definitely not that of a shamed loner. The discourse of Free Ones porn fans clearly has a high degree of sociality, as well as notable elements of confessional culture and identity work. The porn audience is now increasingly social. However, as Stephen Strager contends, "From the frescoes and statuary exhumed from the ashes at Pompeii, to flickering peep shows, 16 millimeter, VCR, CD-ROM, DVD, and DSL lines, new technology has always been adapted to the purpose of disseminating pornographic material" (2003, p. 50) and, despite changes in new technology, masturbation continues to be "pornography's raison d'être" (2003, p. 51). As my study of the Free Ones discussion board shows, this continues to be the case.

The male porn audience is a homosocial audience. Men watch porn to be men, together, in a social and cultural context where the most important elements are—in Strager's words, "masturbation," "male pleasure," and "reductive female categorization" (2003, p. 55). The discursive presence of wives and girlfriends adds support to the findings of the studies by Loftus (2002) and Hardy (1998), indicating that some negotiation of porn use is taking place between the male viewer and the woman with whom he has a real life relationship. Yet even though real-life wives and girlfriends may be present in some sense, their position within this discourse is rather marginal. If we return once again to Figure 1., the connection of the four largest vertices, linked by the strongest lines, supports this argument. What we see is male interaction, mediated by the visuals of a female performer. The "glory holes" of porn theaters supply us with a fitting metaphor for this interaction:

> Men watch pornography to watch each other. ... There are holes ("glory holes') carved through the walls that separate the booths, perfect circles cut so smoothly that one can only conclude they were put in place by the management (or a particularly horny handyman). And, again, this situation, the presence of these glory holes, is remarkable not because it is unique, but because it is quite common. You will find the same in New York and Los Angeles, Paris and Prague. The men come to these stores and enter these booths not to be alone,

but together—divided by a wall with a hole cut into it through which they interact. (Strager, 2003, p. 55)

It is likely that the internet will intensify this, widening the "glory holes" for male masturbation through which individual viewers interact. The men in my study are bonding in the homosocial sense, as much as they are desiring in the heterosexual sense, and it seems that digital technologies, encourage this process. As the participatory potential of the audience grows, the possibility of establishing a globalized networked male porn spectatorship emerges. In the age of the internet, pornography may be undergoing significant changes but, in Free Ones at least, media convergence and the ever-increasing degree of audience participation is leading only to an intensification of previously existing patterns.

Chapter 11
The New World Dream and the Female Itch: Sex Blogging and Lolita Costume Play in Hong Kong, Taiwan, and China
Katrien Jacobs

Most research on pornography focuses on Western cultures and is dominated by Western models of media content and consumption. This chapter takes a novel outlook based on a study of Web cultures in Hong Kong, Taiwan, and Mainland China. In January 2009 it was estimated that there were more than 50 million bloggers in Mainland China.[1] However, the massive population of Chinese internet users has not yet developed an attachment to Western-style internet pornography with streamlined sites for e-commerce or social networking. In Chinese cultures pornography is, in many cases, illegal and is circulated through blogs, bulletin boards, and chat rooms that do not officially distribute or promote pornographic materials. The chapter shows that Chinese Web users are internalizing the lure of overseas porn markets and sex activism, yet framing porn discourses as a mixture of nostalgic grandeur and visionary eccentricity. More specifically, it discusses the erotic discourses of female sex bloggers and Lolita Cosplayers against a backdrop of economic expansionism, urban transformation, and government surveillance.

Netporn Politics in Hong Kong, Taiwan, and the People's Republic of China

In Hong Kong, China, and Taiwan, as in many other countries, online porn, sex products, and social networks are tightly controlled by their respective governments. In my interviews I have found that Chinese people tend to denounce the netporn boom as a "Western" or a "Japanese" obsession. They often mention the existence of a Chinese moral code based on the doctrines of Confucianism to differentiate themselves from overseas cultures. The Confucian doctrines are rarely articulated any further but are used as a basis for formulating disclaimers when openly discussing sexual desires or political changes. All the same, Chinese people have fallen in love with sexually explicit TV programs and movies, such as Ang Lee's *Brokeback Mountain* (2006) and *Lust, Caution* (2007), with the vast gamut of Japanese pornography, and with Western-style online sex and dating sites.

Although the People's Republic of China encourages the use of the internet, it subjects this to heavy censorship and has banned pornography. Online sex work and noncommercial sex practices are strictly monitored by the government and by Internet Service Providers. The government is thought to have a lenient approach toward sex industries, but it carries out random arrests and gives jail sentences to people who have been found to be distributing pornography, whether it is commercial or noncommercial, hardcore or softcore, and whether it is found on local or overseas Web hosts and servers.

In 2005, the EastSouthWestNorth blog published a report about China's "greatest Internet Crime trial,"[2] in which 11 defendants were charged and sent to prison for distributing obscenities. Five of these were university students who had been invited by Fujian resident Wang Rong to help administer an online bulletin board system called 99bbs.com that started as a general interest forum and subsequently offered pornographic content in a separate section to 75,000 fee-paying members. The Web site was hosted on an overseas server, but nevertheless fell under Chinese jurisdiction. The students were not paid for their administrative services, using it instead as a social network to share files and for personal communication. They lived in different parts of the country and knew each other mostly through their nicknames on the bulletin board. One of these, Shao Yong, noted in an interview that she used the Web site to post her writings and journals and "to become immersed in the Internet and to make friends." After Wang Rong fled to the United States, the trial focused on Shao Yong, and she was subsequently sentenced to 12 years in prison.

Taiwan and Hong Kong have less severe forms of criminalization, yet both countries are witnessing the growing power of Christian evangelist organizations that have considerable influence on government bureaucracies and media outlets. These groups also spy and report on Web users and progressive sex activists, sometimes collaborating with the tabloid media and government agencies to control their activities. The most vulnerable sites are those used by sex workers to advertise their services, but conservative groups have also increasingly targeted noncommercial sex activists and bloggers. In 2007, the Mainland Chinese blogger, Romantic Night, was arrested and subsequently vilified in the media. Typically, no detailed information about his blog or the reasons for his arrest were given, and there was no news about other bloggers or sex activists who might have defended him. All that was reported was that Romantic Night had a Web site for "distributing erotica novels" and that he was "caught" by the driver of a well-known CEO and arrested for "distributing erotic culture in Beijing."[3]

These are just two examples of the ways in which Chinese governments are trying to exert influence over the use of new media for sexual purposes. Hong Kong's government-appointed committee, the Obscene Articles Tribunal, is currently swamped and unable to process the number of complaints from citizens about new online sex practices. But Hong Kong also has a tradition of political dissent and laws to protect people who engage in free speech and certain types of political protest. Hong Kong media activist Oiwan Lam has been prominent in challenging the workings of the Obscene Articles Tribunal. In an act of civil disobedience, she urged Web users to post pornographic hyperlinks on the local indie media server, making her own hyperlink to an artistic photograph of a naked woman on the photography sharing site, Flickr. The hyperlink was tracked down by a religious organization who filed a complaint about it to the Obscene Articles Tribunal, and Lam is now facing prosecution for breaking obscenity laws.

Lam's prosecution was set in motion before her activist call had garnered any positive results. However, it has been met with local and international protest and she is meticulously documenting her court case as part of a challenge to the authoritarian upswing in Hong Kong sex culture. In her article, "Don't Turn Hong Kong into a Mono-coloured Ghost City" (2007), she poetically evokes Hong Kong as a gloomy place controlled by an upwardly mobile bourgeoisie and characterized by sex-phobic and xenophobic values. She also argues that over the last decade Hong Kong has lost its identity as a multicultural hub, a meeting point between Eastern and Western cultures, and a free-speech zone (Jacobs, 2008a).

The Taiwanese sex activist Josephine Ho has noted that Chinese societies are setting the example for a citizen-driven "complaint culture" against online sexualities, aided by excessive police surveillance and the mass media. As Ho explains (2005), "Instead of state power being weakened, as most global governance theorists argue, state power has been expanding to ever more social spheres and gaining strength in relation to newly-constructed subjects for rule, and in relation to new spheres where the regulation/surveillance of marginalized populations and their activities carry insurmountable weight, where bodies and everyday life serve as prime targets." Ho's analysis of internet censorship in Taiwan shows that this is not only the result of monopolizing state control, but of the ways in which state power is being transferred to various suprastate international organizations and local or grassroots citizen groups. The groups who have been most eager to introduce censorship legislation are religious groups and child-protection nongovernmental organizations (NGOs) that collaborate with the state, resulting in an expansion of state power and the criminalization of sexual minorities.

There has also been a series of new laws and rules in Taiwan that ban sex-related information, contacts, and enquiries on the internet. For example, an amendment of an antiprostitution law to include all internet-related transactions has worked to heighten Taiwan's sex-phobic atmosphere. The law now states that "those who use advertisement, publication, radio, television, electronic signal and internet, or other media to publish or broadcast messages that induce, broker, imply, or by other means cause one to be involved in sexual transactions shall be punished with imprisonment of no more than five years and alternatively coupled with a fine of no more than one million NT dollars" (Ho, 2005). Thousands of cases have been sent to the Taiwanese court, some targeting Web users who were found playing in sexuality chat rooms or on bulletin board systems.

The Chinese New World Dream and Its Counterpublics

These political developments show that the Chinese netporn era can be tumultuous and violent. They point to a sex-phobic Chinese moral code but are also located within a crude neoliberal transformation of cultures globally. Chinese communism has been transformed by an entrepreneurial capitalism that criminalizes forms of political dissent. As Lisa Rofel has shown, Chinese citizens are encouraged to free themselves of the constraints of hardship and poverty as long as they do this in ways that avoid the "dangerous passions of politics." In the same way, sexual desires and practices which can be interpreted as "benign" forms of consumerism are encouraged and have the added attraction of making China appear cosmopolitan (Rofel, 2007, p. 121).

Chinese citizens are incited to consume products and make art as part of a "new world civilization dream," which in recent government propaganda is characterized as life in a harmonized "world city." Brian Holmes (2008) observes how this mythic city is portrayed in terms of endless construction and expansion, "continuous buildings, endless highways, infinite urbanization, a city beyond the limits of the imagination. Huge urban blocks, surging arteries, expanding ring roads, metros, airports, refineries, power plants, bullet trains, a city that devours the countryside, scraping the mountains and the sky." The process of entering the world city is often described as "jumping in the sea," as a way of expressing how Chinese people are being forced to leave behind the old securities of communist living and begin to conduct themselves as risk-takers.

In Hong Kong there has been a similar trend of corporate-driven government rhetoric about unbridled urbanization, but there is also a tradition of activism which has produced a critique of the gradual destruction of older neighborhoods and heritage sites. Massive protests erupted around the closure and relocation of the historic Queen's Pier in 2007. Thousands of protesters gathered to document the destruction of the building. They shared footage and commentaries about their actions on video blogs, making it clear that they were fed up with the corporate destruction of local culture in favor of the global economy.

Hong Kong artists have also challenged the government's rhetoric of smooth urbanization, using subversive poster campaigns to protest against a proposed land transport link between Hong Kong, Mainland China, and Macao. One anonymous campaign uses slogans such as "Maximum Development in Harmony with Nature!," "Preserve and Destroy!," "Build and Preserve Again!," "2046: 1 Country, 1000 Different Speeds," and "2012 Full Democracy and Full Speed Ahead." These mock Hong Kong's blind surrender to entrepreneurial capitalism, its political insecurities about the handover to Mainland China, and its idle promises of future democracy.

The campaigners echo the writings of Ackbar Abbas (1997), who has criticized Hong Kong's architecture of "placeless landscapes" as the sign of a new colonialism that denies pleasure, contestation, and change. Abbas explores the way Hong Kong's media saturation changes people's experiences of space so that it becomes abstract, dominated by signs and images that dispel memory, history, and presence. However, Lisa Law (2002) has taken issue with this view, arguing that architectural changes do not necessarily extinguish histories of social activism. She has documented how the urban spaces of Hong Kong's downtown area of Central, madeover since the 1970s by global capital, are now used by Filipino domestic workers on their day off to hawk local goods and services, and by migrant workers and other activist organizations to launch protests. She concludes that Hong Kong's inner city is a historically dense and multicoded landscape, characterized by an emergence of counterpublics.

Lolita's Nostalgic Wanderings

Chinese women are among these activist groups, using urban spaces and cyberzones to show glimpses of unorthodox sexual fantasies and to congregate as uncanny counterpublics. They are also developing online self-portraiture to escape from the overly patriotic objectives of the Chinese New World Dream. One way in which they construct joyful, sex-positive personae is through the appropriation of Japanese fashion styles and subcultures. In particular, they draw on a broader Chinese obsession with the Japanese figure of the "pretty girl" (*bishojo*) who dresses in highly feminine costumes and is widely found in the Japanese "Shojo" animations, comics and games marketed to young women. Some critics have reacted strongly to this figure as a sign of weakness related to Japanese consumerism and to the endless distribution and consumption of commodities and images. Young Chinese women who dress as "Lolita" characters—known as costume players or "Cosplayers"—have received particularly negative and sensational coverage in the mass media. The RTHK television documentary, *Pretty Bizarre* (2005), reported outrage at what were described as "psychologically disturbed or oversexed young female members of the community."

However, Orbaugh (2002) argues that Shojo characters can be seen as a tool for the critique of contemporary adult society. For example, the popular "pretty girl" figure can be seen as representing a state of being that is socially unanchored, free of responsibility and self-absorbed—the opposite of the ideal Japanese adult. Japanese girlishness allows women to escape from the Confucian doctrines and censorship politics that frame feminine decorum in terms of responsible citizenship, traditional family values, and rigid gender binaries. Shojo culture offers tropes of exoticism and childishness for unbridled gender play within nostalgic and decadent fantasy settings.

Chinese Cosplayers are mostly young animation, games and comics fans who dress up and make public appearances as their favorite characters. Within the subculture of Cosplayers, there is also a group of "cross-players" who experiment with gender, dressing in the outfits of the opposite sex and posting photographs from their public appearances on online forums such as Crossplay. Yet the site makes no reference to contemporary transgendered subjectivities or queer sexuality and it bans all sexually explicit materials, announcing in the mission statement,

> You agree not to post any abusive, obscene, vulgar, slanderous, hateful, threatening, sexually-oriented or any other material that may violate any applicable laws. Doing so may lead to you being immediately and permanently banned (and your service provider being informed).[4]

Many of the male-to-female cross-dressers upload images of themselves in sexy, ladylike outfits and "pretty girl" poses. The Hong Kong cross-player Martin Leung uses a blog to share his photographs of himself as Princess Princess, a boy who turned into a princess, or as a "Gothic Lolita," an aristocratic young female who wears black lace outfits.[5]

Female costume players also dress as "Lolitas," wearing voluminous lace-covered knee-length dresses, white stockings, and bonnets on their heads. Except for their trendy platform shoes, Lolitas look like Victorian porcelain dolls wearing the clothes of bygone eras. They inhabit a world of presexual adolescence, their innocence emphasized through the heavy layering of vintage clothing and props. They stage city gatherings such as high tea parties where they eat sandwiches using forks and knives and pose for curious Hong Kong photographers and journalists. They are exhibitionistic and media-savvy, but they also act decorously; their aesthetic of nostalgic decadence referring to older feudal bedrooms or secluded rose gardens where sexual moves unfold slowly and with a sense of grace. Modes of well-mannered femininity are taken to an extreme in order to develop erotically charged subjectivities. They suggest a play with dogmatic clichés as means of asserting agency within dominant discourses.

When Lolitas dress up and gather in public settings, they express a nostalgic kind of girlishness to embellish a city dominated by endless shopping malls and anonymous high-rise architecture. They can be seen as figures of consumerism or male sexual fantasy, though they reclaim those figures by making their own outfits, dressing up together and preparing social outings in public spaces. Most Lolita discussions and transactions take place online at blogging sites such as Lolita Online, where members look at each other's photo albums and share experiences. As Lolita Cynthia explained to me, this form of online self-portraiture is undertaken in order to experience an identity transformation: "It makes me more comfortable and makes me want to be in front of the camera more. It is more like a little mask that you wear in front of people. For instance, I smile a lot less usually, but when I am in my character I smile a lot more. It is also how people interpret me" (Jacobs, 2008b). Cynthia explains that her smile is not faked, but is rather part of a dream and an escape from everyday life boredom, from pressures from school, work, family, and friends. Lolitas mimic and rewrite male fantasies of pure girlishness and in this way escape the pressure they experience, both from the rigid rules of Confucianism and the era of soulless economic expansionism.

Sex Bloggers and the Natural Call

Web users in greater China participate in global waves of sex blogging and pornographic video sharing. Indeed, China and Hong Kong can be said to be going through a blogolution and blogs are frequently used to create sex diaries and share information about the sexual adventures of their authors. In Hong Kong and Singapore, Web users also use American-style swingers' sites such as Adult Friend Finder or local sites such as Sexy Wife to share their own brands of homemade pornography.

However, in Mainland China, government propaganda prevents sex bloggers from using sexual commentaries to express anger or dissent. As Aaron Bowen (2007) has pointed out, Chinese censors can and do censor the sexual content of blogs. He argues that the political, social, and sexual spheres cannot be discretely separated from each other, and that posting sexual content online can often be seen as a form of social or political dissent. Some bloggers enthusiastically post government propaganda while spying on those who post sexual content. This is part of a nationwide effort to cleanse the internet of political dissent and pornography, in which agents are hired to troll online, block internet sites, erase commentary and arrest people for being anticommunist or "anti-social" (French, 2005).

While the Chinese blogosphere can be seen as part of a broader progressive Web culture and the development of libertine values, it is clearly less influenced by the online exhibitionism and geeky intellectualism that have defined the Western nets. For instance, American sex bloggers such as Violet Blue (at Tiny Nibbles) and Audacia Ray (at Waking Vixen) operate as accomplished writers whose politicized essays and queer identities are confident, influential, and respected. But it is much more dangerous for Chinese Web users to divulge such political identities, and this awareness has enhanced a dominant blog rhetoric of sexual naïvety or pure lust. This rhetoric reclaims sexual portraiture and storytelling as expressions of "pure" hedonism or a form of sexuality that does not have political or critical ambitions. For example, it is possible for one of the most popular Chinese sex bloggers, Mu Mu, to be a devoted party member and an online exhibitionist at the same time (French, 2006).

Hong Kong Web users tend to maintain blogs to engage in "purely sexual" storytelling that is devoid of cultural reflection. They use the blog format to make their own versions of DIY porn sites, posting detailed confessional stories about sex encounters that blur the boundaries between fact and fiction. These are often accompanied by pornographic photographs that directly or obliquely refer to the story. Even though the stories sometimes deal with taboo subjects such as incest and bestiality, people mostly express themselves within quite conventional limits. And while some of the photographs depict the blogger, many are stolen from commercial porn sites. One popular kind of blog is that of heterosexual swinger couples who post stories with photographs and videos on Sexy Wife, a site that currently has a constituency of 7,000 members in Hong Kong. In these, traditional gender roles are generally maintained. In many cases, the male partner holds the membership and uses the site to brag about and showcase his wife or girlfriend, who is otherwise invisible or absent. In a story posted by hkw200k, a husband describes his wife's feelings and emotions during a visit to a massage parlor where they end up having sex with the parlor's owner. The site also hosts solo bloggers like Naughty Tanya, who posts beautifully framed and decapitated pictures of her voluptuous body in lingerie outfits. The images are designed both to attract comments from other members and to make money by selling the lingerie. Arisa maintains a similar kind of blog, Arisa Sex World, using this as a sex diary that records detailed descriptions of sex positions, illustrated with photographs of her body and face.

Bloggers in Mainland China are more vulnerable than those in Hong Kong. Their work is not only more actively monitored, but they are more often attacked by public commentators. Oftentimes these attacks reveal a patriarchal knee-jerk reaction, as if female sexual agency can only be appreciated if it reveals a pleasant, subdued, and nonconfrontational attitude. For instance, in 2005 the city of Beijing organized Blognight, encouraging female bloggers to upload a selection of their most beautiful photographs and participate in a beauty pageant. Citizens were encouraged to vote on "the most beautiful blogger" who would win a hefty cash award. The jury received about 300 submissions from bloggers in various poses, fetching dresses and lingerie, including one from Hedgehog Mu, who sent in a photograph of herself fully nude. Hedgehog Mu's submission received negative reviews all over the Web, and was voted down by the jury because of her confrontational and lewd attitude.[6] As this incident shows, the female blogosphere is subjected to a specifically Chinese version of patriarchal commentary. It is harder to place female sex bloggers within the lineage of feminist sex activism or sexpertism that has been apparent in the West. The Chinese climate is more hostile, and it is more difficult for bloggers to engage in this kind of art and activism.

The Guandong-based Mu Zimei, who could be described as the mother of Chinese sex blogging, had a very popular blog to describe her social encounters in trendy bars and clubs and the various seduction routines that she uses, resulting in one-night stands. She published the names of the men she slept with and described the fights she had with them in bars, making fun of them and their shortcomings. Her tone was proudly juvenile and she sometimes used erotic prose poetry to mimic the clipped, telescopic communication of the one-night stand. Her accounts openly violated Confucianist morality and conventional notions of romance and love, but they were not politicized in the way that the writings of many Western sex bloggers are. Instead, she produced essays which talk about liberating the "self" or "human nature" from social norms.[7] In short, her blog functioned as a "one-woman liberation movement" centered on a radical and angry defense of casual sex and the ability to separate sex from emotional entanglements (Farrer, 2007).

James Farrer (2007) has described how Mu Zimei teased the patriarchy by requiring journalists to sleep with her before granting an interview, "the longer the sex, the longer the interview." Her blog received millions of hits after it was reported in the news, but the comments were mostly negative and the government finally shut down the mother blog. Other sex bloggers have enthusiastically adopted Mu Zimei's use of humor and bawdiness, receiving many hits and comments, as well as attention from supportive international media organs such as the *Asian Sex Gazette*. Qin Dai created a buzz by posting snapshots of her naked buttocks and back alongside a copy of a romantic novel that she was writing.[8] She responded to negative criticism by comparing her writings to those of Franz Kafka, arguing that being a writer fulfilled her urge to "let her deep-rooted joy and freedom float freely." One of her opponents, Annie Rose, a Kafka connoisseur, attacked Qin Dai, writing, "She can't say how she's like Kafka at all. He was a great writer and had nothing to do with nude ass. Qin just wants to make a name for herself by stripping." She insisted that Qin apologize to her parents and to her buttocks as well. Such conflicts show a deeply rooted sense of conservatism and lack of support and networking between female bloggers.

Another blogger, Mu Mu, posts images of her naked body while refusing to reveal her face, making people speculate about the motives behind her images. She explains that these portraits are a defense of pure sex and designed to prevent people from excessively analyzing her facial expressions and emotional states.[9] Other bloggers have built archives of Chinese people's porn; for example Lost Sparrow has compiled an encyclopedia of lovemaking noises based on the premise that they would sound different in different parts of China (Chien, 2005). Hairong Tian Tian hit the news after she started collecting pictures of men's limp penises. She has explained that she wanted to explore the "the root of Chinese masculinity" by showing the cock in its most mundane state.[10] Just like Hong Kong's Naughty Tanya, Hairong Tian Tian also has an extensive gallery of photographs of herself in fetching lingerie outfits. The amateurish look of these poses is reminiscent of performance art, but like Naughty Tanya she also uses the photos for commercial purposes—in order to sell her lingerie.

In these ways, Chinese bloggers tailor sexual agency to the demand of benign consumerism while engaging in humorous activism on the side. Porn culture in the West is very different, given its geek girl establishment, and run by pro-porn feminists and queer celebrities such as Joanna Angel, Audacia Ray, and Violet Blue who operate in alternative creative industries. The Chinese blogosphere is more vulgar and ephemeral, a bit like a 1960s nudist performance piece or like acts of streaking in public places. As the experience of the "mother of sex blogging," Mu Zimei, shows, if women make bold statements, they have to deal with hostility from other Web users or from the agents of surveillance and censorship. These fights may be signs of sexual and political progress. According to Farrer (2007), it is exactly the social process of debates like this that signifies a threat to communist authorities. However, it is currently uncertain whether a more boisterous and challenging Chinese type of sexual self-presentation will appear.

Performing Sex in Chinese Fashion

As a Belgian sex researcher living and working in Hong Kong, I am constantly made aware of the fact that there is a wide cultural gap between Chinese and non-Chinese forms of sex activism. It is currently unthinkable that Chinese cultures will officially open up internet pornography markets to foster their new economies or that they will tolerate new types of sex activism, particularly given that the new availability of netporn has been matched by an upsurge in religious and conservative citizen movements.

According to Aaron Bowen, China currently has about 162 million internet subscribers, only 12.3 percent of the total population of China, but equivalent to more than 50 percent of the total population of the United States. As internet connectivity in China grows, so too does China's influence over the internet. China has already managed to convince major search engines such as Yahoo and Google to censor its political content. It will be interesting to see whether China will attempt to encourage Web users to adapt their sexual tastes and opinions to a restrictive and patriarchal porn Web in the future.

As Brian Holmes has observed (2008), Chinese media culture and art can be a significant cultural language if it offers a new kind of dreamscape for developing a cultural and critical autonomy:

> Critical interpretations of the new cultural forms, and of the social and political frames in which they create their effects and meanings, will be crucial in opening the imaginary space where people can gain some kind of relative autonomy, some capacity to be their own steersman. But that critique must reach all the way into the images themselves, it must be transformative. The stakes of these new images are tremendous. When state-capitalist power begins manufacturing your dreams, then art becomes the primary process of politics.

There is an emerging wave of sexual storytelling and sexual debate in greater China, which is also nourished by a history of radical-critical visions about the body politic in performance art. Some of this focuses on the coalescence of economic-political growth and death (Berghuis, 2006). In 2000, Zhu Yu created a scandal by taking a number of photographs of himself while eating a fetus as a protest against state abortion as a means of population control. Peng Yu and Sun Yuan extracted fat from a baby's corpse and dumped it into Beijing's most polluted rivers as a commentary on death and looming catastrophe.

Other artists have focused on more intimate issues. Hairong Tian Tian and Ye Fu made a performance art piece, "Living in a Glass House" (2007), in which they lived in a tiny glass room, separated from each other by a transparent wall, for a month. This was intended "to highlight a gender gap in modern family relationships in China," and offered a powerful metaphor of alienation and imprisonment, encouraging viewers to contemplate contemporary Chinese relationships.[11] There have also been performance pieces which operate as forms of self-portraiture, critiquing Confucian gender decorum and commercial images of Asian sexy babes. For example, the Hong Kong artist Phoebe Man produced "A Masquerade on the Internet" (1999–2000), an early cybersex project in which men in a chatroom were asked to describe what kind of ideal online woman they would want to be. Man then materialized their ideals by means of masquerade and photograph. In a later project, she became "Rati," a girl whose face and appearance were invisible inside a gigantic vagina. In a humorous video piece she is shown sitting at home in front of her computer, nervously walking around her apartment and going out on errands.[12]

It is useful to look at intersections between the ephemeral blogosphere and more critical art forms to see how women might construct critical sex imaginaries. Performance artists tend to take a more confrontational approach to the body in challenging consumerism and government surveillance (Jacobs, 2005). Their productions can be seen as an emotive outburst against the new climate of sex surveillance and the new economy's promise of endless consumerism. In contrast, the forms of self-presentation I have outlined here seem to mimic the fantasies of China's utopian New World Dream, the acquisition of individuality through consumption, and the exercise of spoilt or shopaholic femininity, often related to Japanese pop culture. Dressing up as Japanese Lolitas or 18th-century court figures, women make delightful and nostalgic appearances in vintage clothing. The countercultures of Cosplay do not reveal a feminist awareness, although they do maintain supportive

Web zones for romantic fantasies and sexual taboos. Similarly, the feminine self-portraiture found in sex blogs usually focuses on compulsive confessional sex stories. Although a small number of artists and bloggers develop a dark and oppositional philosophy, the majority of Chinese women are developing performative modes of sexuality and gender by obeying patriarchal Confucianist thinking and the paradigm of endless consumerism. This is a kind of collective acting out of hyperfeminine roles and responsibilities that reveal their power over self-portraiture. They reveal their own self-absorbed and playful versions of good decorum or idealized femininity.

Notes

1.   "Mainland Now Home to more than 50M Bloggers," South China Morning Post, 8 January 2009.
2.   "The Greatest Internet Crime Trial in China," EastSouthWestNorth Blog, http:// zonaeuropa.com/20050514_1.htm. Accessed 28 October 2008.
3.   "Romantic Night arrested," Beijng Daily, 17 May 2007, http://news.qq.com/a/200705 18/000934.htm. Accessed 1 January 2008.
4.   Crossplay Mission Statement, http://www.crossplay.net/index.php?name=Your_ Account&file=register. Accessed 28 October 2008.
5.   Leung, Martin, http://album.blog.yam.com/maggieleung71. Accessed 28 October 2008.
6.   "Hedgehog Mu at Blognight," Beijing Daily, 14 May 2006, http://news.sohu.com/ 20060222/n241960175.shtml. Accessed 1 January 2008.
7.   Zimei, Mu, "Left Over Love Letters," http://www.ec35.com/muzimei and http:// comebackgirl.nease.net/mzmwx.html. Accessed 28 October 2008.
8.   "China's Unrepentant Bare-Assed Blogger," Asian Sex Gazette, http://www.asian sexgazette.com/asg/china/china05news92.htm. Accessed 12 November 2007.
9.   "Mu Mu: China's Nude Breed of Blogger," Asian Sex Gazette, http://www.asian sexgazette.com/asg/china/china05news86.htm. Accessed 12 December 2008.
10.   "Hot Chinese Blogger Wants a Photo of Your Penis', Skirmisher, http://skirmisher. org/filth/hot-chinese-blogger-wants-a-photo-of-your-penis/. Accessed 10 December 2008.
11.   "Living in Glass House: China's Version," Skirmisher, http://skirmisher.org/culture /living-in-a-glass-house-chinas-version. Accessed 10 December 2008.
12.   http://www.cyman.net/web.htm. Accessed 11 November 2008.

Chapter 12

"How Do I Rate?": Web Sites and Gendered Erotic Looking Glasses
Dennis D. Waskul and Cheryl L. Radeloff

Launched in 2006, YouPorn is perhaps the pinnacle of internet DIY pornography. Like its sibling, YouTube, YouPorn invites Web surfers to view and upload digital videos of an overwhelmingly homemade assortment—all free of charge, no membership required, and with minimal advertising. The popularity of this homespun internet "reality porn" is remarkable: as of June 2008, YouPorn swanked an astounding global Alexa traffic rank of 35; that means only 34 Web sites in the entire World Wide Web had more traffic than YouPorn—and those were colossal sites such as Yahoo!, Google, Amazon, MySpace, Facebook, eBay, and Wikipedia.

Digital cameras make virtually anyone a potential model or producer of new media erotic images; like its legacy technology, the Polaroid camera, they make possible both instant photography and instant pornography (Edgley & Kiser, 1981). Although there are similarities between "Polaroid sex" (ibid.) and contemporary sexual uses of digital photographic technology, it is hard to deny that digital cameras have profoundly expanded those possibilities, and the internet permits a variety of easy means to distribute those images—instantly, globally, and anonymously. Although much sexual representation on the internet "differs only in its method of distribution," in these kinds of more-or-less interactive DIY sites "individuals are constructing their own sexual representations, in effect re-presenting sexuality. Instead of consuming sexual images, participants act out the construction of sexual imagery" (Kibby & Costello, 2001, p. 354). Consistent with other erotic uses of new media technologies, this kind of "de-eliting" or democratization of technology allows "ordinary" people to display their bodies in a sexual manner and fits with the rise of confessional culture and reality television genres that emerged in the early 21st century (McNair, 2002). It also creates a "fusion of image and act" that "destabilizes the relationship between subject and object" (Kibby & Costello, 2001, pp. 359, 361). Although erotic DIY digital pictures are nothing new, one novel form by which they are distributed is rate-my-erotic-picture Web sites where people post erotic digital pictures (mostly of themselves) for viewers to rate. The sheer variety of these Web sites is amazing and their names offer ample cues to their character: MeNude, RateMeNaked, FloppyDicks, RateMyWedgie, BootyVote, BoobCritic, RateMyMelons, RateMeaBBW, RateLegs, and more. In all of these, viewers are invited to rate submitted images, get a free account, and upload their own pictures for others to see and evaluate. Some of these sites include an obvious mixture of both home made pictures and professional images. Regardless, in virtually all cases they replicate commonly accepted body parts associated with gendered sexuality—breasts, penises, buttocks; body parts generally considered "fetishes," such as knees, elbows, and feet, are not the standard fare.

Rating Web sites typically ask viewers to evaluate people either by certain bodily attributes (overall physical appearance or specific body parts) or occupational performance (professors, lawyers, or doctors). Rate-my-erotic-picture sites are of the former kind and based on the same principle as HotorNot—widely recognized as the site that popularized the "rate-me" phenomenon.[1] Most rating sites also offer "best" and "worst" lists, as well as some forms of social networking such as discussion forums and private messaging. The popularity of rating Web sites has resulted in hundreds of contemporary variations (Lee et al., 2007).

In erotic-rate-me Web sites, men and women submit pictures that are posted for viewers to evaluate. Submitted pictures are typically of various states of nudity and are primarily assessed by standards of direct and explicit sexual aesthetics. As viewers evaluate images, average ratings are immediately calculated. Many of the Web sites also allow viewers to leave comments on the images posted, which are typically short and blunt ("Very sexy," "Gorgeous tits!!," "Nice ass!"). Submitted images are usually reviewed for appropriateness by site administration, presumably to filter out images that are obviously copyright-protected, portray something that poses legal risks, or depict someone who reports or appears to be under legal age. As revealed in their FAQs, Web sites also impose their own additional and varying criteria: some only allow the exposure of women's breasts, some allow genital exposure but not erect penises, some allow images of couples but not penetration, and some seem to have no obvious nonlegal content limits at all[2].

Our analysis examines public domain rate-my-naked-picture data. We illustrate the gendered dynamics by which images are composed and evaluated, as well as the kind and nature of comments they receive. We explore how gender structures both what is seen in these images and how they are rated in ways that are both explicit and subtle. Our data is primarily drawn from one erotic-rate-me Web site. We did not seek permission from the Web site to conduct this research. The data we've gathered is strictly that which is available in the public domain and we've obscured, omitted, or concealed identifying information about participants and the Web site. We drew a random sample of 52 male images and 52 female images. Because participants can post more than one picture, we did get some duplicate subjects, but each picture is unique. Our data also include other public domain information: the reported age of each participant, the number of individual "votes" the image received, average evaluation score, and all comments that other users posted about the picture.

How Do I Rate?

Images posted at rate-my-erotic-picture Web sites are profoundly gendered in the way they are composed and evaluated. This isn't surprising. "The naked body is, in glaring clarity, a *gendered* body. Many social roles can be shed along with the clothing worn to play them, but some roles are permanently fashioned into our skin—and the more of that skin we show, the more salient that role becomes" (Waskul, 2002, p. 220, emphasis in original). In our analysis we focus on the gender dynamics of nudity and identity, how men and women compose their bodies in differing ways, and the differences in the way the images are evaluated by viewers. However, before detailing our analysis, it is important to contextualize our findings relative to two important details.

First, there is a significant reported age difference between the men and women in our sample. 64 percent of the women report an age between 18 and 30, compared to only 26 percent of the men. The men are significantly older; 50 percent of the men sampled report an age between 31 and 40 and 72 percent of the male sample are older than 31. Since reported age may be subject to a fiction makeover, it is possible that women present themselves as younger than they are, and this seems more likely than men reporting an age that is older than they are. But this is mere speculation; on the basis of available data, there is about a decade difference between the reported ages of the majority of men and women in our sample.[3]

Second, it appears that men are more likely to participate in rate-my-erotic-picture Web sites, which is consistent with pornography consumption in general, on the internet and elsewhere. Moreover, Americans are apparently the main participants in the rate-me-naked phenomenon. One rate-me Web site gives some clues: in November 2007 the site included 1,678 men (847 from the United States, the rest small numbers from all over the world), 360 women (190 from the United States), and 192 couples (96 from the United States). These dynamics appear normative in rate-my-erotic picture Web sites; men roughly outnumber women two to one and participation is American dominated.

Peek-a-Boo: Nudity and Identity

Like text and webcam cybersex (Waskul et al., 2000; Waskul, 2002), the majority of participants in rate-my-erotic-picture Web sites strategically conceal their identity in order to circumvent potential stigma. This is no surprise. These are public Web sites that require no membership or fee—anyone could potentially view the pictures posted: lovers, friends, coworkers, neighbors, family members, one's teachers or students, for that matter. For these reasons, participants typically protect their anonymity, and largely by omitting or obscuring their face—a tactic also common in webcam cybersex (see Waskul, 2002). In 67 percent of all the pictures in our sample the subject's face is covered, cropped, blacked-out, blurred, turned from the camera's view, or otherwise concealed. There was a slight gender difference in that 73 percent of the men omitted or obscured their face, while 62 percent of the women did.

Some participants posted pictures in which there was no attempt to conceal or obscure their face. Others showed some portion of their face; perhaps the subject's mouth is visible, or just the eyes have been obscured. Here, again, there are gender differences: 31 percent of images of men reveal some or all of the face compared to 52 percent of images of women. In these images we were able to discern other gender differences in the way men and women both gaze and compose their faces. Sixty-nine percent of the men look directly into the camera with their head positioned squarely as if with poised confidence. In only four images is the man's head tilted to the side. Likewise, in just four images were men looking away from the camera (either a profile view, looking to the side, or gazing at their own bodies). In a mere three images is the man smiling. Instead of a smile, men gazed with "a frozen, summoning look, as though the subject were making eye contact, sometimes collusively, with someone there in the flesh behind the shutter, or with a wider group of these in camera land" (Goffman, 1976, p. 16).

Women composed their faces and gazes quite differently. Seventy-four percent gaze at the camera, but 44 percent tilt their head to the side, giving the appearance of either playfulness or uncertain curiosity. In the remaining pictures, 33 percent are profiles or the woman is looking away from the camera—a "licensed withdrawal" (Goffman, 1976, p. 57) that entails the appearance of a kind of momentary blindness to what is going on and who might be watching. Four images of women show them with their eyes closed (comparatively, only one male image shows closed eyes)—perhaps the most complete form of a licensed withdrawal. It is especially interesting that women are smiling in the majority of images where a face is visible (52 percent, fourteen images) which contrasts sharply with men's images. Indeed, "smiles, it can be argued, often function as ritualistic mollifiers, signaling that nothing antagonistic is intended or invited, that the meaning of the other's act has been understood and found acceptable, that, indeed, *the other is approved and appreciated*" (Goffman, 1976, p. 48, emphasis added).

Body Parts and Flesh Flashing Poses

There are significant differences in what men and women revealed in their erotic pictures. Whereas 77 percent of men posted a picture that reveals their exposed genitals, only 27 percent of women posted a picture with any portion of their vulva visible. Women were more likely to post images of their breasts or buttocks. These dynamics are not particularly surprising, and for two reasons. First, because of the erotic meanings associated with men and women's bodies, women have varying degrees of nude embodiment, but, strictly defined, men are not nude unless their genitals are visible. To be seen "nude," men are essentially required to give the "full Monty." Second, "conventions of heterosexual masculine erotic display"—unlike feminine erotic display—"are not well developed" (Kibby & Costello, 2001, p. 360). Thus women may "draw upon established signifiers of the erotic," but for men the common mode of sexual display is situated squarely between the legs (Kibby & Costello, 2001).

Rate-me participants can tag statements about the pictures they post. Many of these are simple queries such as "Am I hot?," "Do you like my titties?," and so on. Yet the statements women tag onto their pictures differ, depending on what body parts those women are exposing. Thus, for example, when women posted images in which their vulva is visible, they frequently included bawdy statements like:

"waiting and wanting to be fucked"
(a woman wearing nothing except crotchless panties laying on a bed with her legs spread)

"need lickin"
(a topless woman sitting on the edge of a bathtub, with both hands pulling down her shorts and panties to modestly reveal her mons)

"come and get it"
(a nude women standing in a shower)

Breast and buttocks images are more likely to include tag statements that are less sexually explicit and more about aesthetics or playfulness. For example:

"do you like my titties"
(a topless woman lying on a bed looking away from the camera with hair covering most of her face)

"Just me advertising"
(a topless woman in the front passenger seat of a car)

"I love to show off my ass"
(a woman leaning over a balcony and looking over her shoulder toward the camera, her shorts pulled down to the bottom of her buttocks revealing g-string underwear and her fully exposed bum)

There was no similar qualitative relationship in the men sampled.

Self-touching is another relevant dynamic that can be read "as conveying a sense of one's body being a delicate and precious thing" (Goffman, 1976, p. 31). Forty percent of the male pictures and 42 percent of the female images entail some form of self-touching. Although the majority of men's pictures clearly show their genitalia, in only two pictures are men touching them. The same was true for women, where in only three pictures are they touching their vulva in any way.

The self-touching of body parts was characterized by gender differences. Sixty-seven percent of men's images showed them touching knees, chest, or hips. Men touching their knees were universally either seated or lying down; when touching their chest they were usually crossing their arms; hands on the hips was a frequent and bold masculine pose.

In contrast, 59 percent of women's images showed them touching the head, hips, or waist. When their hands were on their heads, women were generally appearing to manage their hair. Women's hands on the hips or waist were most often positioned to frame the genitals or buttocks.

Picture Composition

We presume the majority of participants knowingly and willingly take erotic pictures of themselves for others to see and evaluate. Therefore, we also assume that rate-me participants are highly "dramaturgically aware" (Brissett & Edgley, 1990, p. 5) and have composed their picture(s) with intent, purpose, and at least some measure of planning. In this section, we examine some of those elements of composition, many of which are highly subtle.

Camera angle is an important component of photographic composition. If the subject is shot from below they will appear "larger than life," even powerful. If they are shot from above, the effect is diminutive, even subordinating. If they are horizontal to the camera, the effect is neutral, perhaps equalizing. In a full 90 percent of the male pictures the camera is horizontal to the subject compared to only 48 percent of the female pictures with 40 percent of the total sample of women shot from above and thus resulting in a diminutive or subordinating effect.

Furthermore, in *all* images of the men one can discern a pose. Sixty percent of the men are standing; the others sit or lie, perhaps reflecting how "holding the body erect and the head high is stereotypically a mark of unashamedness, superiority, and disdain" (Goffman, 1976, p. 40). Only 25 percent of women are standing, with the rest sitting, lying, on their knees or in close-up shots, usually of breasts. In contrast to the majority of men's images, the pose is "a classic stereotype of deference" (Goffman, 1976, p. 40).

Because setting is a prominent feature in women's sexual fantasies, but not the fantasies of men (see Kimmel & Plante, 2002), we speculated that the surroundings in which the pictures were taken would illustrate a significant gender difference. For the most part, this wasn't the case. In 38 percent of images of men and 33 percent of images of women there is no identifiable setting whatsoever. In pictures with a visible setting or background, there were no gender differences in the type of settings—bedroom, kitchen, living room, bathroom, on a couch. There is only one category where gender differences are evident: women were more likely to post a picture of themselves in an outdoor setting, most often nude or sunbathing topless.

Ratings and Comments

Women's images clearly receive the bulk of attention on rate-my-erotic-picture Web sites. This is evident in both the number of ratings images receive as well as the comments that viewers post to those images. Furthermore, women's images are almost universally evaluated more positively than men's. In this section we briefly review the findings on ratings and comments.

Images are evaluated on a scale of 0 to 10. The higher the rating, the more attractive, sexy, or desirable the picture was regarded. In our sample, the average rating for male images ranged from 2.6 to 4.6 with the average at 3.4. These low ratings are virtually universal for the men. In November 2007, the top ten most highly evaluated images of men ranged from 3.6 to 4.6.

Women are rated much more positively. The average rating for women's images ranged from 3.7 to 7.8 with the average at 4.9. Indeed the lowest rated female picture was still higher than the average rating for our entire sample of men. Here, again, higher ratings for women are almost universal. In November 2007, the top ten most highly evaluated images of women ranged from 5.9 to 7.0.

Women's images also receive a substantially greater volume of ratings. The average number of votes for the entire sample of men was 1,501, while the average number of votes for the entire sample of women was 5,363.

Women's images also elicit almost all the comments. In our sample of men, there were only three images for which viewers left a comment, one of which was negative. In contrast, only nine images of women *didn't* have at least one comment, and all were positive.[4] The majority of these comments were about the women's breasts, and they were simple if not repetitive:

> "wow great tits very sexy"
> "Great tits, your hot"
> "WoW! Those are Big TiTs alright! Big BEAUTIFUL TiTs!"
> "The most amazing tits I have seen on this site"

Twenty-two percent of the comments on women's pictures were frank but highly general aesthetic remarks:

> "What a pleasant sight"
> "very sexy woman"
> "looks tasty"
> "mmmm what a hottie"

Eighteen percent of the comments on women's pictures were action-related or confessions of what the images allegedly did to (and for) the viewer:

> "Would love to rub you down with oil"
> "I'd be on top of her in an instant! BOING!"
> "Oh Baby! You make me HARD!"
> "I'll climb on that!"
> "I'd love to spread your legs and enjoy your delights."

Just six comments were on the woman's buttocks ("very nice ass," "great ass," "Nice buns, for sure!!"). Five were on the woman's pose or view ("What a fantastic view, would love to see more," "love the pose"). There were a small number of "other" comments ("oh hells yeah," "ooops! Did

I cum on you?," "Lordy! Mother, may I?!"). These comments radically challenge Hughes' (2004) assessment of commercial sex industry Web sites where male participants of brothel Web site message boards are characterized as posting critical reviews of women's bodily appearances and performances. Perhaps the medium of posting (quid pro quo) and the perception of amateur rather than professional status tempers critique and encourages participation through sexual banter.

Erotic Looking Glasses

As we have explored in this chapter, participants in rate-my-naked picture Web sites utilize new media technologies to create novel possibilities for interaction in anonymous, online community forums. Here, subjects occupy a position of being "surveyed" and "surveyor," and their sense of self is informed by acts of seeing, being seen, and being appreciated by both the self and others (also see Kibby & Costello, 2001). From this perspective, the central intrapersonal dynamic is neither new nor unique to these Web sites: a fundamental "looking glass" process (Cooley, 1964) by which we fashion a sense of self in everyday life or online. The key difference, of course, is that these dynamics occur in the context of various states of nudity—they are "erotic looking glasses" that reflect on how participants conceive of the body as an "erotic generator" (Davis, 1983, p. 51)—and by use of a static image.

Indeed, if one's sense of self is constructed by appearance and performance, it is crucial to exert power over the representation process by controlling and internalizing it (Berger, 1972). Bonney (1986) argues that the traditional subject position of women was disrupted as women began to challenge gender conventions during the second wave of the women's movement by engaging as producers of art rather than just as muses. Female participants in rate-my-erotic picture Web sites might well be engendering a similar challenge—even if the form and products of those expressions remain rather traditional.

For men, it is possible that participation in rate-my-erotic Web sites is an extension of the new portrayal of men's bodies in contemporary media culture (Bordo, 2000). Increasingly men are portrayed as both subjects and objects of the erotic gaze of others. As is especially evident in the advertising industry, "beauty has (re)discovered the male body" (Bordo, 2000, p. 168). For men to be seen and appreciated in these ways might be experienced as not only novel, but exciting—albeit something that women routinely manage in their everyday lives, in ways that are not always welcome, and experienced with a certain degree of mundane monotony; this perhaps explains why women are less likely to participate in rate-my-erotic-picture Web sites. For women, being "rated" on the basis of physical appearances might be all too common.

In his analysis of Western tourism, Dean MacCannell (1989) coined the term "staged authenticity" to refer to a simultaneous discontent with Western modernity and the structuring of "exotic" tourism by a longing to momentarily experience the perceived authenticity of non-Western cultures. Rate-my-naked-picture Web sites patently entail the same dynamics of staged authenticity—precisely what Barcan (2004) suggested in her analysis of glamour photography and amateur pornography. As in these, rate-me sites offer a space to act as participants in constructing the self. The more we are encouraged to perform our subjectivity in public, the more strongly fetishized the private becomes, and few things are more personally private than one's own nude embodiment. Yet, at its core, staged authenticity entails a commodification and fetishization of the "real" that provokes a "resignation to the fact that the real is always elusive, fun in fakery, and celebration of the delights of role-play and performance" (Barcan, 2004, p. 255). Likewise, rate-my-naked-picture sites offer a tantalizing means for one kind of experience of authenticity—to intentionally display one's self stripped of the veneers of clothing, but participants necessarily do so by (re)presenting themselves as a mere image for the consumption of others. Thus, there is a fusion of the image and act as participants *perform* nude embodiment to *produce an image for visual consumption*—and that alone challenges (if not undermines) the very assumptions of authenticity altogether; in this case, the literal "naked truth" is patently "staged."

What does the *experience* of rate-my-erotic-picture do to and for participants? That is a subject for other work, but we conclude with some speculation. Participants in rate-me sites explicitly revel in a delighted gaze. They do not challenge standards of beauty and sexual capital. Instead, they willingly offer themselves to a viewing audience who rate those images by such standards. And, as we have illustrated in our analysis, those standards are profoundly gendered. These dynamics have also been documented in webcam cybersex (see Kibby & Costello, 2001; Waskul, 2002) and this suggests that perhaps the central motivating factor and pleasure of participation in rate-my-erotic-picture Web sites is a certain technologically mediated manipulation of the erotic gaze itself: for participants, "the excitement that others receive from seeing them nude is repaid unto the self by the indirect yet comforting knowledge that one's body *is* appealing and desirable" (Waskul, 2002, p. 213).

Indeed, "being admired is very compelling" (Ray, 2007, p. 175), if not intoxicating, and because "participants can control the angle and zoom of the digital camera" they can reap these benefits while also "preserving the integrity and dignity of the self" (Waskul, 2002, p. 216). This is part of the reason the internet has undoubtedly "boosted the freedom with which young women [and men] get naked or pose in sexually suggestive ways" (Ray 2007, p. 174). However, as our analysis indicates these expressions seem to imitate commercial sexiness and hegemonic norms of gendered sexual display. Audacia Ray writes:

> What is unsettling to me is not that women [and men] might consider themselves candidates for porn stardom, or a job as some other kind of sex worker, but that the only space available for them to express their sexuality is through imitating commercial sexiness. The Internet makes commercial sexiness more readily available to women [and men] who are buying into it—even if they're not buying it. (2007, p. 174)

Ray has a fair point, but maybe we are reading these images too seriously. Goffman (1976, p. 12) insightfully wrote, "What Narcissus saw was a reflection, not a photograph ... a photograph does not embody objects that it pictures." While participation in sexual forms of expression like rate-my-naked-picture Web sites generally mimic gender norms and commercial sexiness, nonetheless they *do* bestow agency and that may be as empowering as it is intoxicating. Even though participants in rate-my-erotic-picture Web sites fashion themselves within hegemonic gender dynamics, that sense of empowerment is not *necessarily* alienating, nor "false." Not all emotional labor is alienating (Godwyn, 2006) and that applies equally to erotic labor.

Participants in rate-my-erotic-picture Web sites maintain creative control over the products of their erotic labor and are, therefore, much like the "artisans" that Marx and Engels (1975, p. 46) wrote of. Because the artisan maintains control over the process and product of his or her (erotic) labor, that "work" contributes to social identities and self-images. Rate-my-erotic-picture Web sites are not revolutionary (perhaps just the opposite), yet participants playfully deploy the technology to uniquely fashion creative images and see themselves through the eyes of others—to manipulate erotic looking-glasses to create a sense of their own bodies as erotic generators.

Notes

1.   HotorNot was founded in October 2000 by James Hong and Jim Young (originally titled "AmIHotorNot"). Within a week of launching, it had almost two million page views per day.

2.   Content prohibitions may be based on interpretations of law and policy regarding pornography and obscenity. According to Slade (2000), nude images are often perceived to be acceptable as long as they are not arousing. For example, an erect penis is often taken as evidence of arousal and, therefore, such images could be read as "appealing to prurient interests" (a significant phrase in U.S. definitions of "obscenity"). According to Lacanian theorists, another possibility for the erasure of erections in particular is that Western culture minimizes phallic display as a means of preserving power. Male dominance relies on keeping the symbol of power hidden.

3.   Another possibility for the preponderance of women aged 18 to 30 is a reflection of what Levy (2005) calls the "raunch culture" of pro-sex postfeminism. This emerging form of representation, of which one form is illustrated in this study,

represents a "tawdry, tarty cartoonlike version of female sexuality [that] has become so ubiquitous, it no longer seems particular. What we once regarded as a kind of sexual representation, we now view as sexuality. Spectacles of naked ladies have moved from seedy side streets to center stage, where everyone —men and women—can watch them in broad daylight" (Levy, 2005, p. 5). This is consistent with McNair's 2002) view of "striptease culture," which incorporates the various media forms of sexual revolution and exhibition that thrived and expanded in late capitalism.

4. While the volume of comments that viewers leave on women's pictures is significant, it is also interesting to note that those comments tend to come from just a few participants. Indeed, of the total 74 comments left on women's pictures, 78 percent of them (58 remarks) came from just four participants (all four self-identifying as men).

Chapter 13
Beyond "Key Parties" and "Wife Swapping": The Visual Culture of Online Swinging

Alison Rooke and Mónica G. Moreno Figueroa

They say that love makes the world go 'round ... well in the lifestyle, love has a name and thy name is single bisexual female. Almost everybody in the lifestyle is seeking a bisexual female, and most married and committed women in the lifestyle are bisexual or bi-curious. Think about it: Straight men want women, by definition. The only thing they want more than a woman is two women ... or three or four ... So when you get right down to it, the fantasy for almost everyone in the lifestyle, male or female, is more experiences with women. Single bi-females are also rare, as you can imagine ... An exception is SDC, there are still many bisexual females as members of SDC because they willingly choose to have non committal sexual experiences. See if there is a bisexual female for you: join SDC.[1]

Swinging is a global sexual phenomenon which shares the casual and episodic practices formerly most often associated with gay male sexual subcultures. Swinging Web sites play a key role in the practice of swinging as they become spaces where the relationship between sexual acts and heterosexual identities are simultaneously undone and reestablished as normative. The members of these Web sites produce and consume sexual images; indeed, the virtual display of sexuality is central to online swinging and it is one example of the proliferation of self-authored pornography on the Web. This chapter examines the visual cultures of online swinging as they contribute to the emerging literature on online pornography. It considers how these offer a creative resource for pushing the boundaries of established sexual practices, and for experimentation, sexual identity work, and community formation, while simultaneously producing a stabilizing logic whereby normativity is subtly yet constantly reinstated.

Swinging Subjectivities: "You almost feel like you discovered America"

We begin with the figure of the bisexual female and its importance in swinging cultures. The extract above, taken from the promotional pages of the Swingers Date Club (SDC) Web site, emphasizes this. The following testimony by SDC member, Mickie, makes clear what is at stake in this form of bisexuality:

> So how do you know if you truly are bisexual? Well I can tell you this by experience, you catch yourself watching a girl on girl porn and all of a sudden it seems like the hottest thing you have ever seen in your life. You almost feel like you discovered America. ... At the same time asking myself am I gay? ... In the Lifestyle you are free to be who you want to be and have as much fun as you want to have. So in a sense let's call it Disney land for adults. ... At that point I realized that yes I am a bisexual female because I still love men but being with a woman is so sensual, erotic and sexy. ... I felt like I finally got the approval I was looking for. It's ok to be a bisexual female and it's ok to give into your fantasies. (Mickie, 26 years old, Miami, Florida)[2]

Mickie's story exemplifies a concept that is central to this chapter: that of "heteroflexibility" (Essig, 2000; Diamond, 2005). This concept, alongside "heteronormativity" (Warner, 1991), has been important to debates on sexuality and gendered practices and offers a critical framework for unpacking heterosexuality. Heteroflexibility is the depiction of "presumably heterosexual women hinting at or experimenting with same-sex sexuality" (Diamond, 2005, p. 104) and we argue that it is key to the practice of swinging and its visual representations. As Wilkinson (1996) and Diamond (2005) have suggested, these depictions produce a double-edged effect: trivializing and depoliticizing same-sex sexuality by portraying it as a fashionable "'add on' to otherwise conventional heterosexuality" (Diamond, 2005, p. 105), while undoing the coordinates of the heteronormative consensus. As Richardson has observed, heterosexuality has commonly been defined in terms of difference and sameness, and forms the basis for a "particular form of practice and relationships, of family structure, and identity. [Heterosexuality] is constructed as a coherent, natural, fixed and stable category; as universal and monolithic." It is a "socially constructed institution which structures and maintains male domination, in particular through the way it channels women into marriage and motherhood" (2000, p. 20). Swinging practices lie at the borders of "respectable" heterosexuality and its norms of sexual and emotional monogamy, offering a fertile site for the investigation of the relationship between sexuality, subjectivity, agency, representation, technologies, and performativity.

Here, we focus on the visual cultures of online swinging and ask the following questions: What can a critical examination of swinging offer to theorizations of heterosexuality? Is swinging a new form of heterosexuality? What can theories of postfeminism offer to an analysis of swinging and its visual conventions? Does swinging *queer* heterosexuality? What can an analysis of swinging Web sites add to our understanding of online pornography? We examine one particular swinging Web site, SDC, to explore the relationship between agency and subjectivity in the (re)production of swinging sexual identities. Focusing on swinging as a sexual practice, and specifically on its technological and visual interface in Web sites, we examine the negotiation and presentation of a sexual self at play. The discussion draws on our analyses of the SDC Web site architecture, user profiles and photographs, videos, and chat rooms, as well as contact with individual swingers, some of whom have been participating in this Web community for several years.

We are particularly interested in how the processes of making, presenting, and consuming images "play a major role in identity work" and constitute "a major technology of the self" (Foucault, 1988; Barcan, 2002, p. 3) within the geographies of cyberspace. We consider the processes of building a swinger's profile, the significance of the images displayed within them, and the ways they mirror the visual cultures of pornography. We argue that the specific uses of images in swinging Web sites are an excellent platform for examining the visual, and its relationship to the construction of (hetero)sexual subjectivities within a more general sexualization of contemporary culture (Attwood, 2006; Gill, 2007b) and the "pornographication of the mainstream" (McNair, 2002, p. 60). Furthermore, we explore the implications of this conjunction of processes for an understanding of sexual liberation in the context of postfeminism.

Swinging: The Lifestyle

Literature on swinging tends to focus on heterosexual coupled relationships. This is reflected in definitions of swinging as "comarital sex" (Jenks, 1998, p. 1), as the practice of "married couples exchanging partners solely for sexual purposes" (Buunk & van Driel, cited in Jenks, 1998, p. 1), and as a "non-monogamous sexual activity, treated much like any other social activity, that can be experienced as a couple" (Bergstrand & Williams, 2000, p. 2). Recent studies in social psychology have developed a more elaborated definition; de Visser and McDonald, for example, consider swinging as an activity that "involves consensual mutual involvement in extra-dyadic sex, thereby breaching customary beliefs that marriage (and de facto marriage) should be based on monogamy" (2007, p. 459). SDC's "Swingers Dictionary" section defines swinging as "an alternative lifestyle for consenting adults who enjoy social, recreational sexual activities with others, most often on a couple-to-couple basis, with full knowledge and mutual consent of both partners; single men and women are sometimes involved."[3]

The emergence of swinging can be dated back to the sexual practices amongst American military personnel during the Korean War, when it was dubbed "wife swapping" (Bergstrand & Williams, 2000, p. 3). Since then, swinging has been associated with the "key party" at which the male partner of a couple places their car keys in a bowl and the female partner chooses a set of keys, leaving with their owner to have sex. Today, swinging is a global phenomenon, undertaken by ostensibly heterosexual couples and single men and women, engaging in sexual encounters with other couples or singles. Swinging activities include, but are not limited to: group sex or orgies; exhibitionism; voyeurism; masturbation; cross dressing; soft swinging or "soft swap," which involves the members of one couple having any sexual encounter up to, but not including, intercourse with another person or couple; and full swap, in which one or both members of a couple engage in penetrative sex with another person or couple. Swinging can take place in participants' homes, in hotel rooms, and increasingly, in saunas, at specialist swinging clubs, and at private parties.

Swinging encounters tend to be casual, nonspontaneous, and episodic, with the potential to be sustained on a continuous basis for a length of time. They are facilitated by the use of a variety of technologies whose development is driven by pornography itself (O'Toole, 1999). These include Web sites, chat, and webcam facilities; blogs and e-mail; contact magazines; and mobile phone facilities such as text messaging and photography. The proliferation of swinging Web sites like SDC enables people interested in swinging to meet each other. They facilitate and speed up people's participation in swinging and provide a range of services and information to the potential swinger; tips on how to swing, the etiquette of sex parties, and information about organized swinging trips, workshops, and conventions. They also enable a series of practices that employ technologies of image production and consumption in the formation of swinging identities.

An examination of the SDC Web site shows three main groups interacting: a significant number of single swingers who are not part of a couple; single people that join other singles to present themselves as a couple for swinging purposes; and married or cohabitating couples. Rather than "wife swapping," many couples are seeking singles to have sex with. Indeed one common request on the Web site is from "heterosexual" couples seeking another woman for a "threesome," or for the female partner to explore same-sex sexuality in order to satisfy her, or her partner's, "curiosity," as our opening quotes illustrate. The SDC Web site also illustrates the workings of a "sexual hierarchy of swinging," or what some members describe as "the food chain." This hierarchy is made explicit in several ways: for example, swinging party publicity shows that couples and single females are offered free entry, whereas single men have to pay an entry fee, and SDC profiles show that single, mainly bisexual, women are highly sought after by couples and single males, whereas single men are often explicitly rejected. We have come across some exceptions: one couple explain that they are "not interested in single guys for the moment, we have a few friends that we play with when the need arises ... lol ... unless you're a well endowed black guy!" Here, there is a hint of the racial hierarchy of swinging where "black male and well endowed" is a rare and sought after commodity. While this chapter does not examine the racialization of swinging discourses, crass stereotyping and the eroticization of the exotic racial other are clearly in evidence.

Virtual Space and the Production of the Swinging Online Self

The Swingers Date Club is an extensive global online community. Members register and pay a monthly fee to become part of the "lifestyle"—as swinging is also called. It claims to be the "the world's largest and most active Adult Lifestyle Site," having "over two million real lifestyle couples and singles Worldwide."[4] The Web site is available in several languages and claims to have up to 5,000 members online on a weekday afternoon, increasing at weekends and evenings, with around 250 people in chat rooms at any given time. As with a range of Web 2.0 platforms such as online social networks, wikis, and blogs, the Web site allows the user to choose the level of interaction they desire, for example, availability to chat, instant messaging, use of webcam, selection of favorite members, and the exchange of e-mails with potential swinging couples or singles. SDC members can start a blog or ask "The Counsellor," an experienced member and founder of SDC for advice. A "Swingers Talk" message board provides space for travel tips, swingers' stories, jokes, current events, and political debates.

Within this structure, and central to the SDC Web site, anonymity and community are at work in the construction of the swinger identity. On the one hand, anonymity enables experimentation and encourages the soon-to-be swinger to start the process of getting in touch with others. Simultaneously, anonymity allows swingers to revise the ways they present themselves in their profiles. However, anonymity within the online space is, to some extent, undone by the incitement to "connect" with others. Creating a swinging history, having a long list of friends, and accumulating "validations" from other members certifying reliability, provide a sense of "authenticity" and strengthen the swinger's profile.

As Barcan (2002) notes, the internet "encourages both anonymity … and community (which encourages both the sharing of interests and a consequent push toward moral normalisation)." A push toward the moral normalization of generally unconventional sexual practices is evident in the process of creating a profile on SDC. Users are offered a menu of options that allow them to present an "online self" within preexisting categories. The first step is to indicate the user's "swinging status" such as "Soft Swap Couple"; "Full Swap Couple"; "Bisexual Couple"; "Bisexual Female"; "Couple (Girl & Girl)"; or "She-Male." This list is interesting in its heterosexual and heteroflexible assumptions and in its omissions: there is no option for single gay men, lesbians, or male couples. Here, the process of normalization works both through what is included and excluded, and through the privileging of some swinging identities such as "soft swap" over others such as "she male." The production of the swinger's profile also requires the user to state which kinds of sexual partners they are searching for. Another list of options (set out in the table) describes the user's characteristics:

Bodily appearance	eye and hair color; race; piercing and tattoos; weight; height; and so on
Body type	"nice and slim"; "average"; "absolutely athletic"; "nicely shaped"; "a few extra pounds"; "huggable and heavy"; "disabled"; "other"; and "tell you later"
Sexuality	"straight female"; "straight male"; "bi-sexual"; "bi-curious"; or "prefer not to say"
Level of experience	"no"; "yes"; and "just getting started"
Comfort level	"must use condoms"; "body contact"; "erotic massage"; "kissing & romance"; "giving oral sex"; "receiving oral sex"; "anal sex giving"; "anal sex receiving"; and "polyamory"
Preferred sexual activities	"active involvement"; "passive"; "watching only"; "one on one"; "threesomes"; "group sex"; "masturbation"; and "voyeurism"
Fetishes	"bondage & discipline"; "candle wax"; "cyber sex"; "erotic email or pictures"; "fetish various"; "phone sex"; "porn"; "role playing"; "rubber & latex"; "S & M"; "toys play"; "underwear"; "videos"; "water sports"; "web cams"; and "anything goes"

Drop-down menus offer further opportunities to state other desired characteristics such as level of intelligence, importance of looks, smoking habits, and so on. The only place where the soon-to-be-swinger can write freely is in response to the following questions: "How would you describe yourselves?"; "What are you looking for?"; "Describe your fantasies and desires"; and "Describe your bisexuality ... if applicable."

One of the central logics of the Web site is the (re)production and maintenance of the user's subjectivity and public identity as a swinger: "The personal profile is your swingers ad, and the heart and soul of a Swingers' lifestyle site."[5] Although swinging is referred to as "the life" or "the lifestyle," rather than as an identity, identity work takes place on several levels in this online space. The user is interpolated as a swinger through the production and maintenance of the profile and the ongoing interactions on the Web site such as e-mailing, browsing profiles, choosing "favourite" members, chatting, and validating other members. In the process, users' identities are continuously worked on. The swinging subject is also constituted through the inclusion and exclusion of others as potential partners and through the ongoing discursive work whereby sex with multiple partners is celebrated and the social stigma surrounding it is suspended.

It is worth considering the kinds of sexual subjecthood invoked as users go through this process. Clearly the borders of the heterosexual imaginary are blurred as the links between bodies, acts, identities, and relationship status, which lie at the heart of normative heterosexual monogamy, are undone in the options listed under "swinging status"—"searching for," "comfort level," "sexuality," and "preferred sexual activities." The user's "lifestyle" is separated from questions of identity as sexuality becomes a matter of tastes and preferences for combinations of bodies and acts. The spaces of sex are circumscribed and situated; they become a matter of personal choice and of desiring bodies. At the same time, the swinger is offered the opportunity to narrate the self in a fragmented, predetermined format to an imagined audience. Once members of this audience become known through "real" sexual encounters, the profile might be rewritten. In these ways, the Web site offers its members sexual scripts and a space for sexual self-expression and self-realization, albeit within predetermined frameworks.

The SDC swinger profile is completed when photographs, and in some cases videos and sound recordings, are uploaded. The soon-to-be-swinger can add up to one hundred uncensored photographs and choose different levels of visibility. Images are crucial in reading and decoding a profile. It is the visible evidence of authenticity and the perceived measure of the reliability of the swinger behind it. One couple writes: "we COMPLETELY respect the privacy of other couples, however, we do like to see facial pics of BOTH sexes in your profile. We won't respond to any e-mails if we cannot see your face from your profile!" This highlights the expectations and anxieties around "authenticity" and "real" sexual experiences and encounters that are constraining elements of online swinging spaces. Although the technologies of online swinging offer the possibility of purely online sex, the emphasis is on developing and authenticating the swinging self by moving beyond the virtual into the "real" world of physical sex within the SDC online community. The endorsement of the user's "authenticity," through visual expressions of reciprocal relationships, is central to the Web site's construction as a space that emphasizes sex as "play" and works to construct swingers' online performances as "real" rather than simply "realistic."

Photographs include conventional portraits of couples and singles, either of the head and shoulders or fully clothed body shots; naked or seminaked, cropped and whole body shots featuring lingerie and fetish wear; closeups of vaginal penetration, penises, muscular chests, breasts, and women performing oral sex; cropped naked torsos either facing to, or away from, the camera in a variety of sexual positions; and images of group sex. Although swingers use a range of locations as settings for these images, home interiors and hotel rooms are the most common.

These images demonstrate the prevalence of a "homemade" or amateur porn aesthetic, indicative of a growing preference for "authentic" porn that privileges ordinary and everyday bodies engaging in "real" sex. This search for "authenticity" can be read as part of a wider cultural fascination with "reality" and implies a rejection of the more glamorous "plastic" bodies found in professional texts: perfectly toned, evenly tanned, and cosmetically and surgically modified. The presentation of the sexual self through images and videos is one of the central technologies at work on SDC. Here the user can produce and "broadcast" his or her own pornographic images. They can also view images of others in a process of "prosumption" (Bell, 2006, p. 399), whereby the swinger is simultaneously the spectacle and the spectator. Members can reflexively manage the display of the self, and examine the images of others in the continuous visual play of looking and being looked at.

The architecture and visual culture of the Web site we have described is just one example of the many ways that the internet has transformed the performative possibilities of contemporary swinging. This configuration of possibilities allow, enable, and mediate casual and episodic sexual encounters such as online dating and dogging (Bell, 2006), opening up the possibility of sexualities that have long been associated with gay male subcultures, such as anonymous, recreational, public, and group sex to new global demographics. Moreover, swinging Web sites intersect with the reality genre, working much like reality television and celebrity magazines, which also render the mundane spectacular, in a seemingly unending desire for private, often intimate moments to be broadcast publicly. Like these, they have "helped create new occasions and opportunities for the staging of the self" (Barcan, 2002, p. 5).

Heteroflexibility and Pornonormativity

Swinging Web sites such as SDC can be seen as intersubjective spaces of negotiation, sexual experimentation, and reflexivity. The ways that women are represented, discussed, and interacted with are particularly significant for an understanding of swinging subjectivities in general. These can be framed as expressions of a contemporary cultural sensibility that has been described as postfeminist. This sensibility depends on:

The notion that femininity is a bodily property; the shift from objectification to subjectification; the emphasis upon self surveillance, monitoring and discipline; a focus on individualism, choice and empowerment; the dominance of a makeover paradigm; a resurgence in ideas of natural sexual difference; a marked sexualization of culture; and an emphasis upon consumerism and the commodification of difference. These themes coexist with, and are structured by, stark continuing inequalities and exclusions that relate to "race" and ethnicity, class, age, sexuality and disability—as well as gender. (Gill, 2007b, p. 149)

This postfeminist sensibility and the broader sexualization of popular culture provide a context for making sense of online swinging. In contemporary Western cultures in which sexualized bodies are increasingly on display, there is an "ironic normalisation of pornography" (McRobbie, 2004, p. 8). The sexualizing trend can also be seen in the marketing of the playboy bunny logo to preteens, the softcore aesthetic of lad mags, lifestyle magazines' obsession with the sex lives and bodies of celebrities, and the popularity of pole dancing as a form of exercise (see Gill, 2007b). As Gill notes, in this process women apparently move from being "sex objects to desiring subjects," in control of their sexuality and seeking "to present themselves in a seemingly objectified manner because it suits their liberated interests to do so" (2007b, p. 151). Gill and McRobbie offer a poststructuralist feminist critique of this cultural moment in which sexual subjectivities are produced in highly mediated and circumscribed ways. The postfeminist sexually empowered female subject is a gendered manifestation of the self-monitoring subject of late modernity (see Giddens, 1991 and Beck & Beck-Gernsheim, 2002) who is compelled to make the "right" choices in a process of being reflexive about every aspect of her life. The potential sexual utopia of the SDC lifestyle is clearly an example of the discourses of postfeminism: it is filled with narratives of self-improvement and fulfilment, encapsulated in their banner, "better bodies, better sex." These matters of choice, agency, and the right to act on one's desires, sexual or otherwise, are central to the discursive formulation of the swinging self. By acting on such "right" choices, in a process of self-monitoring, the users of the Web site can improve their sex lives through the presentation of sexually reflexive selves who know what they want. However, the notion of women as autonomous agents is not sufficient to explain swinging as a straightforward expression of sexual agency.

One of the ways in which the apparent heterosexuality of the Web site is maintained is through its visual discourses, which conform to the visual conventions of "pornonormativity." This concept was developed by Slater (1998) in his work on the online exchange of pornographic visual material, and later used by Bell (2006) in his work on dogging, to describe the way that images are "organized and policed according to the conventions of off-line mainstream (heterosexual) pornography" (Slater, 1998, p. 99). Slater, discussing the sharing of explicit images in internet chat rooms describes these as: (1) images that accord with familiar genres and conventions of pornography which are indistinguishable from the categorizations found in sex shops and "top shelf" magazines; (2) self representations that perpetuate gendered conventions; (3) the absence of gay men; (4) the prevalence of the "bisexual female"; and (5) an emphasis on sexual transgression which reinforces rather than challenges normality. Female sexual activity is shown as heterosexual or bisexual, whereas male sexual activity is represented in ways which can only be read as heterosexual. This can be understood as a visual expression of "heteroflexibility," whereby sex between women is coded as a fashionable "add-on" to heterosexuality (Wilkinson, 1996; Diamond, 2005; Gill, 2008).

These conventions are also found in mainstream media where lesbian sex is often represented in ways which remove it from the possibility of identity. In advertising, for example, lesbian themes are used to make products seem edgy and contemporary, yet the presentation of the "hot lesbian" draws on traditional norms of feminine attractiveness, and often displays lesbians in pairs, a form of "doubling," which references what is taken to be "a common male fantasy" (Gill, 2008, p. 50, see also Gill, 2009). As Gill and Slater argue, these kinds of representations conform to mainstream pornographic conventions and play to a heterosexual male imaginary of choice. Although they undo some of the negative associations of lesbianism as failed masculinity or an imitation of heterosexuality, they present lesbian sexuality as occurring within the shadow of heterosexual coupledom. Such depictions are directed at a heterosexual male gaze, as the precursor to the "real sex" of penetration, neutralizing any challenge to heterosexuality. Thus, engaging in same-sex practices can become a means of confirming a seemingly essential heterosexuality through "free" experimentation in which sexual identity is separated from sexual acts.

These conventions are reproduced in the way that images are displayed on the SDC Web site. Swinging couples often only upload images of the female partner on their profile and, as a result, women's faces and bodies predominate. While women are represented as active, empowered, conventionally feminine, and displaying a confident sexual self in photo collections of sexual encounters on SDC, lesbian sex is primarily represented in relation to heterosexuality (hence the Web site's strap line, "*spice up your marriage*"). For example, heterosexual couples often use images of the female partner engaged in sexual acts with another woman, with a male partner looking on. Another common image is of two women having sex with each other, with subsequent shots showing a male joining in or replacing a female. Another indication of the underlying heteronormativity of the Web site is the absence of images of men having sex with each other. Male bisexuality on SDC is often expressed in rather evasive terms such as "not being worried with close contact." Although there are men on SDC who define themselves as "straight but open minded" or "bisexual male," sex between men, unlike lesbian sex, is not visible. Indeed, its absence points to the ways that it disturbs the dominant heteroflexible visual discourse at work. Heteroflexibility works to titillate other couples and encourage the participation of single bisexual and bicurious women while discouraging potential male homosexual and bisexual swingers.

Queer Straights?

However, a postructuralist feminist reading of online swinging as heteroflexible and adhering to the visual conventions of pornonormativity does not do justice to the queer potential of such spaces. We are referring here to Foucault's (1976) theorization of sexuality as a historical organization of power, discourse, and bodies, and to work by Sedgwick (1991 and 1993) and Butler (1990, 1993, and 1997) on the self, performativity, and the discursive production of the categories of sex, gender, and sexuality. A queer reading of online swinging foregrounds the configurations of bodies, acts, desires, and practices that become possible. As Sedgwick states, "one of the things that 'queer' can refer to [is] the open mesh of possibilities, gaps, overlaps, dissonances and resonances, lapses and excesses of meaning when the constituent elements of anyone's gender, of anyone's sexuality aren't made (or can't be made) to signify monolithically" (1993, p. 9).

Swinging practices do not necessarily follow a straightforward trajectory of "sex equals gender equals desire equals identity." Attempting to read the Web site through the trope of identity risks erasing the multiple configurations of sex, gender, acts, bodies, and spaces that swinging practices allow. One of the dangers of a poststructuralist feminist approach to such practices is that it disallows an analysis of the experience of desire and being desired, or a sense of sexual agency, and leads to a reading of female bodies and sex acts merely as examples of the semiotic degradation of women. This risks erasing the ways that the Web site allows women to be desiring subjects in a subculture that accords their sexualities with value. Here, the pleasure-seeking female sexual agent is celebrated and desired rather than condemned as a "slut" for her promiscuity (Attwood, 2007c). Images of women are read by a range of sexual subjects including heterosexual, bisexual, lesbian, and bicurious women. And in contrast to sexualized popular culture in which women who are not considered to be young, slim, white, middle class, or conventionally "beautiful" are ridiculed if they express sexuality, a much wider range of identities and body images are used to enact women's sexual subjecthood. Women may "prosume" images of each other for their own sexual pleasure and engage in practices that can unfix predefined sexual identities. This raises questions about sexual agency and the extent to which the concepts of heteroflexibility and pornonormativity are useful in making sense of online swinging practices.

A queer view of swinging allows a site like SDC to be read as a space where members can explore being desired and desiring subjects. Here they can explore pleasures, bodies, acts, energies, and moments; or specific situational sexualities that might define what they will do at a sex party or in a private encounter in a smaller group. Often these sexual practices lie beyond the norms of acceptable and respectable female sexuality. Being part of "the lifestyle" offers a framework where one can *do* queer things beyond political sexual identities including "queer." Although the identity of "queer" is taken up elsewhere by many people whose genders and sexual practices go beyond a straightforward binary of gay/straight, SDC members are navigating a space between identities and practices, as the following statement illustrates:

> I will go 1 on 1 with a lady as part of our fun and games and have, and will, enjoy being fucked with a strap-on, but I am not interested in having a solo 1 on 1 private liaison with a lady (i.e. in a lesbian relationship).

Here a female SDC member makes clear the extent of her bisexuality. Similarly, a female swinger discusses bisexuality in relation to herself and her partner like this:

> John isn't uncomfortable in the presence of other guys and isn't against fumbling with Mary present (as this would excite her) but the right situation has never occurred, so we would only pursue this if both totally comfortable.

The first statement expresses the limits of bisexuality for one female swinger, while the second suggests that both partners will experiment with bisexuality if they are "both totally comfortable." Heterosexual practices are being queered here. These are spaces outside of sexual (but not emotional) monogamy, which open up the possibilities of antinormative heteroeroticism. However, this is realized in complex ways whereby heterosexual practices and identities are undone and redone in the interplay of images, intersubjective encounters, and embodied connections.

Swinging Paradoxes

The sites most intensely invested in desire always occur at a conjunction, an interruption, a point of machinic connection, always surface effects, between one thing and another—between a hand and a breast, a tongue and a cunt, a mouth and food, a nose and a rose. In order to understand this notion, we have to abandon our habitual understanding of entities as the integrated totality, and instead focus on the elements, the parts, outside of their integration or organization, to look beyond the organism to the organs that compose it (Grosz, 1995, p. 182).

The logics of pornonormativity and heteroflexibility are in evidence in the visual cultures of this online swinging space. There is circularity at play in the symbolic meanings of self-authored photographs and videos. In these images heterosexual desire is constantly reconfigured, even as it is undone through queer bodily acts. This undoing refers to the challenge that heteroflexibility creates. Clearly, the relationship between online self-representation and sociosexual practice is by no means a straightforward one (Bell, 2000; Plant, 2000; Wakeford, 2000). The conventions of heteronormativity are being queered as ostensibly heterosexual couples and individuals seek to experiment with their desires and, in that process, undo the conventions of heterosexual intimacy and the private spaces where this can appropriately take place. Swinging Web sites and the practices that emerge from them are spaces of sexual experimentation in which the user has same-sex sexual partners, multiple sexual partners, engages in fetishes and other kinds of sex play, and develops new friendships, social networks, and sexual spaces. Furthermore, in these spaces and resultant social networks, women can display, enact, and explore their sexualities in ways that go beyond the bounds of heteronormativity.

This case study points toward some of the paradoxes of swinging. Online swinging and the offline interactions that take place in homes and sex clubs are sites where the bounds of normative monogamous heterosexual identities are undone and simultaneously redone. Sexual practices formerly associated with gay subcultures—episodic, casual, with multiple partners, on premises and so on—are performed by those not previously considered queer. In this sense, the Web site and the discourses surrounding it produce new sexual configurations and opportunities for transgression and experimentation. However, this is not a straightforward utopian space of sexual creativity and "liberation" from heteronormativity. Female same-sex sexuality is represented in ways which are circumscribed by the conventions of pornonormativity and heteroflexibility. At the same time, agency and subjectification are both present as possibilities within a discursive field of constraint. Swinging subjectivities produce discourses of sexual experimentation and choice, but, to paraphrase Judith Butler (1993), these are acquired through the discursive regimes of gendered and sexed normativities. The prosumption that the Web site enables for those women who are not represented positively as sexual agents in advertising and popular culture, provides the possibility to express their often unconventional desires, whilst the weight of pornonormativity and heteroflexibility restricts both what can be shown, and how swingers' self-expression is likely to be read and consumed.

We end this chapter with the paradox of acknowledging that the existing theoretical approaches that are used to analyze female sexuality are insufficient for making sense of swinging subjectivities and the cultural significance of swinging in a way that contributes to our understanding of contemporary sexual cultures. This will require analyses that go beyond the visual cultures of swinging Web sites, based on an ethnographic and qualitative methodology and exploring how male and female swingers make sense of themselves and how they navigate questions of gender, sexuality, identity, power, and agency in responding to images, profiles and swinging encounters. Nevertheless, our reading of this site shows how online swinging practices offer women new configurations of sexual subjectivities that go beyond simple dichotomies of respectability and contempt.

Notes

1. "Bisexual Females," http://swingers321.com/bisexualfemales.htm. Accessed 6 January 2009.
2. "Bisexual Females," http://sitemap.sdc.com/sitemap/bisexual-female.htm. Accessed 6 January 2009.
3. "Swinging," http://swingers321.com/swingersdictionary.htm#n124. Accessed 6 January 2009.
4. http://www.sdc.com/. Accessed 6 January 2009.
5. Swingers Personals, http://swingers321.com/swingerspersonals.htm. Accessed 6 January 2009.

Conclusion:
Toward the Study of Online Porn Cultures and Practices
Feona Attwood

More than any other genre, pornography has been reified and instrumentalized, turned into a scary "thing," and portrayed as a stimulus for bad effects or as "the nadir of culture" (Kipnis, 1996, p. 174). Yet media scholars argue that porn should be studied for all kinds of reasons; because it "is an enormous economic force" and has been "a driving force behind the technological development and deployment of almost every media"; because it has "emerged as a key area for feminist scholarship" and public policy debates; because it "poses powerful questions about the relationship between form, content and ideology," "the nature of fantasy," and "emotional investments"; and because of what it reveals about how "categories operate to police taste and to impose ideological constraints' (Jenkins, 2004, pp. 2–3). As Karen Boyle (2006) notes, engaging with porn also makes us reflect on questions about power, tolerance, affective response, and viewing context. The study of porn is uniquely placed to illuminate these important issues, providing "an opportunity to change theoretical directions, to test new paradigms, to challenge tired assumptions, or to return to under-examined areas of investigation' (Gaines, 2004, p. 38).

Forms of popular culture are often seen in terms of the way they repeat and standardize certain aesthetics, narratives, figures, and modes of address, and, on the other, how they become hybridized, break with convention, and provide spaces for innovaiton. Porn is no different in this respect, though until recently in media studies, rather more emphasis has been placed on its formulaic, monolithic quality. However, this kind of homogenization in which "porn" becomes shorthand for "something already known," belies the diversity of porn texts, and, in the process, "queer pornographies and independent productions in particular tend to disappear from view" (Paasonen, 2006, p. 405). The more recent study of online porn emerging from new media studies has worked in the other direction, as Susanna Paasonen notes, where much less attention has been paid to older forms of heteroporn. Here, contrasts are often made between "commercial, predictable and dull" porn and new forms of "netporn" that are seen as "networked, interactive, novel, intellectually and aesthetically challenging' (2007, p. 164). The contrast has been useful as a way of identifying the variety of features of production, style, and distribution that new pornographies employ. However, an overemphasis on this distinction can work to collapse the variety of online porn into a simple opposition of "old" and "new" and to make invisible the ways that particular forms of style and content may straddle "old" and "new," "online" and "offline," "mainstream" and "alternative" pornographies. In the process, any sense of the differences within the types and subgenres of porn is repressed (see Jancovich, 2001).

Indeed, the extent to which either set of elements is foregrounded often takes on a particularly political significance. To emphasize what is typical, generic, and traditional in porn is often to make an argument about its heteronormativity, whereas to highlight the novel and the different may be linked to arguments about porn's radical potential. Certainly, many online porn sites still "reinforce traditional constructions of men's power over women" (Heider & Harp, 2002, p. 297). As Susanna Paasonen's discussion of pornographic spam email shows, this construction relies on focusing attention on the bodies of thin, young, blonde, white women (2006, p. 406), and on a series of binary oppositions (hard/soft, dominant/submissive, aggressive/passive) in order to establish a view of sexuality as based on different but complementary bodies and temperaments, often in an excessive way that "seems to stretch heterosexual morphology to its extremes" (2006, p. 407). Yet this representational regime of "pornonormativity" is not necessarily distributed neatly between "old" and "new" or "mainstream" or "alternative" forms of porn.

Instead, there is a variety of porn styles and sensibilities, forms of address and means of expression. Porn texts may be professional, amateurish, glossy, raw, excessive, decorous, dirty, naïve, knowing, mundane or spectacular. Older sexual practices such as swinging are reproduced online in ways that queer norms of straight sexuality to some extent, while newer practices of self-display in erotic rate-me sites draw on some very familiar and traditional conventions of gender presentation. Even the most standard and familiar of porn scenarios shift as they emerge in different forms and contexts. Thus, *Debbie Does Dallas* is repurposed as couples porn, is turned into a musical, becomes the subject of a documentary, is given the alternative treatment and ends up as reality TV. Elsewhere, familiar concepts of what porn is and is for are problematized by shock imagery that focuses on extremity and abnormality. As porn mutates and proliferates, we need new ways of thinking about porn texts.

Technologies of Sex

As Henry Jenkins has argued (2007), "the evolution of pornography can show us how different media can change our relationship to the same (very) basic content." This is most clearly discernible in the technological shifts by which "...print made sexual imagery more democratic ... photography made it real ... film made it a spectacle ... and video made it private"; and how more recently, the internet has enabled "near-infinite choice in the selection of images," increased porn's "democratic potential ... exponentially," provided a new space for "whole new sexual subcultures," and amplified its "appeal of the real" by making it possible to interact with people (Tang, 1999, p. 167).

These themes—accessibility, diversity, the public and the private—and, above all, "the real," recur throughout discussions of sex and technology; predictably perhaps, given the trajectory which media imagery has taken since the mid-19th century. As Walter Kendrick has noted, in "the pornographic era" representations of all kinds have multiplied "at a wildly accelerating pace," becoming steadily more detailed and explicit until "it has become possible to photograph the earth from outer space, a fetus in the womb, and Vietnamese children in the process of dying" (1996, p. 221). Technological processes have worked "to bring the experience of represented events ever closer to their real experience," providing "the most vivid possible equivalent of sensory stimuli" (1996, p. 248).

Yet what counts as "real" changes over time. The realism of photographic and cinematic porn depended heavily on its claim to capture evidence of pleasure, documenting authentic acts of sexual arousal and satisfaction and reproducing these as responses in its audience. Here, knowledge of sex was constructed through what Linda Williams (1989) has called "the frenzy of the visible," played out through highly-lit closeups of body parts, moving through "thousands of scenarios, angles, positions, and partners in its tireless search" (Gaines, 2004, p. 34), and later elaborated through a set of conventions based around sexual "numbers" and the money shot.

Since the golden age of film porn, technologies have continued to extend the way we are able to see and represent the world, to rework the way we understand and interact with representations, and to reconstruct our ideas about seeing, knowledge, and reality. In the process the older version of the pornographic "real" has come to be understood as formulaic and predictable (Paasonen, 2006, p. 411), becoming associated with performance, the spectacular and artificiality, unconvincing representation and "fake" sex.

A newer strategy of authentification, most notable within the gonzo and amateur pornographies of the 1990s and 2000s, draws on a concept of the real demonstrated by liveness, presence, immediacy, and spontaneity; characteristics associated with television rather than cinema (Levin Russo, 2007, pp. 244–245). This real, developing further as a corollary of reality genres more generally, has increasingly seemed to bridge the gap between the fantasy world of sex that porn represents and everyday life (Paasonen, 2006, p. 413), between the spectacular and the mundane, the world of celebrity performances and ordinary routines, and between the public and the private. The contemporary real also increasingly incorporates contradictions; "desire for the real, fetishization of the real, resignation to the fact that the real is always elusive, fun in fakery, and celebration of the delights of role-play and performance" (Barcan, 2004, p. 255).

More recently still, accompanying the new diversity of porn texts, there has been a proliferation of different versions of the "real" of porn. Realness may be expressed by the extent to which the action is divorced from emotion or everyday life, or conversely the extent to which it is connected to these; it may be held to depend on the authenticity of the producers or the direct responses of the consumer; on conventions of "liveness," "nastiness," or lack of aesthetic and technical varnish; on the effective staging of conventional and recognizable porn elements; on psychologization, personalization, or politicization; on how faithfully it represents the desires of individual performers, communities or subcultures; on interactivity; on how boldly it asserts or refuses sex and gender difference, or on how dramatically it upholds or transgresses representational and sexual norms and categories.

Porn as Work, Porn as Leisure, Porn as Sex

Online, the real of porn draws not only on newer and more diverse iconographies of authenticity, but on the facilitative nature of the internet as host and stage for the recombination of new and old sexual representations and practices, thereby breathing new life into existing forms of role-play, sexual communication and commercial sex work. Films and videos, erotica and other forms of sexual narrative, art works and cartoons, vintage and contemporary photography, gaming and other playful forms and performances are drawn together with the modes of camming, chatting and messaging, in blogs and contact pages, dating and networking sites, or through links and framings that connect the sexual and nonsexual: the "fusion of image and act" (Kibby & Costello, 2001, p. 359) giving rise to a pornucopia of practices. As media have become part of a cyborg reality in which representations and practices, bodies and technologies are combined, porn practices no longer take place in physical spaces but at "nodes in a part-physical, part-immaterial, part-phantasmatic webwork of economic and subjective transactions," across real and virtual environments and with "diminishing boundaries between online porn and real life sexuality" (Arvidsson, 2007, p. 74).

The sexual is "increasingly lived in worlds of mediated forms" (Plummer, 2008, p. 10), while the significance of "porn" shifts as "kinky" iconography and practices become more visible in a wider range of sites, porn itself is more accessible, and mainstream texts are more explicit. The capture, production, and circulation of images of all kinds as modes of record, self-expression, communication, interaction, production, and consumption has become an important, though increasingly mundane, part of many people's lives. This extension of what Brian McNair (2002) has called the "striptease culture" of public and mediated intimacy increasingly depends not only on the production and consumption of explicit representations, or ordinary people's appearance in these, but on the multiplication of a range of practices that work to constitute the "real."

The shift toward a diverse set of porn practices is significant for understanding the ways in which we represent, express and experience sexuality in the 21st century, but it only makes sense when placed in the broader context of contemporary technology and media use, work and leisure practices, and changing conceptions of what sex and sexuality are. It problematizes older notions of how a porn "industry" might operate and points to new forms of porn production and new economies of sex; some of which can be glimpsed in the casual labor performed by amateurs on tube sites, the artisanal work on rate-me sites, the critical exchanges of pro-am writers on erotica sites, and the precarious erotic labor of new porn professionals.

Elsewhere, cultural work, or the labor of "becoming" in fan commentary, sex blogging and porn activism, is evident in the use of new media to produce self, connection, affect, and meaning. Modes of expression and response go beyond the seduction and arousal frequently attributed to pornographic texts and their consumption. Porn is the site of reflexivity and critique, playfulness and pleasure, disgust and desire. It is also increasingly difficult to distinguish labor from play in some forms of porn production and other forms of online sexual activity. New porn professionals form networks which link together the private worlds of individuals with writerly ambitions, artistic production, education and political activism. Porn fans congregate to discuss the conventions and pleasures of their collections and more besides, amateur writers and readers engage in interactions which are at once mutually arousing and culturally appreciative, while elsewhere the sexual display of the body becomes the focus of commentary and assessment or the prelude to more material kinds of sexual encounters.

Online Porn Studies

These developments in porn practices are not unique to porn but are part of the broader transformations in the economy and in culture in which the relations between production and consumption, work and leisure, public and private are being redrawn according to a paradigm of service work, the pursuit of "creative" and "flexible" labor, recombinant families, isolable individuals, and a sexual ethic of "bounded authenticity" in which commerce and intimacy coexist (Bernstein, 2007, p. 173). Indeed, while porn is interesting for its generic specificities and peculiarities, it is the broader significance of online porn practices—their staging of different notions of sex and self, the real and the body, culture and commerce—that make them particularly fascinating as a site of contemporary study.

We live in contradictory times characterized by a new sense of responsibilization where we are expected to bear the burden of our own choices in relation to sex and representation (Buckingham & Bragg, 2004), cut across with moves toward remoralization and regulation, and amidst a more general confusion of the material and the immaterial that has shaken up "the most basic presuppositions of traditional thinking about images of all sorts" (Kendrick, 1996, pp. 251–252). A contemporary view of the self as reflexive and self-regulating jostles with older notions of the individual as susceptible to "effects" and in need of policing. New paradigms for studying sex media, evident in the development of porn studies, compete with the recycling of tired antiporn discourses in popular writings and government reports. These fret about the mainstreaming and normalization of sexually explicit media, and about the internet as a conduit of perverse imagery and sexual deviation. Familiar anxieties about childhood, commodification, technology, representation, and desire are rearticulated as contemporary issues: addictive behavior, women's collusion with their own objectification, adults preying on children, the blurring of boundaries between cultural forms, the plasticity of sexuality.

In this context it is perhaps not surprising that the term, "porn" has gradually come to mean an increasingly wide range of things, to indicate in a much muzzier way the variety of things that may turn us on, and to suggest a sense of unease with the way that sex and media now appear to be everywhere and nowhere, unconfinable and uncategorizable. In this sense, porn has come to stand for the vague sense that we are a society haunted by the "spectre of sex" (Bauman, 1999, p. 30) and the fear that Kendrick described as "older than Plato," "that images will invade reality and warp it" (Kendrick, 1996, p. 226). If these fears were contained by the "neat compromise" of privatized media consumption, which until recently worked to preserve public decency whilst ensuring the ever wider distribution of porn (Kendrick, 1996, p. 250), they appear to be no longer so, unsurprisingly perhaps, given the increasing interrelationship of the real and representational, the material and immaterial. In this context, we need to pay much closer attention to the specific practices and cultures of porn that are emerging online, while becoming much more imaginative in the way we conceptualize these. Neither fear, nor unease, nor fretting are good starting points for either of these tasks, but the new wave of research into sex and the media, of which this collection is a part, provides us with a space for the dialogue we need to make sense of online pornography.

References

Film and TV

Art School Sluts 2004. Dir. Eon McKai.
Bend over Boyfriend 1998. Dir. Shar Rednour.
Boogie Nights 1997. Dir. Paul Thomas Anderson.
Bridget Jones's Diary 2001. Dir. Sharon Maguire.
Brokeback Mountain 2006. Dir. Ang Lee.
Contract Killers 2005. Dir. Dez.
Debbie Does Dallas 1978. Dir. Jim Clark.
Debbie Does Dallas 2 1981. Dir. Jim Clark.
Debbie Does Dallas 3 1985. Dir. Joseph F. Robinson.
Debbie Does Dallas 4 1988. Dir. Ron Jeremy.
Debbie Does Dallas 99 1999. Dir. Paul Thomas.
Debbie Does Dallas: The Revenge 2003. Dir. Paul Thomas.
Debbie Does Dallas: The Musical 2001. Dir. Peter Ross.
off-Broadway version 2002. Dir. Brock Enright.
Debbie Does Dallas Uncovered 2005. Dir. Francis Hanley
Debbie Does Dallas 2007. Dir. Paul Thomas.
Debbie Loves Dallas 2007. Dir. Eon McKai.
Debbie Does Dallas ... Again (2007).
Gag Factor 2000. Dir. Jim Powers.
Getting Stoned 2007. Dir. Lee Stone.
Hard Love 2000. Dir. Shar Rednour & Jackie Strano.
Hong Kong Connection: Pretty Bizarre (2005).
Jackass (2000-2002).
Justine's Red Letters 2005. Dir. Shy Love.
Lust, Caution 2007. Dir. Ang Lee.
Narcassist 2004. Dir. Ariana Jollee.
Pansexual Public Porn 1997. Dir. Del La Grace Volcano.
Pornography: The Secret History of Civilisation (1999).
Riot Sluts 2004. Dir. Mason.
Secret Diary of a Call Girl (2007-).
Sex and the City (1998–2004).
Sex Fest 2006. Dir. Kylie Ireland.
Showgirls 1995. Dir. Paul Verhoeven.
Skeeter's Fresh Asses 2006. Dir. Skeeter Kerkove.
Skin Flick 1999. Dir. Bruce LaBruce.
Squirt Factor 2005. Dir. Vincent Voss.
Striptease 1996. Dir. Andrew Bergman.
The Crash Pad 2005. Dir. Shine Louise Houston.
The *Girl Next Door* 2004. Dir. Luke Greenfield.

The Whore Next Door 2008. Dir. Kylie Ireland.
Whale Tale 3 2006. Dir. Mike Metropolis.
Who Let the Whores Out 2005. Dir. Kami Andrews.
Zack and Miri Make a Porno 2008. Dir. Kevin Smith.

Websites

Adult Friend Finder, http://adultfriendfinder.com/go/p231918. Accessed 14 January 2009.
All Lesbian Nation, http://alllesbiannation.com/. Accessed 21 March 2009.
Altporn, http://altporn.net/. Accessed 21 March 2009.
Arisa Sex World, http://hk.myblog.yahoo.com/arisa2007001. Accessed 28 October 2008.
Asian Sex Gazette, http://www.asiansexgazette.com/. Accessed 21 March 2009.
AVN, http://www.avn.com/. Accessed 21 March 2009.
Audacia.Ray, http://www.audaciaray.com/. Accessed 21 March 2009.
Backlash, http://www.backlash-uk.org.uk/. Accessed 21 March 2009.
Bella Vendetta, http://www.bellavendetta.com/v2/index.php. Accessed 20 January 2009.
BoobCritic, http://www.boobcritic.com/. Accessed 21 March 2009.
BootyVote, http://www.bootyvote.com/. Accessed 21 March 2009.
Brooklynbizarro, http://www.brooklynbizarro.com/. Accessed 8 October 2007.
Buck Angel, http://www.buckangel.com/. Accessed 20 June 2009.
Consumption-junction, http://www.consumptionjunction.com/. Accessed 8 October 2007.
Crash Pad Series, http://crashpadseries.com/. Accessed 25 April 2009.
Crossplay, www.crossplay.net. Accessed 14 January 2009.
Cupchicks, http://www.cupchicks.com/. Accessed 8 October 2007.
Cyber-Dyke, http://www.cyber-dyke.net/. Accessed 25 April 2009.
Deviant Nation, http://www.deviantnation.com/. Accessed 25 November 2008.
Downloadpass, http://www.downloadpass.com/ft=pimp2261-ccfcf3d9/pp=13/cf=1/index.
    html?. Accessed 21 March 2009.
Ducky Doolittle, http://www.duckydoolittle.com/. Accessed 20 June 2009.
Extreme-board, http://www.extreme-board.com/. Accessed 8 October 2007.
FloppyDicks, http://www.floppydicks.com/. Accessed 21 March 2009.
Freegaypornfinder, http://www.freegaypornfinder.com/. Accessed 20 June 2009.
FreeOnes, http://www.freeones.com/. Accessed 21 March 2009.
Furry Girl, http://furrygirl.com/. Accessed 20 January 2009.
GayBlackHardcore, http://www.gayblackhardcore.com/index.html. Accessed 20 June 2009.
Gaydar, http://gaydar.co.uk/. Accessed 20 June 2009.
Gaymoviedome, http://www.gaymoviedome.com/. Accessed 20 June 2009.
GayVN Online, http://gay.avn.com/. Accessed 25 April 2009.
Gurochan, http://gurochan.net/. Accessed 8 October 2007.
HisFirstGaySex, http://www.hisfirstgaysex.com/gay-sex/?revid=40050&s=1&nopop=1.
Accessed 20 June 2009.

Hogtied, http://www.hogtied.net/. Accessed 20 July 2009.

HotBareBacking, http://HotBareBacking.com/. Accessed 25 April 2009.

HotorNot, http://www.hotornot.com/. Accessed 21 March 2009.

Internet Filter Review, http://internet-filter-review.toptenreviews.com/internet-pornography-statistics. Accessed 14 January 2009.

Internet Watch Foundation, http://www.iwf.org.uk/. Accessed 21 March 2009.

I Feel Myself, http://www.ifeelmyself.com/public/main.php. Accessed 20 June 2009.

I Shot Myself, http://www.ishotmyself.com/public/main.php. Accessed 20 June 2009.

Kink, http://www.kink.com/. Accessed 20 July 2009.

Lemon Party, http://www.lemonparty.org/. Accessed 8 October 2007.

Live Girl Review, http://livegirlreview.com/. Accessed 22 January 2009.

Literotica, http://www.literotica.com/. Accessed 21 March 2009.

Liveleak, http://www.liveleak.com/. Accessed 8 October 2007.

Lolita Online, http://www.lolionline.net. Accessed 14 January 2009

Meatspin, http://meatspin.com/. Accessed 8 October 2007.

MegaPorn, http://www.megaporn.com/. Accessed 21 February 2009.

MeNude, http://www.menude.com. Accessed 21 March 2009.

Naughty Tanya, https://sexywife.kennedy2046.com. Accessed 28 October 2008.

Networkcultures, http://www.networkcultures.org/clickme/. Accessed 30 April 2009.

No Fauxxx, http://www.nofauxxx.com/. Accessed 20 January 2009.

PayOnes, http://www.payones.com/warning.seam. Accessed 21 March 2009.

Playbutch, http://www.playbutch.com/. Accessed 20 June 2009.

PornoTube, http://www.pornotube.com/. Accessed 21 March 2009.

Postpornpolitics, http://www.postpornpolitics.com/ Accessed 10 July 2009.

RateLegs, http://www.ratelegs.com/. Accessed 21 March 2009.

RateMeaBBW, http://www.ratemeabbw.com/. Accessed 21 March 2009.

RateMeNaked, http://www.ratemenude.com/. Accessed 21 March 2009.

RateMyMelons, http://ratemymelons.com. Accessed 21 March 2009.

RateMyWedgie, http://ratemywedgie.com/. Accessed 21 March 2009.

RedTube, http://www.redtube.com/. Accessed 20 December 2008.

Rich Snob, http://www.richsnob.com/. Accessed 24 November 2008.

RoseBud Bar, http://www.cyber-dyke.net/public/gallery/rosebud/. Accessed 25 April 2009.

Rotten, http://www.rotten.com/. Accessed 8 October 2007.

Sappho's Girls, http://www.sapphosgirls.com/. Accessed 20 June 2009.

Scarleteen, http://www.scarleteen.com/. Accessed 10 July 2009.

Sexerati, http://melissagira.com/sexerati/. Accessed 21 March 2009.

Sex Work 101, http://www.sexwork101.com/. Accessed 22 January 2009.

Sex Work Awareness, http://sexworkawareness.org/. Accessed 25 January 2009.

Sexy Wife, https://sexywife.kennedy2046.com. Accessed 28 October 2008.

Sharing is Sexy, http://sharingissexy.org/node/2. Accessed 25 November 2008.

$pread magazine, http://www.spreadmagazine.org/. Accessed 21 March 2009.

Suicide Girls, http://suicidegirls.com/. Accessed 21 March 2009.

SDC, http://www.sdc.com/index.aspx?ref=RMID24&gclid=CNztkaKbtJkCFU2K3godw E3eGQ. Accessed 21 March 2009.

Tinynibbles, http://www.tinynibbles.com/. Accessed 22 January 2009.
Tube8, http://www.tube8.com/. Accessed 20 December 2008.
VideosZ, http://www.videosz.com/index.php?link_id=2539&tracker_
  id=2076&gclid=CO2M1cuZtJkCFYQ-3godkj3d6g. Accessed 21 March 2009.
Vivid Corporate, http://www.vividentertainment.com/. Accessed 15 January 2009.
Voyeurweb, http://www.voyeurweb.com/. Accessed 21 March 2009.
Waking Vixen, http://www.wakingvixen.com/. Accessed 22 January 2009.
WeLiveTogether, http://www.welivetogether.com/mainhtm?id=googlerk&p=clean&cmp=we2_
  we%20live%20together/. Accessed 24 November 2008.
XBiz World Magazine, http://www.xbizworld.com/. Accessed 21 March 2009.
XTube, http://www.xtube.com/index.php?ref=&cache=1237644588&ww=1. Accessed 21 March 2009.
XXXChurch, http://xxxchurch.com/. Accessed 15 January 2009.
YouPorn, http://youporn.com/. Accessed 21 March 2009.

Bibliography

Abbas, Ackbar (1997) *Hong Kong: Culture and the Politics of Disappearance*. Hong
  Kong: Hong Kong University Press.
Adams, Eddie (2007) "Vivid-Alt Releases Debbie Loves Dallas Blu-ray Disc, http://
  www. avn.com/video/articles/4589.html. Accessed 20 January 2009.
Adler, Amy (2001) "The Perverse Law of Child Pornography," *The Columbia Law Review*
  101(2): 209–273.
Adler, Amy (2006) "Child Pornography Law and the Proliferation of the Sexualized
  Child," in Robert Atkins & Svetlana Mintcheva (eds.) *Censoring Culture:
  Contemporary Threats to Free Expression*. New York: The New Press: 228–240.
Adorno, Theodor & Horkheimer, Max (1973/1993) "The Culture Industry:
  Enlightenment as Mass Deception," in Simon During (ed.) *The Cultural Studies
  Reader. London & New York*: Routledge: 31–41.
Agustin, Laura (2007) *Sex at the Margins: Migration, Labor Markets and the Rescue
  Industry*. London & New York: Zed Books.
Akdeniz, Yaman (1999) *Sex on the Net: The Dilemma of Policing Cyberspace*. Reading:
  South Street Press.
Akdeniz, Yaman (2002) "Anonymity, Democracy, and Cyberspace,' *Social Research*
  69(1): 223–238.
Akdeniz, Yaman (2008) *Internet Child Pornography and the Law*. Hampshire: Ashgate.
Albury, Kath (2002) "Getting to Yes: From Compulsory Heterosexuality to Ethical
  Hetero-Sex," in *Yes Means Yes: Getting Explicit About Heterosex*. Crows Nest:
  Allen & Unwin: 170–192.
Albury, Kath (2003) "The Ethics of Porn on the Net," in Catherine Lumby & Elspeth
  Probyn (eds.) *Remote Control: New Media, New Ethics*. Cambridge: Cambridge
  University Press: 196–211.
Albury, Kath (2008) "DIY Porn: Fans, Amateurs and Cottage Industries," in Alan
  McKee et al. *The Porn Report*. Melbourne: Melbourne University Press: 128–148.

Albury, Kath (2009) "Reading porn reparatively," *Sexualities* 12(5): 647–53.

Andrews, David (2006) *Soft in the Middle: The Contemporary Softcore Feature in Its Contexts*. Columbus: Ohio State University Press.

Angelides, Steven (2005) "The Emergence of the Paedophile in the Late Twentieth Century," *Australian Historical Studies* 37: 272–295.

Archibald, Timothy (2005) *Sex Machines: Photographs and Interviews*. Los Angeles, CA: Process Books.

Armstrong, Isobel (2000) *The Radical Aesthetic*. Oxford: Blackwell.

Arvidsson, Adam (2007) "Netporn: The Work of Fantasy in the Information Society?," in Katrien Jacobs et al. (eds.) *C'lick Me: A Netporn Studies Reader*. Amsterdam: Institute of Network Cultures: 69–76.

Attwood, Feona (2002) "Reading Porn: The Paradigm Shift in Pornography Research," *Sexualities* 5(1): 91–105.

Attwood, Feona (2006) "Sexed Up: Theorizing the Sexualization of Culture," *Sexualities* 9(1): 77–94.

Attwood, Feona (2007a) "'Other' or 'One of Us'? The Porn User in Public and Academic Discourse," *Participations: Journal of Audience and Reception Studies* 4(1), http://www.participations.org/. Accessed 5 January 2009.

Attwood, Feona (2007b) "No Money Shot? Commerce, Pornography and New Sex Taste Cultures," *Sexualities* 10(4): 441–456.

Attwood, Feona (2007c) "Sluts and Riot Grrrls: Female Identity and Sexual Agency," *Journal of Gender Studies* 16(3): 233–247.

Attwood, Feona (ed.) (2009) *Mainstreaming Sex: The Sexualization of Western Culture*. London & New York: I.B.Tauris.

Attwood, Feona & Hunter, I.Q. (eds.) (2009) "Researching and Teaching the Sexually Explicit Issue," *Sexualities* 12(5).

Barber, J. Matt (2008) "Hard-Core Pornography Isn't Free Speech," http://www.cwfa.org/articledisplay.asp?id=14527&department=CFI&categoryid=pornography. Accessed 1 February 2008.

Barcan, Ruth (2002) "In the Raw: 'Home-made' Porn and Reality Genres," *Journal of Mundane Behaviour* 3(1), http://mundanebehavior.org/index2.htm. Accessed 27 March 2008.

Barcan, Ruth (2004) *Nudity: A Cultural Anatomy*. New York: Berg.

Barker, Martin & Petley, Julian (2001) *Ill Effects: The Media/Violence Debate*, second edition. London and New York: Routledge.

Barthes, Roland (1993/1973) *Mythologies*. London: Paladin.

Baudrillard, Jean (2004) "War Porn," *International Journal of Baudrillard Studies* 2(1), http://www.ubishops.ca/baudrillardstudies/vol2_1/taylor.htm. Accessed 2 August 2008.

Bauman, Zygmunt (1999) "On Postmodern Uses of Sex," *Theory, Culture & Society* 15: 3–4.

Baym, Nancy K. (2000) *Tune in, Log on: Soaps, Fandom, and Online Community*. Thousand Oaks, CA: Sage.

Beck, Ulrich & Beck-Gernsheim, Elisabeth (2002) *Individualization: Institutionalized Individualism and its Social and Political Consequences*. London: Sage.

Bell, David (2000) *An Introduction to Cybercultures*. London: Routledge.

Bell, David (2006) "Bodies, Technologies, Spaces: On 'Dogging'," *Sexualities* 9(4):

387–407.

Belle du Jour (2005) *The Intimate Adventures of a London Call Girl*. London: Phoenix.

Bennett, David (2001) "Pornography-Dot-Com: Eroticising Privacy on the Internet," *The Review of Education, Pedagogy & Cultural Studies* 23(4): 381–391.

Berger, John (1972) *Ways of Seeing*. New York: Penguin Group.

Berghuis, Thomas (2006) *Performance Art in China*. Hong Kong: Time Zone 8.

Bergstrand, Curtis & Williams, Jennifer B. (2000) "Today's Alternative Marriage Styles: The Case of Swingers," *Electronic Journal of Human Sexuality* 3, http://www.ejhs. org/volume3/swing/body.htm. Accessed 6 January 2009.

Bernardi, Daniel (2006) "Interracial Joysticks: Pornography's Web of Racist Attractions," in Peter Lehman (ed.) *Pornography: Film and Culture*. New Brunswick, NJ: Rutgers University Press: 220–243.

Bernstein, Elizabeth (2007) *Temporarily Yours: Intimacy, Authenticity, and the Commerce of Sex*. Chicago & London: The University of Chicago Press.

Best, David (2006) "Web 2.0 Next Big Thing or Next Big Internet Bubble?" http://page. mi.fu-berlin.de/best/uni/WIS/Web2.pdf. Accessed 12 May 2008.

Blue, Violet (2007) "Eon McKai's Altporn Liberation Army," SFGate, http://sfgate.com/cgi-bin/article.cgi?file=/gate/archive/2007/02/08/violetblue.DTL. Accessed 10 May 2007.

Blue, Violet (2008) "Sex Doesn't Sell," SFGate, http://www.sfgate.com/cgi-bin/article. cgi?f=/g/a/2008/10/09/violetblue.DTL. Accessed 24 November 2008.

Bogue, Ronald & Conis-Pope, Marcel (1996) "Introduction: Paradigms of Conflict and Mediation in Literary and Cultural Imagination," in Ronald Bogue & Marcel Conis-Pope (eds.) *Violence and Mediation in Contemporary Culture*. Albany: State University of New York Press: 1–18.

Bonney, Claire (1986) "The Nude Photograph: Some Female Perspectives," *Women's Art Journal* 6(2): 9–14.

Bordo, Susan (2000) *The Male Body: A New Look at Men in Public and Private*. New York: Farrar, Straus, & Giroux.

Borenstein, Eliot (2008) *Overkill: Sex and Violence in Contemporary Russian Popular Culture*. Ithaca: Cornell University Press.

Borgman, Christine L. (1990) *Scholarly Communication and Bibliometrics*. London: Sage.

Bowen, Aaron "Sex, Blogs, and the Great Firewall Part I—Censorship," http://www. neasist.org/icisc/blog/?p=38. Accessed 28 October 2008.

Boyer, Quentin (2008) "Vivid vs. Pornotube," *XBiz World Magazine*, http://www.xbiz. com/articles/91710/vivid+vs.+pornotube). Accessed 9 November 2008.

Boyle, Karen (2006) "The Boundaries of Porn Studies: On Linda Williams' *Porn Studies*," *New Review of Film and Television Studies* 4(1): 1–16.

Brents, Barbara G. & Hausbeck, Kathryn (2007) "Marketing Sex: US Legal Brothels and Late Capitalist Consumption," *Sexualities* 10(4): 425–439.

Brewer, Kathee (2008) "Down the Tubes," http://www.avn.com/internet/articles/5774. html. Accessed 14 January 2009.

Bright, Susie (1999) *Full Exposure: Opening Up to Sex and Creativity*. San Francisco: Harper.

Brissett, Dennis & Edgley, Charles (1990) *Life as Theater: A Dramaturgical Source*

Book. New York: Aldine de Gruyter.

Brooks, David (2000) *Bobos in Paradise: The New Upper Class and How They Got There*. New York: Simon and Schuster.

Bruns, Axel (2008) *Blogs, Wikipedia, Second Life, and Beyond: From Production to Produsage*. New York: Peter Lang.

Buckingham, David & Bragg, Sara (2004) *Young People, Sex and the Media: The Facts of Life?* Basingstoke & New York: Palgrave Macmillan.

Burchell, Graham (1996) "Liberal Government and Techniques of the Self," in Andrew Barry et al. (eds.) *Foucault and Political Reason: Liberalism, Neo-liberalism and Rationalities of Government*. London: UCL Press: 19–36.

Burger, John R. (1995) *One-Handed Histories: The Eroto-Politics of Gay Male Video Pornography*. New York: Haworth Press.

Butkas, Claire (2004) "Female Porn Providers and Internet Services," *Convergence: The International Journal of Research into New Media Technologies* 10(1): 10–22.

Butler, Heather (2004) "What Do You Call a Lesbian with Long Fingers?: The Development of Lesbian and Dyke Pornography," in Linda Williams (ed.) *Porn Studies*. Durham & London: Duke University Press: 167–197.

Butler, Judith (1990) *Gender Trouble: Feminism and the Subversion of Identity*. New York: Routledge.

Butler, Judith (1993) *Bodies That Matter: On the Discursive Limits of "Sex."* London & New York: Routledge.

Butler, Judith (1997) *Excitable Speech: A Politics of the Performative*. New York: Routledge.

Butler, Judith (2004) *Undoing Gender*. New York & London: Routledge.

Califia, Pat (2000) *Public Sex: The Culture of Radical Sex*. San Francisco, CA: Cleis Press.

Cameron, Deborah & Frazer, Elizabeth (2000) "On the Question of Pornography and Sexual Violence: Moving Beyond Cause and Effect," in Drucilla Cornell (ed.) *Feminism and Pornography*. Oxford: Oxford University Press: 240–53.

Cante, Rich C. & Restivo, Angelo (2004a) "The Cultural-Aesthetic Specificities of All-male Moving Image Pornography," in Linda Williams (ed.) *Porn Studies*. Durham: Duke University Press: 142–166.

Cante, Rich C. & Restivo, Angelo (2004b) "The 'World' of All-Male Pornography: On the Public Place of Moving-Image Sex in the Era of Pornographic Transnationalism," in Pamela Church Gibson (ed.) *More Dirty Looks: Gender, Pornography and Power*. London: BFI Publishing: 110–126.

Carnes, Michelle (2007) "Bend Over Boyfriend: Anal Sex Instructional Videos for Women," in Susanna Paasonen et al. (eds.) *Pornification: Sex and Sexuality in Media Culture*. Oxford: Berg: 151–160.

Carter, Angela (1979) *The Sadeian Woman: An Exercise in Cultural History*. London: Virago.

Carter, Cynthia & Weaver, C. Kay (2003) *Violence and the Media*. Philadelphia: Open University Press.

Castells, Manuel (1996) *The Rise of the Network Society*. Oxford: Blackwell.

Champagne, John (1997) "'Stop Reading Films!': Film Studies, Close Analysis, and Gay Pornography," *Cinema Journal* 36(4): 76–97.

Chien, Eugenia, "Chinese Women Bloggers Explore Unchartered Territories," *Pacific*

News Blog, http://news.pacificnews.org/news/view_article.html?article_id=30576ff1d d2beb5da172e6a41ffe5f33. Accessed 28 October 2008.

Chun, Wendy Hui Kyong (2006) *Control and Freedom: Power and Paranoia in the Age of Fiber Optics*. Cambridge, MA: MIT Press.

Church Gibson, Pamela & Gibson, Roma (eds.) (1993) *Dirty Looks: Women, Pornography. Power*. London: BFI Publishing.

Church Gibson, Pamela (ed.) (2004) *More Dirty Looks: Gender, Pornography and Power*. London: BFI Publishing.

Citizen Lab, The (2007) *Everyone's Guide to By-Passing Internet Censorship: For Citizens Worldwide*, http://deibert.citizenlab.org/Circ_guide.pdf. Accessed 8 January 2009.

Cochrane, Kira (2007) "For Your Entertainment: The Rise of Torture Porn," *G2: A Guardian Supplement*, May 1: 4–7.

Cohen, Henry (2002) "Obscenity, Child Pornography and Indecency: Recent Developments and Pending Issues," in Matthew D. Clark (ed.) *Obscenity, Child Pornography and Indecency*. New York: Novinka: 1–8.

Cooley, Charles (1964/1902) *Human Nature and Social Order*. New York: Charles Scribner's Sons.

Cooper, Al (1998) "Sexuality and the Internet: Surfing into the New Millenium," *Cyberpsychology and Behaviour* 1(2): 181–187.

Cooper, Sharon W. (2005) "A Brief History of Child Sexual Exploitation," in Sharon W. Cooper et al. (eds.) *Medical, Legal, & Social Science Aspects of Child Sexual Exploitation: A Comprehensive Review of Pornography, Prostitution and Internet Crimes*. St. Louis: GW Medical Publishing Inc: 1–24.

Coopersmith, Jonathan (2000) "Pornography, Videotape, and the Internet," *IEEE Technology and Society Magazine*, Spring: 27–34.

Cornell, Drucilla (ed.) (2000) *Feminism and Pornography*. Oxford: Oxford University Press.

Coté, Mark & Pybus, Jennifer (2007) "Learning to Immaterial Labour 2.0," *Ephemera* 7(1): 88–106.

Craig, Thomas & Petley, Julian (1998) "Invasion of the Internet Abusers," in Martin Barker & Julian Petley (eds.) *Ill Effects: The Media Violence Debate*, second edition, London: Routledge: 186–201.

Cramer, Florian (2007) "Sodom Blogging: Alternative Porn and Aesthetic Sensibility," in Katrien Jacobs et al. (eds.) *C'Lick Me: A Netporn Studies Reader*. Amsterdam: Institute of Network Cultures: 171–175.

Cramer, Florian & Home, Stuart (2007) "Pornographic Coding," in Katrien Jacobs et al. (eds.) *C'Lick Me: A Netporn Studies Reader*. Amsterdam: Institute of Network Cultures: 159–170.

Creed, Barbara (1993) *The Monstrous-Feminine: Film, Feminism, Psychoanalysis*. London & New York: Routledge.

Critcher, Chas (2003) *Moral Panics and the Media*. Buckingham: Open University Press.

Cronin, Blaise & Davenport, Elisabeth (2001) "E-Rogenous Zones: Positioning Pornography in the Digital Economy," *The Information Society* 17: 33–48.

Cumberland, Sharon (2004) "Private Uses of Cyberspace: Women, Desire, and Fan Culture," in David Thorburn & Henry Jenkins (eds.) *Rethinking Media Change:*

The Aesthetics of Transition. Cambridge, MA: MIT Press: 261–279.

Curry, Ramona (1996) "Media Scholars Teaching Pornography: Stepping Across Broadway," *Jump Cut* 40: 114–118.

Dahlberg, Lincoln (2001) "The Habermasian Public Sphere Encounters Cyber-Reality," in *Javnost—The Public* 8(3): 83–96.

Davis, Murray (1983) *Smut: Erotic Reality/Obscene Ideology*. Chicago: University of Chicago Press.

deGenevieve, Barbara (2007) "Ssspread.com: The Hot Bods of Queer Porn," in Katrien Jacobs et al. (eds.) *C'lick Me: A Netporn Studies Reader*. Amsterdam: Institute of Network Cultures: 233–238.

Deleuze, Gilles (1992) "Postscript on the Societies of Control," *October* 59 (Winter): 3–7.

Dery, Mark (2007), "Naked Lunch: Talking Realcore with Sergio Messina," in Katrien Jacobs et al. (eds.) *C'Lick Me: A Netporn Studies Reader*. Amsterdam: Institute of Network Cultures: 17–30.

de Visser, Richard & McDonald, Dee (2007) "Swings and Roundabouts: Management of Jealousy in Heterosexual 'Swinging' Couples," *British Journal of Social Psychology* 46: 459–476.

deVoss, Danielle (2002) "Women's Porn Sites—Spaces of Fissure and Eruption or 'I'm a Little Bit of Everything'," *Sexuality and Culture* 6(3): 75–94.

Diamond, Lisa (2005) "'I'm straight, but I kissed a girl': The Trouble with American Media Representation of Female-Female Sexuality," *Feminism & Psychology* 15(1): 104–110.

Donnerstein, Edward et al. (1987) *The Question of Pornography: Research Findings and Policy Implications*. New York: Macmillan/Free Press.

Douglas, Mary (1966) *Purity and Danger: An Analysis of Concepts of Pollution and Taboo*. London: Routledge & Kegan Paul.

Drezner, Daniel W. & Farrell, Henry (2004) "Web of Influence," *Foreign Policy* 145: 32–40.

Driscoll, Catherine (2006) "On True Pairing: The Romance of Pornography and the Pornography of Romance," in Karen Hellekson & Kristine Busse (eds.) *Fan Fiction and Fan Communities in the Age of the Internet*. Jefferson: McFarland: 79–96.

Driver, Susan (2004) 'Pornographic Pedagogies?: The Risk of Teaching 'Dirrty' Popular Cultures," *M/C Journal* 7(4), http://journal.media-culture.org.au/0410/03_teaching. php. Accessed 2 December 2008.

Durham, Meenakshi Gigi (2008) *The Lolita Effect: The Media Sexualization of Young Girls and What We Can Do About It*. Woodstock & New York: The Overlook Press.

Durkin, Keith (2004) "The Internet as a Milieu for the Management of Stigmatized Identity," in Dennis D. Waskul (ed.) *Net.seXXX: Readings on Sex, Pornography and the Internet*. New York: Peter Lang: 131–147.

Dworkin, Andrea (1979) *Pornography: Men Possessing Women*. London: The Women's Press.

Dworkin, Andrea (2000) "Pornography and Grief," in Drucilla Cornell (ed.) *Feminism and Pornography*. Oxford: Oxford University Press: 39–44.

Dyer, Richard (1989) "A Conversation about Pornography," in Simon Shepherd & Mick Wallis (eds.) *Coming On Strong: Gay Politics and Culture*. London: Unwin Hyman:

198–212.

Dyer, Richard (1992) *Only Entertainment*. London: Routledge.

Dyer, Richard (1992) "Coming to Terms: Gay Pornography," in *Only Entertainment*. London & New York: Routledge: 121–134.

Dyer, Richard (2002) "Idol Thoughts: Orgasm and Self-Reflexivity in Gay Pornography, in *The Culture of Queers*. London & New York: Routledge: 187–203.

Easton, Dossie & Liszt, Catherine, A. (1998) *The Ethical Slut: A Guide to Infinite Sexual Possibilities*. Greenery Press: San Francisco.

Edelstein, David (2006) "Now Playing at Your Local Multiplex: Torture Porn," *New York Magazine*, http://nymag.com/movies/features/15622/. Accessed 12 February 2009.

Edgley, Charles & Kiser, Kenneth (1981) "Polaroid Sex: Deviant Possibilities in a Technological Age," *Journal of American Culture* 5(1): 59–64.

Eglash, Ron (2002) "Race, Sex, and Nerds: From Black Geeks to Asian American Hipsters," *Social Text* 20: 49–64.

Elias, Norbert (2000) *The Civilizing Process*. Oxford: Blackwell.

Ellis, Kate et al. (1986) *Caught Looking: Feminism, Pornography, and Censorship*. Seattle: The Real Comet Press.

Esch, Kevin & Mayer, Vicki (2007) "How Unprofessional: The Profitable Partnership of Amateur Porn and Celebrity Culture," in Susanna Paasonen et al. (eds.) *Pornification: Sex and Sexuality in Media Culture*. Oxford: Berg: 99–111.

Essig, Laurie (2000) "Heteroflexibility, http://dir.salon.com/story/mwt/feature/2000/11/15/heteroflexibility/. Accessed 6 January 2009.

Falk, Pasi (1993) "The Representation of Presence: Outlining the Anti-aesthetics of Pornography," *Theory, Culture & Society* 10: 1–42.

Farrer, James (2007) "China's Women Sex Bloggers and Dialogic Sexual Politics on the Chinese Internet," *China Aktuell* 36(4): 9–45.

Foucault, Michel (1976) *The History of Sexuality: Vol.1: An Introduction*. London: Penguin.

Foucault, Michel (1979) *Discipline and Punish: the Birth of the Prison*. Transl. by Allan Sheridan. London: Penguin Books.

Foucault, Michel (1984) "Truth and Power," in Paul Rabinow (ed.) *The Foucault Reader*. New York: Pantheon Books: 51–75.

Foucault, Michel (1988) *Technologies of the Self: A Seminar with Michel Foucault*. Amherst, MA: University of Massachusetts Press.

Frank, Thomas (1998) *The Conquest of Cool: Business Culture, Counterculture, and the Rise of Hip Consumerism*. Chicago & London: University of Chicago Press.

Free Speech Coalition (2007) "State-of-the-Industry Report 2007–2008," http://www.freespeechcoalition.com/webdocs/FSC_SoI_Report_Final_12_2007.pdf. Accessed 28 February 2008.

French, Howard (2005) "A Party Girls Leads China's Online Revolution," *New York Times*, http://www.howardwfrench.com/archives/2005/11/24/a_party_girl_leads_chinas_online_revolution/. Accessed 10 October 2008.

French, Howard (2006) "As Chinese Students Go Online, Little Sister Is Watching," *New York Times*, http://www.nytimes.com/2006/05/09/world/asia/09internet.html?_r=1&oref=slogin. Accessed 10 October 2008.

Fulton, Deidre (2005) "SuicideGirls Revolt," http://www.portlandphoenix.com/features/other_stories/documents/05018238.asp. Accessed 23 October 2006.

Fung, Richard (2005) "Looking for My Penis: The Eroticized Asian in Gay Video Porn," in Kent A. Ono (ed.) *A Companion to Asian American Studies*. New York: Blackwell Publishing: 234–251.

Gaines, Jane (2004) "Machines That Make the Body Do Things," in Pamela Church Gibson (ed.) *More Dirty Looks: Gender, Pornography and Power*. London: BFI: 31–44.

Gastil, Raymond D. (1976) "The Moral Right of the Majority to Restrict Obscenity and Pornography Through Law," *Ethics* 86(3): 231–240.

Gauntlett, David (2007) "Media Studies 2.0," http://www.theory.org.uk/mediastudies2.htm. Accessed 26 July 2008.

Giddens, Anthony (1991) *Modernity and Self-Identity: Self and Society in the Late Modern Age*. Cambridge: Polity.

Gill, Rosalind (2007a) *Technobohemians or the New Cybertariat?* Amsterdam: Institute of Network Cultures.

Gill, Rosalind (2007b) "Postfeminist Media Culture: Elements of a Sensibility," *European Journal of Cultural Studies* 10(2): 147–166.

Gill, Rosalind (2008) "Empowerment/Sexism: Figuring Female Sexual Agency in Contemporary Advertising," *Feminism & Psychology* 18: 35–60.

Gill, Rosalind (2009) "Beyond the 'Sexualization of Culture' Thesis: An Intersectional Analysis of 'sixpacks,' 'midriffs' and 'hot lesbians' in Advertising," *Sexualities* 12(2): 137–160.

Gill, Rosalind & Pratt, Andy (2008) "In the Social Factory? Immaterial Labour, Precariousness and Cultural Work," *Theory, Culture & Society* 25(7–8): 1–30.

Gillespie, Alisdair A. (2008) *Child Exploitation and Communication Technologies*. Dorset: Russell House Publishing.

Gilmore, Leigh (2005) "How We Confess Now: Reading the Abu Ghraib Archive," in Jo Gill (ed.) *Modern Confessional Writing: New Critical Essays*. London: Routledge: 180–92.

Gira, Melissa (2008a), "The Future of Sexerati," http://melissagira.com/sexerati/2008/01/07/the-future-of-sexerati/. Accessed 24 November 2008.

Gira, Melissa (2008b) "The End of Sexpertise," http://melissagira.comsexerati/2008/10/10/the-end-of-sexpertise/. Accessed 24 November 2008.

Godwyn, Mary (2006) "Using Emotional Labor to Create and Maintain Relationships in Service Interactions," *Symbolic Interaction* 29(4): 487–506.

Goffman, Erving (1976) *Gender Advertisements*. New York: Harper Colophon.

Goldstein, Leigh (2009) "Documenting and Denial: Discourses of Sexual Self-Exploitation," *Jump Cut* 51: http://www.ejumpcut.org/currentissue/goldstein/text.html. Accessed 30 March 2009.

Gonsalves, Antoine (2007) "Adult Video Maker to Ship First Movie on Blu-ray Disk," *Information Week*,http://www.informationweek.com/news/management/showArticle.jhtml?articleID=197002968. Accessed 16 January 2009.

Gossett, Jennifer Lynn & Byrne, Sarah (2002) "'Click Here': A Content Analysis of Internet Rape Sites," *Gender and Society* 16(5): 689–709.

Graham, Phil (2000) "Hypercapitalism: A Political Economy of Informational Idealism," *New Media and Society* 2(2): 131–156.

Gray, Jonathan et al. (2007) *Fandom: Identities and Communities in a Mediated World.* New York: New York University Press.

Greenfield-Sanders, Timothy (2004) *xxx 30 Porn-Star Portraits.* New York: Bullfinch Press.

Grenzfurthner, Johannes et al. (2008) *prOnnovation: Pornography and Technological Innovation.* San Francisco: RE/Search Publications/Monochrom.

Griffin, Susan (1981) *Pornography and Silence: Culture's Revenge against Nature.* New York: Harper & Row.

Griffin-Shelley, Eric (2003) "The Internet and Sexuality: A Literature Review—1983–2002," *Sexual and Relationship Therapy* 18(3): 355–370.

Grossman, Lev (2006) "Time's Person of the Year: You," *Time*, http://www.time.com/time/magazine/article/0,9171,1569514,00.html. Accessed 10 January 2009.

Grosz, Elizabeth (1995) *Space, Time and Perversion.* London, Routledge.

Hacking, Ian (1999) *The Social Construction of What?* Cambridge, MA: Harvard University Press.

Halavais, Alexander C. (2006) *Cyberporn and Society.* Dubuque, Iowa: Kendall/Hunt Publishing Company.

Hardy, Simon (1998) *The Reader, the Author, His Woman and Her Lover: Soft-Core Pornography and Heterosexual Men.* London: Cassell.

Hardy, Simon (2004) "Reading pornography," *Sex Education* 4(1): 3–18.

Hardy, Simon (2008) "The Pornography of Reality," *Sexualities* 11(1–2): 60–64.

Harkin, James (2006) "War Porn," *The Guardian*, August 12: 27.

Harris, Cheryl & Alexander, Alison (1998) *Theorizing Fandom: Fans, Subculture, and Identity.* Cresskill, NJ: Hampton Press.

Hartley, Nina (1997) "In the Flesh: A Porn Star's Journey," in Jill Nagle (ed.) *Whores and Other Feminists.* New York: Routledge: 57–65.

Healy, Margaret A. (1996) *Child Pornography: an International Perspective.* World Congress Against Commercial Sexual Exploitation of Children: Stockholm.

Heath, Joseph & Potter, Andrew (2005) *Nation of Rebels: Why Counterculture Became Consumer Culture.* Albany, OR: Capstone Publishing.

Heider, Don & Harp, Dustin (2002) "New Hope or Old Power: Democracy, Pornography and the Internet," *The Howard Journal of Communication* 13: 285–299.

Heins, Marjorie (2001) *Not In Front of the Children: 'Indecency', Censorship and the Innocence of Youth.* New York: Hill & Wang.

Heins, Marjorie (2006) "Media Effects," in Robert Atkins & Svetlana Mintcheva (eds.) *Censoring Culture: Contemporary Threats to Free Expression.* New York: The New Press: 173–184.

Higonnet, Anne (1998) *Pictures of Innocence: The History and Crisis of Ideal Childhood.* New York: Thames and Hudson.

Hills, Matt (2002) *Fan Cultures.* London: Routledge.

Hite, Shere (1981) *The Hite Report on Male Sexuality.* New York: Knopf.

Ho, Josephine (2005) "Queer Existence Under Global Governance: A Taiwan Exemplar,"

Keynote speech, Beyond the Strai(gh)ts: Transnationalism and Queer Chinese Politics, Institute of East Asian Studies, UC Berkeley, April 29–30.

Hodgkinson, Tom (2008) "With Friends Like These," *The Guardian*, 14 January: 6.

Hoffman, Claire (2007) "Obscene Losses," *Portfolio Magazine*, http://www.portfolio. com/culture-lifestyle/culture-inc/arts/2007/10/15/YouPorn-Vivid-Entertainment-Profile. Accessed 11 January 2009.

Holland, Gemma (2005) "Identifying Victims of Child Abuse Images: An Analysis of Successful Identifications," in Ethel Quayle & Max Taylor (eds.) *Viewing Child Pornography on the Internet: Understanding the Offence, Managing the Offender, Helping the Victims*. Dorset: Russell House Publishing: 75–90.

Holmes, Brian (2008) "One World, One Dream: China at the Risk of New Subjectivities," http://brianholmes.worldpress.com. Accessed 8 January 2008.

Home Office (2006) *Consultation on the Possession of Extreme Pornographic Material: Summary of Responses and Next Steps*. http://www.homeoffice.gov.uk/documents/ cons-extreme-porn-3008051/Gvt-responseextreme-porn2.pdf?view=Binary. Accessed 1 February 2008.

Horeck, Tanya (2004) *Public Rape: Representing Violation in Fiction and Film*. London: Routledge.

Howitt, Dennis (1995) *Paedophiles and Sexual Offences Against Children*. West Sussex: John Wiley & Sons.

Hughes, Donna (2004) "The Use of New Communications and Information Technologies for the Sexual Exploitation of Women and Children," in Christine Stark & Rebecca Whisnant (eds.) *Not for Sale: Feminists Resisting Prostitution and Pornography*. North Melbourne: Spinifex Press: 38–55.

Hunt, Lynn (ed.) (1993) *The Invention of Pornography, 1500–1800: Obscenity and the Origins of Modernity*. New York: Zone Books.

Hunter, Ian et al. (1993) *On Pornography: Literature, Sexuality and Obscenity Law*. New York: St. Martin's Press.

Hutcheon, Linda (1995) *Irony's Edge: The Theory and Politics of Irony*. London: Routledge.

Jackson, Stevi (1996) "Heterosexuality and Feminist Theory," in Diane Richardson (ed.) *Theorising Heterosexuality: Telling it Straight*. Buckingham: Open University.

Jacobs, Katrien (2004a) "Pornography in Small Places and Other Spaces," *Journal of Cultural Studies* 18(1): 67–83.

Jacobs, Katrien (2004b) "The New Media Schooling of the Amateur Pornographer: Negotiating Contracts and Singing Orgasm," http://www.libidot.org/katrien/tester/ articles/negotiating-print.html. Accessed 2 June 2006.

Jacobs, Katrien (2005) *Libi_doc: Journeys in the Performance of Sex Art*. Ljbuljana: Maska Productions.

Jacobs, Katrien (2007) *Netporn: DIY Web Culture and Sexual Politics*. Rowman & Littlefield.

Jacobs, Katrien et al. (eds.) (2007) *C'lick Me: A Netporn Studies Reader*. Amsterdam: Institute of Network Cultures.

Jacobs, Katrien (2008a) Interview with media activist Oiwan Lam. 15 November 2007.

Jacobs, Katrien (2008b) Interview with Lolita Cynthia. 17 August 2006.

Press: 21–38.

Jameson, Jenna (2004) *How To Make Love Like A Porn Star: A Cautionary Tale.* New York: Regan Books.

Jenks, Richard (1998) "Swinging: A Review of the Literature," *Archives of Sexual Behaviour* 27: 507–521.

Jenkins, Henry (2004) "Foreword: So You Want to Teach Pornography?," in Pamela Church Gibson (ed.) *More Dirty Looks: Gender, Pornography and Power.* London: BFI Publishing: 1–7.

Jenkins, Henry (2006) *Convergence Culture: Where Old and New Media Collide.* New York: New York University Press.

Jenkins, Henry (2007) "Porn 2.0," http://henryjenkins.org/2007/10/porn_20.html. Accessed 20 January 2009.

Jenkins, Henry & Dueze, Mark (2008) "Editorial—Convergence Culture," *Convergence: The International Journal of Research into New Media Technologies* 4(1): 5–12.

Jenkins, Philip (1998) *Moral Panic: Changing Concepts of the Child Molester in Modern America.* New Haven, CT: Yale University Press.

Jenkins, Philip (2001) *Beyond Tolerance: Child Pornography on the Internet.* New York & London: New York University Press.

Jensen, Robert (2007) *Getting Off: Pornography and the End of Masculinity.* Cambridge: South End Press.

Johnson, Peter (1996) "Pornography Drives Technology: Why Not to Censor the Internet," *Federal Communications Law Journal* 49(1), http://www.law.indiana.edu/fclj/pubs/v49/no1/johnson.html. Accessed 14 January 2009.

Jones, Steven & Mowlabocus, Sharif (2009) "Hard Times and Rough Rides: The Legal and Ethical Impossibilities of Researching 'Shock' Pornographies," *Sexualities* 12(5): 613–628.

Juffer, Jane (1998) *At Home with Pornography: Women, Sex, and Everyday Life.* New York: New York University Press.

Kappeler, Suzanne (1986) *The Pornography of Representation.* Cambridge: Polity Press.

Keegan, Paul (2003) "Prime-Time Porn Borrowing Tactics from the Old Hollywood Studios, Vivid Entertainment Has Ditched the Plain Brown Wrapper and Is Taking the Multibillion-Dollar Sex-Film Industry Mainstream," *Business 2.0 Magazine,* http://money.cnn.com/magazines/business2/business2_archive/2003/06/01/343376/index.htm. Accessed 14 January 2009.

Kendrick, Walter (1996/1987) *The Secret Museum: Pornography in Modern Culture.* Berkeley, LA & London: University of California Press.

Kerekes, David & Slater, David (1995) *Killing for Culture—An Illustrated History of Death Film from Mondo to Snuff.* London: Creation Books.

Kernes, Mark (2007) "Piracy Conference Could Be the Start of Something Big," http://www.avn.com/index.cfm?objectid=70F9F731-B1EE-818D-931BEAF17B36C7C6&articleid=DD5F351A-D142-6198-043BDF47539D8467. Accessed 1 February 2008.

Kernes, Mark (2009) "Max Hardcore Surrenders to U.S. Marshals," http://avnmag.avn.com/articles/34339.html. Accessed 4 February 2009.

Kerr, Darren & Hines, Claire (eds.) (2010) *Hard to Swallow: Reading Pornography On Screen*. London: Wallflower Press.

Kibby, Marj & Costello, Brigid (1999) "Displaying the Phallus: Masculinity and the Performance of Sexuality on the Internet," *Men and Masculinities* 1(4): 352–364.

Kibby, Marj & Costello, Brigid (2001) "Between the Image and the Act: Interactive Sex Entertainment on the Internet," *Sexualities* 4(3): 353–369.

Kibby, Marjorie (2001) "Women and Sex Entertainment on the Internet: Discourses of Gender and Power," *Mots Pluriels* 19, http://www.arts.uwa.edu.au/MotsPluriels/ MP1901mk.html. Accessed 4 March 2008.

Kimmel, Michael (ed.) (1990) *Men Confront Pornography*. New York: Crown Publishers.

Kimmel, Michael & Plante, Rebecca (2002) "The Gender of Desire: The Sexual Fantasies of Women and Men," in Patricia Gagne & Richard Tewksbury (eds.) *Advances in Gender Research: Gendered Sexualities* 6: 55–77.

Kincaid, James R. (1998) *Erotic Innocence: The Culture of Child Molesting*. Durham, NC: Duke University Press.

Kipnis, Laura (1996) *Bound and Gagged: Pornography and the Politics of Fantasy in America*. New York: Grove Press.

Kipnis, Laura (1999) "The Eloquence of Pornography," Frontline: American Porn— Special Reports, http://www.pbs.org/wgbh/pages/frontline/shows/porn/specialeloqu ence.html. Accessed 1 February 2008.

Kirkham, Pat & Skeggs, Beverley (1996) "Pornographies, Pleasures and Pedagogies in U.K and U.S," *Jump Cut* 40: 106–113.

Kirkup, James & Martin, Nicole (2008) "MPs Attack 'Dark Side' of YouTube," *The Daily Telegraph*, 31 July: 1.

Kitzinger, Jenny (2004) *Framing Abuse: Media Influence and Public Understanding of Sexual Violence Against Children*. London: Pluto Press.

Kitzmann, Andreas (2004) *Saved from Oblivion: Documenting the Daily from Diaries to Web Cams*. New York: Peter Lang.

Klastrup, Lisbeth (2007) "Telling & Sharing: Understanding Mobile Stories & the Future of Narratives," in Andrew Hutchinson (ed.) Proceedings of perthDAC 2007, The 7th International Digital Arts and Culture Conference. Perth: Curtin University of Technology.

Klein, Marty (1999) "The History & Future of Sex," *Electronic Journal of Human Sexuality* 2, http://www.ejhs.org/volume2/history.htm. Accessed 14 January 2009.

Kleinhans, Chuck (1996) "Teaching Sexual Images: Some Pragmatics," *Jump Cut* 40: 119–122.

Kleinhans, Chuck (2004) "Virtual Child Porn: The Law and the Semiotics of the Image," in Pamela Church Gibson (ed.) *More Dirty Looks: Gender, Pornography and Power*. London: BFI Publishing: 71–84.

Knight, Brooke A. (2000) "Watch Me! Webcams and the Public Exposure of Private Lives," *Art Journal* 59(4): 21–25.

Knopper, Steve (2009) *Appetite for Self-Destruction: The Spectacular Crash of the Record Industry in the Digital Age*. New York: Free Press.

Knudsen, Susanne V. et al. (2007) *Generation P? Youth, Gender, and Pornography*.

Copenhagen: Danish School of Education Press.

Koontz, Linda D. (2003) "File Sharing Programs: Child Pornography Is Readily Accessible over Peer-to-Peer Networks," in Walker T. Halliday (ed.) *Governmental Principles and Statutes on Child Pornography*. New York: Nova Science Publishers Inc: 79–97.

Kristeva, Julia (1982) *Powers of Horror: An Essay on Abjection*. Trans. Leon S. Roudiez. New York: Columbia University Press.

Kuntsman, Adi (2007) "Belonging through Violence: Flaming, Erasure, and Performativity in Queer Migrant Community," in Kate O'Riordan & David J. Phillips (eds.) *Queer Online: Media, Technology and Sexuality*. New York: Peter Lang: 101–122.

Labelle, Beverly (1992) "Snuff—The Ultimate in Woman Hating," in Jill Radford & Diana E. H. Russell (eds.) *Femicide: The Politics of Woman Killing*. Buckingham: Open University Press: 189–194.

LaBruce, Bruce (1997) *The Reluctant Pornographer*. Toronto: Gutter Press.

Laclau, Ernesto & Mouffe, Chantal (1985) *Hegemony & Socialist Strategy*. London Verso.

LaGrace Volcano, Del (2005) *Sex Works*. Berlin: Konkursbuchverlag.

Lam, Oiwan (2007) "Don't Turn Kong Kong into a Mono-Colour Ghost City," www.interlocals.net/?q=node/9. Accessed 18 October 2008.

Lane, Frederick S. (2001) *Obscene Profits: the Entrepreneurs of Pornography in the Cyber Age*. New York: Routledge.

Langman, Lauren (2004) "Grotesque Degradation: Globalization, Carnivalization and CyberPorn," in Dennis D. Waskul (ed.) *Net.seXXX: Readings on Sex, Pornography, and the Internet*. New York: Peter Lang: 193–216.

Laqueur, Thomas W. (2003) *Solitary Sex: A Cultural History of Masturbation*. New York: Zone Books.

Law, Lisa (2002) "Defying Disappearance; Cosmopolitan Public Spaces in Hong Kong," *Urban Spaces* 39(9): 1625–1645.

Lazzarato, Maurizio (2001) "Toward an Inquiry into Immaterial Labour," *Makeworlds* 1, http://makeworlds.org/node/141. Accessed 27 March 2009.

Leadbeater, Charles & Miller, Paul (2004) *The Pro-Am Revolution: How Enthusiasts Are Changing Our Economy and Society*. London: Demos.

Lee, Leonard et al. (2007) "If I'm Not Hot, are You Hot or Not? Physical Attractiveness Evaluations and Dating Preferences as a Function of Own Attractiveness," *Social Science Research Network*, http://papers.ssrn.com/sol3/papers.cfm?abstract_id=950782. Accessed 20 April 2008.

Lee, Yi-Lin & Li, Yung-Ming (2007) "Pricing Web 2.0 Related Services: Peer Production," ACM International Conference Proceeding Series, http://portal.acm.org/citation.cfm?id=1282183. Accessed 7 August 2008.

Lehman, Peter (ed.) (2006) *Pornography: Film and Culture*. New Brunswick, NJ & London: Rutgers University Press.

Lehman, Peter (2006) A Dirty Little Secret: Why Teach and Study Pornography?, in Peter Lehman (ed.) *Pornography: Film and Culture*. New Brunswick, NJ & London: Rutgers University Press: 1–21.

Lehman, Peter (2007) "You and Voyeurweb: Illustrating the Shifting Representation of the Penis on the Internet with User-Generated Content," *Cinema Journal* 46(4): 108–116.

Leiblum, Sandra Risa (2001) "Review: Women, Sex and the Internet," *Sexual and Relationship Therapy* 16(4): 389–405.

Levin Russo, Julie (2007) "'The Real Thing': Reframing Queer Pornography for Virtual Spaces," in Katrien Jacobs et al. (eds.) (2007) *C'lick Me: A Netporn Studies Reader.* Amsterdam: Institute of Network Cultures: 239–252.

Levine, Judith (2002) *Harmful to Minors: The Perils of Protecting Children from Sex.* Minneapolis and London: University of Minnesota Press.

Levy, Ariel (2005) *Female Chauvinist Pigs: Women and the Rise of Raunch Culture.* London: Simon and Schuster.

Lévy, Pierre (1999) *Collective Intelligence: Mankind's Emerging World in Cyberspace.* Cambridge: Perseus Books.

Livingstone, Sonia (2008) "Taking Risky Opportunities in Youthful Content Creation: Teenagers' Use of Social Networking Sites for Intimacy, Privacy and Self Expression," *New Media and Society* 10(3): 393–411.

Lloyd, Richard (2005) *Neo-Bohemia: Art and Commerce in the Postindustrial City.* London & New York: Routledge.

Lockwood, Dean (2009) "All Stripped Down: The Spectacle of 'Torture Porn'," *Popular Communication* 7(1): 40–48.

Loftus, David (2002) *Watching Sex: How Men Respond to Pornography.* New York: Thunder's Mouth Press.

Lumby, Catharine (1997) *Bad Girls: The Media, Sex and Feminism in the 90s.* St Leonards: Allen & Unwin.

Lyman, Jay (2006) "Priority for Internet Users: Porn," http://www.technewsworld.com/story/34233.html. Accessed 26 July 2008.

Lynn, Regina (2007) "Web 2.0 Leaves Porn Behind," http://www.wired.com/culture/lifestyle/commentary/sexdrive/2007/08/sexdrive_0809?currentPage=all. Accessed 14 January 2009.

MacCannell, Dean (1989) *The Tourist: A New Theory of the Leisure Class.* New York: Schocken.

MacKinnon, Catherine (1993) *Only Words.* Cambridge, MA: Harvard University Press.

MacLeod, Murdo (2007) "Police Target YouTube Over Copycat Crimes," *Scotland on Sunday,* 25 November: 5.

MacRae, Shannon (1997) "Flesh Made Word: Sex, Text and the Virtual Body" in David Porter (ed.) *Internet Culture.* London & New York: Routledge: 73–86.

Maddison, Stephen (2004) "From Porno-Topia to Total Information Awareness, or What Forces Really Govern Access to Porn?," *New Formations* 52: 35–57.

Maddison, Stephen (2007) "The Biopolitics of the Penis," *Cultural Studies Now,* http://www.uel.ac.uk/ccsr/documents/TheBiopoliticsofthePenisCSNowweb.pdf. Accessed 8 January 2009.

Magnet, Shoshana (2007) "Feminist Sexualities, Race and the Internet: an Investigation of Suicidegirls.com," *New Media and Society* 9(4): 577–602.

Marcus, Steven (1964) *The Other Victorians: A Study of Sexuality and Pornography in Mid-Nineteenth-Century England.* New York: Basic Books.

Marr, David (2008) *The Henson Case.* Melbourne: Text Publishing.

Marshall, Barbara L. (2002) "'Hard Science': Gendered Constructions of Sexual Dysfunction in the 'Viagra Age'," *Sexualities* 5(2): 131–158.

Marshall, Barbara L. (2006) "The New Virility: Viagra, Male Aging and Sexual Function," *Sexualities* 9(3): 345–362.

Marx, Karl & Engels, Frederick (1975/1848) *Manifesto of the Communist Party.* Peking: Foreign Languages Press.

Mavor, Carol (1995) *Pleasures Taken: Performances of Sexuality and Loss in Victorian Photographs.* Durham, NC: Duke University Press.

McAfee, Noelle (2004) *Julia Kristeva.* London: Routledge.

McCarthy, John "Managing the Risks to Children Posed by the Internet," SAFE Network, http://www.safenetwork.co.nz/Downloads/Stranger%20Danger%20in%20the%20 Home.pdf. Accessed 1 March 2008.

McCullagh, Declan (2005) "Your ISP as Net Watchdog," http://www.news.com/2100– 1028_3–5748649.html. Accessed 1 February 2008.

McCullagh, Declan (2006) "Lawmakers Take Aim at Social-networking sites," http:// www.news.com/2100–1028_3–6071040.html. Accessed 1 March 2008.

McCullagh, Declan (2007a) "Net Porn Ban Faces Another Legal Setback," http:// www.news.com/Net-porn-ban-faces-another-legal-setback/21001030_3–6169621. html?tag=item. Accessed 1 February 2008.

McCullagh, Declan (2007b) "Wi-fi 'Illegal Images' Politician Defends Legislation," http://www.news.com/8301–13578_3–9830648–38.html?tag=bl. Accessed 1 March 2008.

McGavin, Harvey (2002) "Man Ordered Film of Pets Being Killed for Kicks," *The Independent*, 16 November: 13.

McKee, Alan et al. (2008) *The Porn Report.* Melbourne: Melbourne University Press.

McLelland, Mark (2005) "The World of Yaoi: The Internet, Censorship and the Global 'Boys' Love' Fandom," University of Wollongong Faculty of Arts Papers, http:// ro.uow.edu.au/artspapers/147. Accessed 28 April 2009.

McNair, Brian (1996) *Mediated Sex: Pornography and Postmodern Culture.* London & New York: Arnold.

McNair, Brian (2002) *Striptease Culture: Sex, Media and the Democratisation of Desire.* London & New York: Routledge.

McRobbie, Angela (2004) "The Rise and Rise of Porn Chic," *Times Higher Education*, http://www.timeshighereducation.co.uk/story.asp?storyCode=182087&sectioncode=2 6. Accessed 20 January 2009.

Mercer, Kobena (2000) "Just Looking for Trouble: Robert Mapplethorpe and Fantasies of Race," in Drucilla Cornell (ed.) *Feminism and Pornography.* Oxford: Oxford University Press: 460–476.

Merck, Mandy (1993) "*More of a Man*: Gay Porn Cruises Gay Politics," in *Perversions: Deviant Readings.* London: Virago: 217–235.

Messina, Sergio (n.d) "Realcore: the Digital Porno Revolution," http://realcore. radiogladio.it/. Accessed 11 October 2006.

Meyer, Anneke (2007) *The Child at Risk: Paedophiles, Media Responses and Public Opinion.* Manchester & New York: Manchester University Press.

Mies, Ginny (2006) "A New Erotica? Alternative Culture and the Porn Industry," *American Sexuality*, http://nsrc.sfsu.edu/article/new_erotica_alternative_culture_and_porn_industry. Accessed 25 January 2009.

Miller, Jason Lee (2007) "Search Overtakes Porn in the UK," http://www.webpronews.com/topnews/2007/01/31/search-overtakes-porn-in-the-uk. Accessed 26 July 2008.

Milne, Carly (ed.) (2005) *Naked Ambition: Women Who Are Changing Porn*. New York: Carroll & Graf.

Morgan, Robin (1980) "Theory and Practice: Pornography and Rape," in Laura Lederer (ed.) *Take Back the Night: Women on Pornography*. New York: Morrow.

Morrison, Jack (2007) "Porn 2.0: Giving Way to a New Method for Attracting—and Retaining—Consumers," http://www.avn.com/video/articles/6912.html. Accessed 14 January 2009.

Mowlabocus, Sharif (2007) "Gay Men and the Pornification of Everyday Life," in Susanna Paasonen et al. (eds.) *Pornification: Sex and Sexuality in Media Culture*. London: Berg: 61–72.

Mühleisen, Wencke (2007) "Mainstream Sexualisation—Backlash or Experimentation," in Susanne V. Knudsen et al. (2007) *Generation P?: Youth, Gender, and Pornography*. Copenhagen: Danish School of Education Press: 47–65.

Mühleisen, Wencke (2007) "Mainstream Sexualization and the Potential for Nordic New Feminism," *Nora: Nordic Journal of Women's Studies* 15(2): 172–189.

Mulvey, Laura (1975) "Visual Pleasure and Narrative Cinema," *Screen* 16(3): 6–18.

Nagle, Jill (ed.) *Whores and Other Feminists*. New York: Routledge.

Nead, Lynda (1992) *The Female Nude: Art, Obscenity and Sexuality*. London & New York: Routledge.

Negra, Diane (2009) *What a Girl Wants? Fantasizing the Reclamation of Self in Postfeminism*. London & New York: Routledge.

Nicol, Mark (2007) "REVEALED: The British Links to Internet Rape Site Viewed by this Girl's Sex Attacker," *Mail on Sunday*, 17 June: 34.

Nikunen, Kaarina & Paasonen, Susanna (2007) "Porn Star as Brand: Pornification and the Intermedia Career of Rakel Liekki," *The Velvet Light Trap* 59: 30–41.

Noam, Eli M. (2007) "The Dismal Economics of Virtual Worlds," ACM SIGMIS Database 38(4), http://delivery.acm.org/10.1145/1320000/1314255/p106-noam.pdf?key1=1314255&key2=4267227021&coll=GUIDE&dl=GUIDE&CFID=62189425&CFTOKEN=56208121. Accessed 12 May 2008.

Nooy, Wouter de et al. (2005) *Exploratory Social Network Analysis with Pajek*. New York: Cambridge University Press.

O'Brien, Jodi & Shapiro, Eve (2004) "'Doing It' on the Web: Emerging Discourses on Internet Sex," in David Gauntlett & Ross Horsley (eds.) *Web Studies*. London: Arnold: 114–126.

O'Donnell, Ian & Milner, Claire (2007) *Child Pornography: Crime, Computers and Society*. Devon: Willan Publishing.

Orbaugh, Sharalyn (2002) "Shojo," in Sandra Buckley (ed.) *Encyclopedia of Contemporary Japanese Culture*. London & New York: Routledge: 458–459.

O'Reilly, Tim (2005) "What is Web 2.0: Design Patterns and Business Models for the

Next Generation of Software," http://www.oreillynet.com/pub/a/oreilly/tim/news/2005/09/30/what-is-web-20.html. Accessed 6 May 2008.

O'Toole, Laurence (1998) *Pornocopia: Porn, Sex, Technology and Desire.* London: Serpents Tail.

Owens, Tuppy (1998) "The Oxford Union Debate—Tuppy's Contribution," http://www.sfc.org.uk/oxford-debate2.html. Accessed 1 February 2008.

Paasonen, Susanna (2006) "Email from Nancy Nutsucker," *European Journal of Cultural Studies* 9(4): 403–420.

Paasonen, Susanna et al. (eds.) (2007a) *Pornification: Sex and Sexuality in Media Culture.* Oxford: Berg.

Paasonen, Susanna et al. (2007b) "Pornification and the Education of Desire," in Susanna Paasonen et al. (eds.) *Pornification: Sex and Sexuality in Media Culture.* Oxford: Berg: 1–20.

Paasonen, Susanna (2007) "Porn Futures," in Susanna Paasonen et al. (eds.) *Pornification: Sex and Sexuality in Media Culture.* Oxford: Berg: 161–170.

Palac, Lisa (1998) *On the Edge of the Bed: How Dirty Pictures Changed My Life.* Boston, MA: Little, Brown & Company.

Papacharissi, Zizi (2002) "The Virtual Sphere: The Internet as Public Sphere," *New Media and Society* 4(1): 9–27.

Parent, W. A. (1990) "A Second Look at Pornography and the Subordination of Women," *Journal of Philosophy* 87(4): 205–211.

Pasquinelli, Matteo (2007) "Warporn! Warpunk: Autonomous Videopoesis in Wartime," in Katrien Jacobs et al. (eds.) (2007) *C'lick Me: A Netporn Studies Reader.* Amsterdam: Institute of Network Cultures: 149–158.

Passette, Gracie (2008) "The Clash of the Sex Writers: Should We Stay Or Should We Go?," http://marketingwhore.naughtyblog.net/2008/10/clash-of-sex-writers-should-we-stay-or.html. Accessed 24 November 2008.

Patterson, Zabet (2004) "Going on-line: Consuming Pornography in the Digital Era," in Linda Williams (ed.) *Porn Studies.* Durham, NC: Duke University Press: 105–123.

Paul, Pamela (2005) *Pornified: How Pornography Is Transforming Our Lives, Our Relationships, and our Families.* New York: Times Books.

Pendleton, Eva (1997) "Love for Sale; Queering Heterosexuality," in Jill Nagle (ed.) *Whores and Other Feminists.* New York & London: Routledge: 73–82.

Penley, Constance (1997) *NASA/Trek: Popular Science and Sex in America.* London: Verso.

Perdue, Lewis (2002) *EroticaBiz: How Sex Shaped the Internet.* New York: Writers Club Press.

Perdue, Lewis (2004) "EroticaBiz: How Sex Shaped the Internet," in Dennis D. Waskul (ed.) *Net.seXXX: Readings on Sex, Pornography, and the Internet.* New York: Peter Lang: 259–294.

Phillips, Dougal (2005) "Can Desire Go on Without a Body? Pornographic Exchange and The Death of the Sun," *Culture Machine: Interzone,* http://www.culturemachine.net/index.php/cm/article/view/236/217. Accessed 12 January 2008.

Plant, Sadie (2000) "Coming across the Future," in David Bell & Barbara M. Kennedy (eds.) *The Cybercultures Reader.* London: Routledge: 460–470.

Plummer, Kenneth (2003) *Intimate Citizenship: Private Decisions and Public Dialogues.* Seattle & London: University of Washington Press.

Plummer, Kenneth (2008) "Studying Sexualities for a Better World? Ten Years of *Sexualities,*" *Sexualities* 11(1-2): 7–22.

Postman, Neil (1994) *The Disappearance of Childhood.* New York: Vintage/Random House.

President's Commission on Obscenity and Pornography (1970) *Report of the Commission on Obscenity and Pornography.* Washington, DC: U.S. Government Printing Office.

Projansky, Sarah (2001) *Watching Rape: Film and Television in Postfeminist Culture.* New York: New York University Press.

Quan, Tracy (2001) *Diary of a Manhattan Call Girl.* New York: Three Rivers Press.

Quayle, Ethel et al. (2008) *Child Pornography and Sexual Exploitation of Children Online.* ECPAT, http://www.ecpat.net/WorldCongressIII/PDF/Publications/ICT_Psychosocial/Thematic_Paper_ICTPsy_ENG.pdf. Accessed 28 April 2009.

Queen, Carol (1997) "Sex Radical Politics, Sex-Positive Feminist Thought, and Whore Stigma," in Jill Nagle (ed.) *Whores and Other Feminists.* New York: Routledge: 125–135.

Queenan, Joe (2007) "Slash and Burn," *The Guide: A Guardian Supplement,* June 2–8: 16–17.

Ray, Audacia (2004) "A Beginning," July 28, http://www.wakingvixen.com/blog/2004/07/28/a-beginning/. Accessed 17 November 2008.

Ray, Audacia (2007a) *Naked on the Internet; Hookups, Downloads and Cashing in on Internet Sexploration.* Emeryville, CA: Seal Press.

Ray, Audacia (2007b) "Rated: Alt Porn," *Kunsetbeeld,* English version at http://docs.google.com/View?docid=ah95q5gc8qv9_193ck8rhsf6. Accessed 17 November 2008.

Ray, Audacia (2008a) "Notes for My Sex 2.0 Keynote," 14 April, http://www.wakingvixencom/blog/2008/04/14/notes-for-my-sex-20-keynote/. Accessed 24 November 2008.

Ray, Audacia (2008b) "It's My Blogoversary: Four Years!," 28 July, http://www.wakingvixen.com/blog/2008/07/28/its-my-blogoversary-four-years/. Accessed 24 November 2008.

Ray, Audacia (2008c) "How I Get it All Done: A Slightly Unflattering Self-Portrait," 14 December, http://www.wakingvixen.com/blog/2007/12/14/how-i-get-it-all-done-a-slightly-unflattering-self-portrait/. Accessed 24 November 2008.

Ray, Audacia (2008d) "Frustration, Overload and a Little Panic," 10 June, http://www.wakingvixen.com/blog/2008/06/10/frustration-overload-and-a-little-panic/. Accessed 24 November 2008.

Ray, Audacia (2008e) "The End of the Sex Writer," 3 October, http://www.wakingvixen.com/blog/2008/10/03/the-end-of-the-sex-writer/. Accessed 24 November 2008.

Ray, Audacia (2008f) "Commerce, Activism, and the Frivolous World of Sex," 10 October, http://www.wakingvixen.com/blog/2008/10/10/commerce-activism-and-the-frivolous-world-of-sex/. Accessed 24 November 2008.

Read, Jacinda (2000) *The New Avengers: Feminism, Femininity and the Rape-Revenge Cycle.* Manchester: Manchester University Press.

Reading, Anna (2005) "Professing Porn or Obscene Browsing? On Proper Distance in The University Classroom," *Media, Culture & Society* 27(1): 123–130.

Rheingold, Howard (1993/1995) *Virtual Community: Finding Connection in a Computerized World*. London: Minerva.

Rich, Adrienne (1980) "Compulsory Heterosexuality and Lesbian Existence," *Signs* 5 (4): 631–660.

Richards, Edwina (2002) *People I Don't Know in Photographs I Took of Something Else*. Sydney: Peninsula Paper.

Richardson, Diane (2000) *Rethinking Sexuality*. London: Sage.

Rival, Laura et al. (1999) "Sex and Sociality: Comparative Ethnographies of Sexual Objectification," in Mike Featherstone (ed.) *Love & Eroticism*. London: Sage: 295–322.

Robinson, Kerry (2008) "In the Name of 'Childhood Innocence': A Discursive Exploration of the Moral Panic," *Cultural Studies Review* 14 2): 113–129.

Rofel, Lisa (2007) *Desiring China: Experiments in Neoliberalism, Sexuality, and Public Culture*. Durham, NC: Duke University Press.

Rosoff, Matt (1999) "An Inside Look at the Net Porn Industry," http://home.cnet.com/internet/0–3805-7-280110.html. Accessed 15 October 2003.

Rose, Nikolas (1996) "Governing 'Advanced' Liberal Democracies," in Andew Barry et al. (eds.) *Foucault and Political Reason: Liberalism, Neo-Liberalism and Rationalities of Government*. London: UCL Press: 37–64.

Ross, Andrew (2004) *No-Collar: The Humane Workplace and Its Hidden Costs*. Philadelphia: Temple University Press.

Ross, Andrew (2008) "The New Geography of Work: Power to the Precarious?," *Theory, Culture & Society* 25(7–8): 31–49.

Rubin, Gayle (1984) "Thinking Sex: Notes for a Radical Theory of the Politics of Sexuality," in Carole S. Vance (ed.) *Pleasure and Danger: Exploring Female Sexuality*. Boston, MA: Routledge & Kegan Paul: 267–319.

Rubin, Marian et al. (2006) "Not a Pretty Picture: Four Photographers Tell Their Personal Stories about Child 'Pornography' and Censorship," in Robert Atkins & Svetlana Mintcheva (eds.) *Censoring Culture: Contemporary Threats to Free Expression*. New York: The New Press: 213–227.

Rush, Emma & La Nauze, Andrea (2006) *Corporate Paedophilia*. The Australia Institute, Discussion Paper 90, https://www.tai.org.au/file.php?file=DP90.pdf. Accessed 28 April 2009.

Ryan, Paul (2007) "Australia to Spend $189 Million on Anti-Porn Tech Initiative," 189-million-on-anti-porn-initiative.html. http://arstechnica.com/news.ars/post/20070814-australia-to-spend. Accessed 1 February 2008.

Sabbagh, Dan (2007) "Gangs and Gun Crime Rekindle the Debate on Tighter Internet Regulation," *Times*, 31 August: 59.

Schindler, Stephan K. (1996) "The Critic as Pornographer: Male Fantasies of Female Reading in Eighteenth-Century Germany," *Eighteenth Century Life* 20(3): 66–80.

Schlosser, Eric (1997) "The Business of Pornography," *US News and World Report*, 10 February: 42–50.

Scully, Matthew (2006) "The Playboy Legacy," *Wall Street Journal*, http://www.matthewscully.com/playboy_lagacy.htm. Accessed 1 February 2008.

Sedgwick, Eve K. (1991) *The Epistemology of the Closet*. London: Harvester Wheatsheaf.

Sedgwick, Eve K. (1993) *Tendencies*. London: Routledge.

Segal, Lynne (1993) "Does Pornography Cause Violence? The Search for Evidence," in Pamela Church Gibson and Roma Gibson (eds.) *Dirty Looks: Women, Pornography, Power*. London: BFI Publishing: 5–21.

Segal, Lynne & McIntosh, Mary (eds.) (1992) *Sex Exposed: Sexuality and the Pornography Debate*. London: Virago.

Selke, Lori (ed.) (2001) *The Very Best of Literotica.com*. San Francisco, CA: Black Books.

Senft, Teresa M. (2008) *Camgirls: Celebrity and Community in the Age of Social Networks*. New York: Peter Lang.

Seto, Michael C. et al. (2006) "Child Pornography Offenses are a Valid Diagnostic Indicator of Paedophilia," *Journal of Abnormal Psychology* 115(3): 610–615.

Seto, Michael C. (2008) *Pedophilia and Sexual Offending Against Children: Theory, Assessment and Intervention*. Washington DC: American Psychological Association.

Shaw, Susan M. (1999) "Men's Leisure and Women's Lives: The Impact of Pornography on Women," *Leisure Studies* 18(3): 197–212.

Sheldon, Kerry & Howitt, Dennis (2007) *Sex Offenders and the Internet*. West Sussex: John Wiley & Sons Ltd.

Sher, Julian (2007) *Caught in the Web: Inside the Police Hunt to Rescue Children from Online Predators*. New York: Carroll & Graf Publishers.

Silverman, Jon & Wilson, David (2002) *Innocence Betrayed: Paedophilia, the Media and Society*. Cambridge: Polity Press.

Simpson, Nicola (2005) "The Money Shot: The Business of Porn," *Critical Sense*, http://criticalsense.berkeley.edu/archive/spring2005/simpson.pdf. Accessed 14 January 2009.

Sinfield, Alan (2004) *On Sexuality and Power*. Columbia: Columbia University Press.

Skiba, Brian et al. (2006) *Web 2.0: Hype or Reality ... and how will it play out? A Strategic Analysis* (White Paper), http://www.armapartners.com/files/admin/uploads/W17_F_1873_8699.pdf. Accessed 5 August 2008.

Slade, Joseph W. (2000) *Pornography in America: A Reference Handbook*. Santa Barbara, CA: ABC-CLIO.

Slater, Don (1998) "Trading Sexpics on IRC: Embodiment and Authenticity on the Internet," *Body and Society* 4(4): 91–117.

Smith, Clarissa (2007) *One for the Girls! The Pleasures and Practices of Reading Women's Porn*. Bristol: Intellect.

Snitow, Ann et al. (eds.) (1983) *Powers of Desire: The Politics of Sexuality*. New York: Monthly Review Press.

Sobchack, Vivian (2005) *Carnal Thoughts: Embodiment and Moving Image Culture*. Berkeley: California University Press.

Sofia, Zoë (1999) "Virtual Corporeality: A Feminist View," in Jenny Wolmark (ed.) *Cybersexualities: A Reader on Feminist Theory, Cyborgs and Cyberspace*. Edinburgh: Edinburgh University Press: 55–68.

Sontag, Susan (1969) "The Pornographic Imagination," in *Styles of Radical Will*. New York: Dell: 35–73.

Sprinkle, Annie (1998) *Post-Porn Modernist: My 25 Years as a Multimedia Whore*.

Pittsburgh, PA: Cleis Press.

Stern, Steven E. & Handel, Alysia D. (2001) "Sexuality and Mass Media: The Historical Context of Psychology's Reaction to Sexuality on the Internet," *Journal of Sex Research* 38: 283–291.

Stoltenberg, John (1999) *Refusing to Be a Man: Essays on Social Justice*. New York: Routledge.

Stone, Allucquère Rosanne (1998) *The War of Desire and Technology at the Close of the Mechanical Age*. Cambridge, MA: MIT Press.

Straayer, Chris (1993) "The Seduction of Boundaries: Feminist Fluidity in Annie Sprinkle's Art/Education/Sex," in Pamela Church Gibson & Roma Gibson (eds.) *Dirty Looks: Women, Pornography, Power*. London: BFI: 156–175.

Strager, Stephen (2003) "What Men Watch When They Watch Pornography," *Sexuality & Culture* 7(1): 50–61.

Sullivan, David (2007) "Vivid Entertainment Ships Debbie Does Dallas...Again," *AVN*, http://www.avn.com/video/articles/8171.html. Accessed 14 January 2009.

Swartz, Shauna (2006) "XXX Offender: Reality Porn and the Rise of Humilitainment," in Lisa Jervis & Andi Zeisler (eds.) *Bitchfest*. New York: Farrar: 318–321.

Tang, Isabel (1999) *Pornography: The Secret History of Civilization*. London: World of Wonder/Channel 4 Books.

Tate, Tim (1990) *Child Pornography: An Investigation*. London: Methuen.

Taylor, Max et al. (2001) "Typology of Paedophile Picture Collections," *The Police Journal* 74(2): 97–107.

Taylor, Max & Quayle, Ethel (2003) *Child Pornography: An Internet Crime*. East Sussex: Brunner-Routledge.

Thomas, Terry (2005) *Sex Crime: Sex Offending and Society*. 2nd ed. Cullompton: Willan Publishing.

Thompson, Bill & Williams, Andy (2004) "Virtual Offenders: The Other Side of Internet Allegations," in Calder, Martin C. (ed.) *Child Sexual Abuse and the Internet: Tackling the New Frontier*. Dorset: Russell House Publishing: 113–132.

Thompson, Clive (2008) "Brave New World of Digital Intimacy," *New York Times*, http://www.nytimes.com/2008/09/07/magazine/07awareness-t.html. Accessed 21 March 2009.

Thompson, Tony (2002) "Cruelty Fears over Cult of 'Crush Videos'," *The Observer*, 19 May: 15.

Thurman, Neil (2008) "Forums for Citizen Journalists? Adoption of User-Generated Content Initiatives by Online News Media," *New Media & Society* 10(1): 139–157.

Tola, Miriam (2005) "Re-routing the (a)sex Drives of Big Dickie: An Interview with Katrien Jacobs about Netporn and Identity," http://www.networkcultures.org/netporn/index.php?onderdeelID=1&paginaID=13&itemID=70. Accessed 8 June 2008.

Tong, Rosemarie (1992) *Feminist Thought: a Comprehensive Introduction*. London: Routledge.

Trainer, Russell (1966) *The Lolita Complex*. New York: The Citadel Press.

Travers, Ann (2003) "Parallel Subaltern Feminist Counterpublics in Cyberspace," *Sociological Perspectives* 46(2): 223–237.

Trifiletti, Christopher D. (2005) "Investigating Internet Child Exploitation Cases," in Sharon W. Cooper et al. (eds.) *Medical, Legal, & Social Science Aspects of Child Sexual Exploitation: A Comprehensive Review of Pornography, Prostitution and Internet Crimes*. St. Louis: GW Medical Publishing Inc: 609–634.

Vance, Carole S. (ed.) (1984) *Pleasure and Danger: Exploring Female Sexuality*. Boston, MA: Routledge & Kegan Paul.

Wakeford, Nina (2000) "Cyberqueer," in David Bell & Barbara M. Kennedy (eds.) *The Cybercultures Reader*. London: Routledge: 403–415.

Warf, Barney & Grimes, John (1997) "Counterhegemonic Discourses on the Internet," *Geographical Review* 87(2): 259–274.

Warner, Michael (1991) "Introduction: Fear of a Queer Planet," *Social Text* 29: 3–17.

Waskul, Dennis D. (2002) "The Naked Self: Being a Body in Televideo Cybersex," *Symbolic Interaction* 25(2): 199–227.

Waskul, Dennis D. (ed.) (2004) *Net.seXXX: Readings on Sex, Pornography, and the Internet*. New York: Peter Lang.

Waskul, Dennis D. (2004) "Introduction: Sex and the Internet: Old Thrills in a New World; New Thrills in an Old World," in *Net.Sexxx: Readings on Sex, Pornography, and the Internet*. New York: Peter Lang: 1–8.

Waskul, Dennis D. et al. (2000) "Cybersex: Outercourse and the Enselfment of the Body," *Symbolic Interaction* 23(4): 375–397.

Watney, Simon (1987) *Policing Desire: Pornography, AIDS and the Media*. London: Methuen/Comedia.

Watson, Paul "alternaporn: We Sing the Body Politic," http://www.lazaruscorporation. co.uk/v4/articles/alternaporn.php. Accessed 23 November 2006.

Waugh, Thomas (1985) "Men's Pornography: Gay vs. Straight," *Jump Cut* 30: 420–425.

Waugh, Thomas (1996) *Hard to Imagine: Gay Male Eroticism in Photography and Film from Their Beginnings to Stonewall*. New York: Columbia University Press.

Weeks, Jeffrey (1999) "The Sexual Citizen," in Mike Featherstone (ed.) *Love and Eroticism*. London, Thousand Oaks, New Delhi: Theory, Culture & Society/Sage: 35–52.

Weeks, Jeffrey (2007) *The World We Have Won*. London & New York: Routledge.

White, Michelle (2003) "Too Close To See: Men, Women, and Webcams," *New Media and Society* 5(1): 7–28.

White, Michelle (2006) *The Body and the Screen: Theories of Internet Spectatorship*. Cambridge, MA: MIT Press.

Wicke, Jennifer (2004) "Through a Gaze Darkly: Pornography's Academic Market," in Pamela Church Gibson (ed.) *More Dirty Looks: Gender, Pornography and Power*. London: BFI: 176–187.

Wild, Rex & Anderson, Patricia (2007) *Little Children Are Sacred*, http://www.nt.gov. au/dcm/inquirysaac/pdf/bipacsa_final_report.pdf. Accessed 20 January 2009.

Wilkinson, Sue (1996) "Bisexuality 'a la mode'," *Women's Studies International Forum* 19(3): 293–301.

Williams, Christopher R. (2004) "Reclaiming the Expressive Subject: Deviance and the Art of Non-Normativity," *Deviant Behavior* 25(3): 233–254.

Williams, Linda (1989) *Hard Core: Power, Pleasure and the "Frenzy of the Visible."* London: Pandora.

Williams, Linda (1992) "Pornography on/scene or Diff'rent Strokes for Diff'rent Folks," in Lynne Segal & Mary McIntosh (eds.) *Sex Exposed: Sexuality and the Pornography Debate.* London: Virago: 233–262.

Williams, Linda (1993) "A Provoking Agent: The Pornography and Performance of Annie Sprinkle," *Social Text* 37 (Winter): 117–133.

Williams, Linda (ed.) (2004a) *Porn Studies.* Durham, NC: Duke University Press. Berkeley, CA: University of California Press.

Williams, Linda (2004b) "Porn Studies: Proliferating Pornographies On/Scene: An Introduction," in Linda Williams (ed.) *Porn Studies.* Durham, NC & London: Duke University Press: 1–23.

Williams, Linda (2004c) "Second Thoughts on Hard Core: American Obscenity Law and the Scapegoating of Deviance," in Pamela Church Gibson (ed.) *More Dirty Looks: Gender, Pornography and Power.* 2nd edition. London: BFI: 165–175.

Williams, Linda (2008) *Screening Sex.* Durham, NC & London: Duke University Press.

Wittig, Monique (1992) *The Straight Mind and Other Essays.* Boston, MA: Beacon Press.

Wolak, Janis et al. (2005) "The Varieties of Child Pornography Production," in Ethel Quayle & Max Taylor (eds.) *Viewing Child Pornography on the Internet: Understanding the Offence, Managing the Offender, Helping the Victims.* Dorset: Russell House Publishing: 31–48.

Zillmann, Dolf & Bryant, Jennings (eds.) (1989) *Pornography: Research Advances and Policy Considerations.* Hillsdale, NJ: Lawrence Erlbaum.

Zimmermann, Patricia (1995) *Reel Families: A Social History of Amateur Film.* Bloomington: Indiana University Press.

Zizek, Slavoj (1997) *The Plague of Fantasies.* London & New York: Verso.

List of Contributors

Feona Attwood is a principal lecturer in Media and Communication Studies at Sheffield Hallam University, UK. Her research focuses on controversial images, online sexualities, and mediated intimacy. Recent publications include articles in *Sexualities, International Journal of Cultural Studies,* and *Journal of Gender Studies,* and book chapters on pornography, sexual agency, and research methods. She is the editor of *Mainstreaming Sex: The Sexualization of Western Culture* (2009).

Sanna Härmä is a Media Studies postgraduate student at the University of Turku, Finland. Her dissertation examines mainstream pornography within the context of cultural and media studies, feminist and queer theory, and the "pornification of popular culture." Her recent publications include a chapter in *Pornoakatemia* (ed. Harri Kalha, 2007) and an article in *Feminist Media Studies.*

Katrien Jacobs is a scholar, curator, and artist in the field of new media and sexuality and works as assistant professor at City University of Hong Kong. She organized netporn conferences with the Institute of Network Cultures in Amsterdam in 2005 and 2007. Her publications include *Libi_doc: Journeys in the Performance of Sex Art.* (2005), *C'lick Me: A Netporn Reader* (2007), and *Netporn: DIY Web Culture and Sexual Politics* (2007).

Steven Jones teaches in the department of Film and Media at the University of Sussex, UK. His research centers upon the disruptions to selfhood and moralities of victimization posed by horror film and literature. Other research interests include pornography, gender studies, feminism, post-structuralism, discourses of the body, and existential philosophy.

Simon Lindgren is associate professor of Sociology at Umeå University, Sweden. His research interests include the sociology of culture, media studies, discourse analysis, popular culture, semiotics, Web studies, and critical theory. His publications include two textbooks within these fields, *Populärkultur: Teorier, metoder och analyser* (2005) and *Sociologi 2.0: Samhällsteori och samtidskultur* (2007), as well as a number of articles in international journals. He is currently leading two research projects about media discourses on crime victims and online piracy.

Stephen Maddison is a principal lecturer in Cultural Studies at the University of East London, UK. He is the author of *Fags, Hags and Queer Sisters: Gender Dissent and Heterosocial Bonds in Gay Culture* (2000) and has written widely about questions of gender identity and gay culture. His recent work has been concerned with the political and economic infrastructure of porn, and he is currently working on a book, *The Myth of Porn*. He co-runs a Web site, OpenGender.org, that publishes work on sexuality, gender, and new technologies.

Jennifer Moorman is a doctoral candidate in Cinema and Media Studies at the University of California, Los Angeles, USA. Her dissertation, tentatively titled "The Softer Side of Hardcore? Women Filmmakers, Pornography, and Sexperimental Film," is an industrial and contextual analysis, as well as an alternative historiography of U.S. pornographic film and video production, focusing on the above-the-line and behind-the-camera contributions of women. Her other publications include chapters in *Televising Queer Women: A Reader* (ed. Rebecca Beirne, 2007) and *A Dragon Wrecked My Prom: Teen Wizards, Mutants, and Heroes* (ed. Jes Battis, forthcoming).

Mónica G. Moreno Figueroa is a lecturer in Sociology at Newcastle University, UK. Her research is concerned with contemporary practices of racism in relation to mestizaje (racial mixing), visibility, and emotions, with a specific focus on Mexico. Her work has appeared in journals such as *History of the Human Sciences* and the *Journal of Intercultural Studies*, as well as in *Raza, Etnicidad y Sexualidades: Ciudadanía y Multiculturalismo en América* (ed. Peter Wade et al., 2008).

Sharif Mowlabocus is a lecturer in Media and Digital Media and a member of the research centre for Material Digital Culture at the University of Sussex, UK. His research explores sexual representation and sexual subcultures, primarily within digital environments. He has written on a variety of subjects including amateur pornography, dating/ sex Web sites, barebacking, and cybercruising. His book *Gaydar Culture* is due to be published in 2010.

Susanna Paasonen is a research fellow at the Helsinki Collegium for Advanced Studies, University of Helsinki, Finland, where she is currently preparing a book on online pornography, affect, and feminist methodology. She is the author of *Figures of Fantasy: Internet, Women and Cyberdiscourse* (2005) and coeditor of *Women and Everyday Uses of the Internet: Agency & Identity* (2002), *Pornification: Sex and Sexuality in Media Culture* (2007), and the forthcoming *Working with Affect in Feminist Readings: Disturbing Differences*. Susanna's research on pornography has appeared in *Feminist Theory, European Journal of Cultural Studies,* and *The Velvet Light Trap.*

Cheryl L. Radeloff is an assistant professor of Women's Studies at Minnesota State University, Mankato, USA. Her published work examines feminist curriculum initiatives in the geosciences, safer sex and feminist methodology. Her teaching and research interests are prostitution, sex work, pornography, and sexualities. She is currently studying gender and work issues within the sex and body industry and preparing her Ph.D. dissertation on HIV testing laws and policies in Nevada's sex industry for publication.

Alison Rooke is a lecturer in Sociology at Goldsmiths University, UK. Her work explores the philosophical underpinnings of sociological representation, and the ways that understandings of representation inform the epistemology of ethnographic social research. Her Ph.D. research used photo elicitation to explore the everyday temporality and spatiality of London as experienced by lesbian and bisexual women. More recently, her research has included developing ways of using visual sociology in the evaluation of social and arts policy.

David Slayden is an associate professor at the School of Journalism and Mass Communications at the University of Colorado at Boulder, USA. He has worked as an editor, scriptwriter, creative director, and professor of communication arts. He is the author of *Hate Speech* (1995) and *Soundbite Culture* (1999), and winner of the Gustavus Myers Center Award for the Study of Human Rights in North America (1995).

Adam Stapleton is a PhD student at the University of Western Sydney, Australia, where he is a lecturer and research assistant in the School of Communication Arts and a member of the Centre for Cultural Research and the Writing and Society Group. His research interests include erotica, pornography, and obscenity; and particularly the emergence of child pornography as a form of obscenity. His other research interests involve fan communities, the contemporary horror film genre, and emotional contagion.

Joakim Stolpe is a Philosophy postgraduate student and lecturer at Åbo Akademi University, Finland. His dissertation focuses on the understanding of human actions in their (f)actual surroundings. Through his involvement with Women's Studies at the University of Turku, he also has a long-standing interest in media studies and feminist ontology, focusing mostly on pornography, music, class, and cleanliness. He is a contributor to the quarterly philosophical publication, *Ikaros*, and to the www.filosofia.fi philosophical archives.

Dennis D. Waskul is an associate professor of Sociology at Minnesota State University, Mankato, USA. He is the production editor for *Symbolic Interaction* journal. He is author of *Self-Games and Body-Play: Personhood in Online Chat and Cybersex* (2003), editor of *Net.*

seXXX: Readings on Sex, Pornography, and the Internet (2004) and, with
Phillip Vannini, editor of *Body/Embodiment: Symbolic Interaction and
the Sociology of the Body* (2006). His published research has explored
internet sex, sexual embodiment, sociology of the body, sociology of the
senses, fantasy role-playing games, and chronic illness.

Index

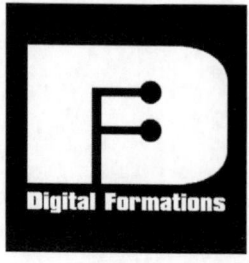

Digital Formations

General Editor: Steve Jones

Digital Formations is an essential source for critical, high-quality books on digital technologies and modern life. Volumes in the series break new ground by emphasizing multiple methodological and theoretical approaches to deeply probe the formation and reformation of lived experience as it is refracted through digital interaction. Digital Formations pushes forward our understanding of the intersections—and corresponding implications—between the digital technologies and everyday life. The series emphasizes critical studies in the context of emergent and existing digital technologies.

Other recent titles include:

Felicia Wu Song
  Virtual Communities: Bowling Alone, Online Together

Edited by Sharon Kleinman
  The Culture of Efficiency: Technology in Everyday Life

Edward Lee Lamoureux, Steven L. Baron, & Claire Stewart
  Intellectual Property Law and Interactive Media: Free for a Fee

Edited by Adrienne Russell & Nabil Echchaibi
  International Blogging: Identity, Politics and Networked Publics

Edited by Don Heider
  Living Virtually: Researching New Worlds

Edited by Judith Burnett, Peter Senker & Kathy Walker
  The Myths of Technology: Innovation and Inequality

Edited by Knut Lundby
  Digital Storytelling, Mediatized Stories: Self-representations in New Media

Theresa M. Senft
  Camgirls: Celebrity and Community in the Age of Social Networks

Edited by Chris Paterson & David Domingo
  Making Online News: The Ethnography of New Media Production

To order other books in this series please contact our Customer Service Department:
(800) 770-LANG (within the US)
  (212) 647-7706 (outside the US)
  (212) 647-7707 FAX

To find out more about the series or browse a full list of titles, please visit our website:
WWW.PETERLANG.COM